A Destiny Apart

A Destiny Apart

NEW ZEALAND'S SEARCH FOR NATIONAL IDENTITY

Keith Sinclair

UNWIN PAPERBACKS
IN ASSOCIATION WITH
THE PORT NICHOLSON
PRESS

First published in 1986
by Allen & Unwin New Zealand Ltd,
in association with the Port Nicholson Press,
60 Cambridge Terrace, Wellington, New Zealand

Allen & Unwin Australia Pty Ltd, NCR House,
8 Napier Street, North Sydney, NSW 2060, Australia

Allen & Unwin (Publishers) Ltd,
40 Museum Street, London WC1, England

National Library of Australia Cataloguing-in-Publication Entry
Sinclair, Keith, 1922-
A destiny apart: the search for New Zealand's national identity.
Includes index.
ISBN 0 86861 690 7.
ISBN 0 86861 682 6 (pbk.).
1. New Zealand – History. 2. National characteristics, New Zealand.
3. Nationalism – New Zealand – History. I. Title.
993.1

Acknowledgements

Several librarians and others gave valuable assistance in obtaining illustrations. The publishers and the author are grateful to them, and to the following for permission to reproduce the images: Alexander Turnbull Library, Wellington; *Auckland Star*; Auckland Public Library; Australian War Memorial, Canberra; Peter Bromhead; Canterbury Public Library, Christchurch; E. H. Minhinnick; National Archives, Wellington; National Museum, Wellington; *New Zealand Herald*/Wilson & Horton, Auckland.
Particular thanks are due to Heather Chandler for picture research.
The publishers also wish to thank Colin McCahon and Marti Friedlander for permission to reproduce their work.

Front cover: *A Southern Landscape* by Colin McCahon
Back cover: Keith Sinclair by Marti Friedlander

Typeset by Graphicraft Ltd, Hong Kong
Printed by Asquith House New Zealand Ltd, Auckland

TIME: *National, the word, is a sign among you,*
Everywhere nation is talked and taught;
In one-man schools, at public luncheons,
They speak of a nation, never of islands,
As if by repeated incantation
Some god might be persuaded
To descend and transfigure,
Making every man bigger.

ISLAND: *The third and fourth generations*
Begin to speak differently,
Suffering mutations,
Cannot help identity;
Nation's their only sign
Meaning man and brother . . . .

Allen Curnow, 'Dialogue of Island & Time' (1941)

Ben Comerford and I had known each other a long time; or what one thinks of as a long time when young. Come to that, 'knowing' needs a qualifier too: in New Zealand everyone knows everyone more or less: those you don't know personally you might just as well because they're bound to be very like the people you know already; or think you know, because of course everyone's different deep down but in New Zealand the stereotype that controls what you can say or be seen to do is very strong. Whether that's a good or bad thing in peacetime, I wouldn't like to say – couldn't, even, because once you've been in a serious war there's never really peacetime for you again . . . .

Dan Davin, 'Cassino Casualty', *Islands*, 34 (1984)

Contents

PREFACE

This study is the first to examine New Zealand nationalism at any length. Written for the general reader rather than for specialist historians, it is nevertheless based on extensive research in primary sources. Some chapters rest upon my research over many years. My *Imperial Federation. A Study of New Zealand Policy and Opinion 1880–1914* was published in London in 1955. In the 1960s I investigated and published several articles on Australia–New Zealand relations. My Pelican *History of New Zealand* (1959) was, in part, a preliminary look at New Zealand nationalism. When I lectured on that theme in Dublin in 1978, my Australian friend, Dr Noel McLachlan, then a lecturer there, suggested that I should write a book on the subject.

The New Zealand Social Science Research Committee, to which I am greatly indebted, awarded me a generous grant to pay for research assistance. Dr Jane Thomson and Ms Sue Glazebrook, worked successively with me, part-time, in the years 1982–84. Between us we read every New Zealand literary periodical and journal of comment that we could find in the period 1865–1940. We also read some professional journals, such as those of the nurses' and teachers' organisations. We read newspapers from the main towns selectively, with close attention to certain events such as the war in South Africa, but very extensively in total. I was fortunate to have the help of two such expert research workers.

I make some brief remarks in this book on New Zealand speech. Those familiar with that dialect of English will often be able to 'hear' New Zealanders speaking. At least, it has been my aim to let New Zealand voices be heard. In certain sections of the book, notably those discussing the South African war, the First World War and the writers of the 1930s, I have made extensive use of letters, usually in manuscript. In studying the influence of the Great War on nationalism I read numerous soldiers' diaries and letters in New Zealand, in Canberra and in London. Mr Peter Liddle, of the Sunderland Polytechnic, generously gave me access to his extensive collection of New Zealand soldiers' correspondence, etc. Most of these have not previously been cited. I am indebted to Mr Liddle, not least for the hospitality of his wife and himself.

This study concentrates on the period when New Zealand nationalism arose, about 1880 to 1940. However, it looks back to the 1860s and concludes with a look ahead to the 1980s. This arrangement, which is partly chronological, partly topical, posed certain problems for the author. Many pieces of information could have been referred to in several places. Flag-raising, for instance, could be discussed in relation to the 'Boer' war or to the role of children in the nation. The climate or the physique of New Zealanders, similarly, could appropriately be discussed in several sections. A certain amount of repetition was unavoidable. To me, the interconnectedness of the data and themes gave assurance that the pattern was not in my head but in an historical reality. The pieces of data fit together in a structure of time, not of mind.

In any survey of this sort, relevant topics must be omitted or lightly touched on – for instance, the Jubilee and Centennial celebrations of 1890 and 1940, or the great Exhibitions. Obviously much more could be said about painting. On some subjects, such as the role of Maoris, women and children, or the tragedies of Gallipoli and Flanders, no discussion could claim to be definitive. On a few topics, however – for instance, the New Zealand Natives Associations – there is probably less left for future scholars to say.

In addition to those already acknowledged, I have incurred many debts in working on this study. My wife, Dr Raewyn Dalziel, helped in numerous ways, notably by giving me material (for instance, about the 1860s) which she had discovered in the course of her own historical research. Colleagues in Australia, Canada, Great Britain and South Africa, as well as in New Zealand, discussed colonial nationalism with me and suggested various approaches. At Auckland, Dr Margaret Lamb was helpful in talking about the history of nationalism. I am much indebted to the University of Auckland for giving me leave in 1983 to visit universities in Great Britain and the other three former Dominions, and to the British Council and the Australian National University for giving financial assistance. Barbara Batt, Ruth Brown and Freda Christie struggled to type my increasingly untidy hand-written manuscript. I am greatly in their debt. In the New Zealand room of the university library, Theresa Graham and Elspeth Bailey were of constant and unfailing assistance. So were the librarians in the Alexander Turnbull Library, Wellington.

The sources of this study appear in the references but no bibliography is included. My study of this subject began so long ago that any bibliography would be pretentious and probably useless. For instance, an extended reading of the files of one newspaper may have yielded only a reference or two in the text.

Keith Sinclair, Auckland, 1986

I

Ideas About Nations

Bush-felling, Taranaki, 1857 (pencil and watercolour), by William Strutt. *Turnbull*

Chapter One

NATIONAL MODELS

During the nineteenth and twentieth centuries people have been most commonly identified by reference to their nation. Moreover, that is how they have generally identified themselves. There have been rival associations of family, tribe, region or religion, but the idea of the nation has become predominant, even in communist countries where Marxists preached internationalism.

Yet what a nation actually is has always been a puzzle. It is not a race, with identifiable physical characteristics, such as skin colour, though many people have thought so. In a very low-powered definition, it is a group of people many or most of whom think that they are a nation. Not infrequently, when a speaker or writer refers to a nation, someone in that group says, 'we're not a nation', or 'I don't belong.' Holding up a nation for scrutiny is like picking up a jelly-fish.

The question is, why do members of a group believe that they are a nation? This book is not a theoretical, philosophical or comparative study: indeed it is based upon research into and concentration upon New Zealand history. Nevertheless, experience in other countries will often be referred to, and it is necessary to begin with some discussion of the ways in which nations have been imagined, or thought of, so that we may survey the territory we are about to enter. What have people supposed a nation to be, and what have they thought are the causes of national identity?

The idea of nationalism is relatively recent, dating only from the late eighteenth century and not widely accepted until long after New Zealand became a British colony in 1840. Indeed, the idea became almost universal only after the Second World War when decolonisation led to the problem, over large parts of the globe, of what system was to follow imperialism, a question which received many nationalist answers.

It has often, in intellectual short-hand, been said that the idea of nationalism comes from the French revolution. The Declaration of the Rights of Man roundly declared in 1789 that 'The principle of all sovereignty resides essentially in the nation. . . .' Possibly that term meant the citizens as a whole, for often the word 'nation' signified no more than all the people subject to the same government and laws. But what was at first a name, a word, came to be a political ideal. By the early nineteenth century the doctrine of national self-determination was widely advocated. The idea was that a nation was the natural unit of population; each nation should have its own country and government and be independent; the people should possess power.

This idea was preached in Europe but not at first much practised there. In Great Britain and France the monarchies had, over a long period of time, helped to create a partial sense of unity among the people, while standing in the way of some potential nations, such as the Scots or Provençals. But most of Europe was controlled by imperial governments, Russian, Austro-Hungarian or Turkish, which blocked all nationalisms. The Greeks, Italians, Germans, Poles, Rumanians and many other groups had a long wait before achieving nationalist goals.

Only a minority of people in such communities believed in nationalism. The idea scarcely touched the uneducated peasantry. In many countries the first nationalists were a minority of the educated and especially the intelligentsia. Writers, historians, linguists and other scholars almost everywhere in Europe played a major role in spreading nationalist ideas, indeed, in creating nations.

It was widely held that, to be regarded as a nation, a people must have a common, usually long history, a common language, a common culture and its own country. These requirements posed great problems, for some supposed nations had no obvious territorial boundaries, the ways of rivers and mountain ranges not always conforming to language zones, while some languages were demotic, 'peasant', not yet literary phenomena.

Some European nationalists claimed that nations were natural units, created by God. This doctrine, too, involved problems. Mazzini, who believed it, held that each nation had a divinely inspired mission: 'a nation is a living task, her life is not her own, but a force and a function in the universal Providential scheme'. The Germans, for instance, belonged to thought; the French to action. The Irish and Hungarians, he believed, had no missions and hence were not nations.[1]

The idea of nationalism was at first most widely adopted not in Europe but in the Americas. By the time of the American revolution, in 1776, some Americans were asserting that they belonged to a nation; that they were Americans, not British. The state was, as George Washington called it, a 'national union'.[2] In South America too, at about that time, many of the local-born Europeans, the Creoles, were boasting that the New World was their homeland, not Spain; that they were Americans, not Spaniards. They were often hostile to the Spanish-born immigrants, for whom almost all the jobs in the administration were reserved. They began to demand the right to political independence and broke away from the Spanish Crown during the period of the Napoleonic wars and the French occupation of Spain.[3]

Despite some common and contemporary origins, the American nationalisms differed in important ways from those in Europe. Except in Canada (a later creation), language was not an issue: it neither distinguished them from the people in the imperial country nor, in the Spanish-speaking areas of South America, from one another. Nor were American nationalisms to a significant degree literary creations. The new nations had only tiny intelligentsia. They were examples of creole nationalisms; the nationalisms of the native-born Europeans, not all of whom were purely European in descent. In this respect, of course, they were very different from European language-groups who could claim ancient lineage and history. In South America their national countries were former imperial administrative divisions, now some three hundred years old. Almost all of them thought that nationalism meant revolt against monarchy and must lead to republics.[4]

Nationalism in the later British colonies of settlement, which were called the 'Dominions' between the two world wars, was at a further remove from the European model. The new nations in Canada, Australia and New Zealand did not have to fight a war of independence; the Americans had fought that for them. Nor were any of these nations united by hostility to the imperial powers, though anti-British feeling was at times important. Nor did they become republics. Nevertheless, the nationalisms in the so-called 'white' dominions were creole: the nationalism of the native-born Europeans. Although of course he did not invent the expression, Kipling used it in his poem about the 'Four New Nations', 'The Native-born' (1894). In proposing a toast to them, he wrote that their parents' claim to their new countries was 'by purchase', but theirs

. . . by the right of birth;
Our heart's where they rocked our cradle,
Our love where we spent our toil,
And our faith and our hope and our honour,
We pledge to our native soil!

South Africa was in one respect an exception. The Afrikaners did have to fight for survival, against a foreign imperial power. They were not native English-speakers. But it was possible for them, too, to stay within the (British) Commonwealth of Nations, under a monarch, until 1961. How far the English-speaking South Africans belong to the same nation, both groups debate.

The first book on nationalism in the British colonies of settlement was Richard Jebb's *Studies in Colonial Nationalism*, published in London in 1905. It was written by a young Englishman who had travelled extensively in Canada, Australia and New Zealand. His basic idea, which he seems to have been the first clearly to enunciate, was that people in all of the settlement colonies, including the New Zealanders, were becoming new nations. This observation held significant lessons for the future of the Empire. He thought it should become not a political unit, an imperial federation, but an alliance.[5]

Jebb probably invented the term 'colonial nationalism', but he did not put the idea into people's heads. Many native-born New Zealanders had believed for many years that they were becoming a new nation. In the same year, in 1905, the New Zealand feminist reformer and novelist, Edith Searle Grossmann, published an article in the English *Empire Review* on 'The Growth of a Colonial Sentiment'. She wrote that all of the ideals of the first settlers had been English, to carve out a new England in a new land.

Gradually a great change has come over the national sentiment of colonials. The imaginative dependence on the Old World lingers still, but it is dwindling away. We still keep 'the vision splendid' of Europe, but it no longer occupies the foreground in our minds. A strong patriotic feeling has grown up for the land of our birth. We recognise it as our Motherland and our Fatherland. The sentiment for England has receded into the background. It is not unlike the veneration felt for the late Queen by her grandchildren. England is our ancestress, and we venerate it not only for that reason, but because it is a sovereign amongst the nations, and we are proud to belong to its family. But the most close and intimate love is kept as it should be for our own country.

Englishmen and Englishwomen scarcely understand how deep and sincere the new patriotism is amongst colonials. Our personal experiences are stronger than inherited traditions. The bush is no longer an empty and lifeless waste; it is haunted by the memories of our childhood. 'Bird ye never heeded, Oh she calls her dead to him!' We have cause to be proud of our progress. We have limitless hopes for our social future. The New Zealanders of to-day feel that they have a 'goodly heritage' in a country unsurpassed in the world for natural beauty and variety of scenery.

She went on to say that

The New Zealander who at last visits the old country of his childish dreams finds himself almost a foreigner. He has become an alien in the land of his forefathers, but in compensation he is no longer an exile in the land of his birth. The true colonial, however staunch an imperialist he may be, feels that he has now a character, a status, and a country of his own.[6]

In her article Edith Searle Grossmann expresses one of the central beliefs of creole nationalism, that it is the experience of growing up in a particular country that moulds our identities. It is as though we have been imprinted by images of our land. So, in a new land, a new nation becomes differentiated from the parent nation.

This belief has been movingly expressed by later New Zealand writers. The poet, Charles Brasch, wrote about his boyhood:

I grew to know most of the country about Dunedin, in all its variousness. It impressed itself on me so strongly that it seemed to accompany me always, becoming an interior landscape of my mind or imagination, unchanging, archetypal, the setting of what I read about as well as of all the life of the present. The shapes, textures, scents, sounds of all its landscapes grew into me and grew with me.[7]

A contemporary novelist, John Mulgan, wrote, referring to William Wordsworth:

I came in the end to know that much of what he wrote was true, and that, in particular, the land and the people whom we know when we are young stay with us and haunt us until we die. I don't know that this proves anything about immortality or reincarnation, but it is a fact. If you try to fight against this truth, and forget the country of your youth, as I did for a long time, you will lose the fight and wither internally of homesickness.[8]

Several influences were believed to be at work creating new nations. The idea of a nation that is native-born obviously implies some kind of environmental model: the nation is moulded by the place. This model was seized upon with enthusiasm by all new English-speaking nations. The best-known American version is Frederick Jackson Turner's 'frontier thesis', which held that the conditions of frontier life produced a national outlook: the real American was born on the frontier, not on the eastern coast. The main features of American society arose on the wild frontier. The Canadians have embraced the same kind of idea. Canadian democracy was 'forest born'. A similar Australian view will be referred to later.

Breaking in the land, Taranaki. *McAllister Collection, Turnbull*

In New Zealand the idea of a 'moving frontier' of settlement had little relevance. The settlers did not spread out across the country, but inland and along the coast from several coastal settlements. Nevertheless, New Zealanders, too, looked to a rural experience for their roots.

In New Zealand it was the work of clearing the bush and 'breaking in' the land which was seen as central to the process of building a nation. The pioneers, who appeared to people in the late nineteenth century as cast in a heroic mould, were the founding fathers and mothers, the equivalent of the American frontiersman, or the Australian stock-drover or 'selector'. The New Zealand experience was seen as harsh, tough and lonely, and indeed it was. Few jobs can have been harder than clearing the dense North Island bush. The history of settlement cannot be reviewed here. Suffice it to say that everyone was expected to work hard. Here is a quotation from a handbook on *Rural New Zealand. The Britain of the South* (1893):

The labour required for dairying is not of an exhausting nature. A boy of fourteen can milk a dozen cows, a man fifteen, drive the cart, and then have no

The Gate family, Taranaki. *McAllister Collection, Turnbull*

more to do than will keep him out of mischief. Women and old or weakly men can milk, and the latter can drive a steady old horse; and if a man has no labour in his family, contracts can be made with men with families for ld. per gallon, or one-third of total proceeds, to take all the trouble off the owner's hands, milk the cows, drive the cart, and attend to the rearing of the pigs and calves, while the owner of the property can himself be at the plough, or attend to other matters on the farm, as looking after his orchard or poultry ....[9]

That certainly sounds tiring enough to the present writer! It was believed that breaking in the land required a superhuman effort which had formed the national character.

Very often the environmental emphasis was placed not on the land but on the climate. In Canada and Australia the harshness of the environment was regarded as character-forming. In New Zealand it was alleged to be the mildness of the climate which allowed a year-long open air life, so the *New Zealand Herald* boasted in 1910. Sport was a necessity for a people who simply could not remain indoors; indeed, it occupied 'almost the whole attention of New Zealanders'.[10] There was much speculation in the press and in Parliament on the influence of climate on character.

In a book on Canadian nationalism the historian, Carl Berger, wrote that the weather and the climate had seldom 'been exalted as major attributes of nationality'.[11] In New Zealand they were discussed obsessively in that connection. It was widely believed that a climate ranging from bracing to temperate produced the strongest physical and moral character.

Some Australian writers have taken up versions of the frontier theory of national origins with great enthusiasm, despite the fact that so few Europeans lived in the great 'outback'. The most important of these is the historian, Russel Ward, whose book, *The Australian Legend* (1958), seeks to combine a class with a rural origin for a 'specifically Australian outlook'. The 'typical Australian' originated among the early convicts, many of whom became outback employees. They were the first 'Aussies'. The 'bush ethos' which arose among them was spread by the 'nomad tribe' of stock drovers and shearers. Later it was popularised by the *Bulletin* school of writers, like 'Banjo' Paterson. Thus Ward discovers a lower-class origin for Australian national identity.

Some other Australian historians have criticised this theory, which always faced severe difficulties. Australia had about the most urbanised population of any country in the world by the late nineteenth century. Moreover, the trade unions played little part in the national movement which led to federation. A comparison with New Zealand makes the theory even less plausible.

In the preface to his book Russel Ward described the characteristics of the Australian stereotype: he is rough and ready, a great improviser, a hard swearer but taciturn, fiercely independent; he is not only as good as his master but probably better; above all, he sticks to his mates. All of these and other supposedly Australian characteristics were frequently attributed to New Zealanders, who did not have convict origins and had only a small 'nomad tribe'. Similar qualities were attributed to English-speaking settlers in the USA and later British colonies too.

Governor Gore Browne wrote in 1859 that there was a New Zealand opinion 'racily expressed in a vulgar saying that "every man is not only as good as his neighbour, but a great deal better"'. Henry Sewell, soon to be premier, wrote in 1853 that the colonists were 'mightily republican. The fashion of servants is to speak of their fellow-servants and labourers as "Mr." and "Mrs." but of gentlefolks by their surnames only.' Visitors commented on the independent manners of the people and the absence of the 'too often cringing servility' found in England. A Canterbury settler wrote that 'no man who can think at all, is anything but an ultra radical – all for free institutions, free trade, free church, and I never heard a solid or serious objection raised to *universal suffrage*! For indeed you quickly see here that one man is as good as another . . . .'[12]

As for 'mateship', often alleged to be almost an Australian monopoly, it was commonly praised and practised across the Tasman. A New Zealand soldier wrote in 1918 that a man was expected to look after his mate before himself.[13] Mateship was saluted in sentimental verse:

Give me the man as'll share his weed, or his tucker and cash with a pal;
That'll carry his own and a weak chum's 'drum';
That'll shut his napper and keep dead mum
When he's bustin' to tell it all;
That'll race for the 'cobbler' and give it up to his pen-mate that's racing too;*
That'll go dead slow on the johnny-cake,
And kid he's sick o' the sight of steak,
So his cobber'll have a chew.

This verse finishes up, 'Give me, in fact – my mate'.[14] It was written by Claude Jewell, a man born in England who migrated to New Zealand, after a time in Australia, as a young man. He was a well-known writer after the South African war (where he served with the New Zealanders). It might be supposed that his notions of 'mateship' came from Australia. But the praises of mates were also sung by David McKee Wright, an Irishman who migrated to New Zealand when young, and went to Australia later. He sang of 'Old Mates' and 'The Men from the Tussocks' in Australian (or Irish) style *before* he went to Australia.

Nothing in this study will suggest that New Zealand nationalism had its origins specifically within the working class. Rather, as in Australia, the leadership of the national movement was, at least at first, middle class or professional. This is not, however, meant to imply that Pakeha culture was not predominantly British working class in origin. Many New Zealand – and Australian – attitudes must have been imported with the immigrants.

It should be added that there were some differences between New Zealand and eastern Australian points of view. For instance, there does not seem to have been in New Zealand the hostility to the police,

*The last sheep shorn.

indeed to authority, often remarked upon in Australia. The few New Zealand bush-rangers did not, like Ned Kelly, attract admiration: they were regarded as murderers. Presumably that Australian tradition had a convict origin.

The second popular model for explaining the supposed characteristics of the New Zealanders was genetic. This took several forms. It was often said that they were descended from 'the best colonizing stock. They had courage and initiative and displayed untiring industry and unwavering tenacity of purpose. Braving, in meagre craft, the perils of their far voyage, they came to a life poor and mean in all material things, but this they faced with hearts rich in mingled fortitude and hope.'[15]

This version implies that they were of the best stock because they had been selected by distance: only the brave and hardy could face the longest migration route on earth. Dr Duncan Macgregor, a leading medical administrator, wrote in the *New Zealand Magazine* in 1876 that 'our people, in so far at least as they have neither been *assisted* nor *forced* to come hither, have run the gauntlet of a natural selection, which only the fittest survive.' His Darwinian doctrine gave great offence to some Presbyterians.[16]

The other popular version was that the original New Zealand Company and other Wakefieldian settlers had been rigidly selected so that New Zealand received only the highest quality immigrants. R. F. Irvine and O. T. J. Alpers wrote in 1902, that 'The stock from which New Zealanders are sprung is not only British, but the best British.'[17] This coin had another side. To say 'the best British' meant better than the Australian founders. New Zealanders hinted darkly that no 'birth stains' marked their appearance on earth. Julius Vogel ranted about the 'crime stained instincts' in Australia which would produce 'future generations of lawless peoples'.[18]

The emphasis on British origins could be imperialistic or colonial in tone, and often was, but it was perfectly compatible with nationalism. Many Canadians, New Zealanders and Australians, as well as Americans in the eighteenth century, had claimed to be 'native-born Britons', 'British Americans', 'New Zealanders and Britons' and the like. In a book entitled *Nation Making. A Story of New Zealand. Savagism v. Civilization*, a prominent Auckland settler, J. C. Firth, wrote that 'the English race' had been the pre-eminent 'Mother and Maker of Nations' in modern times. That enabled him to combine New Zealand nationalism with British origins.

New Zealand, the youngest of England's Nation Makers, the Britain of the South, is now engaged in the heroic work of Nation Making. Her area, it is true, is small, being only a little larger than Great Britain. But this smallness of area, offers the advantage of enabling us to measure the progress of the Nation Making now going on, better than if our energies were expended on a continental area.[19]

New Zealanders' national self-image has been extremely physical, emphasising hard work, athletic prowess. There has been a constant demand for fitness, not only for sport and war, but in education; an affirmation of health and efficiency. Sometimes this was accompanied by some contempt for intellectual achievements. Themes related to fitness arise constantly in any consideration of New Zealand nationalism. Associated with fitness was a strong emphasis upon military training, which will receive later comment.

A number of other themes will be examined. One was the confident knowledge of the New Zealanders, as early as in the 1860s and 1870s, and again by 1900, that they had a very high standard of living; that one of the goals of the pioneers had been achieved. This was something to boast about; it distinguished them from most of the people in Great Britain, and, indeed, in the world. As the Americans have been called, they were a 'people of plenty'.[20] Wealth was a sign of success and a cause of national pride.

The European nationalists believed that nations were natural divisions of humanity but there is another idea, certainly more generally valid, that nations had to be invented. Ernest Gellner wrote that 'Nationalism is not the awakening of nations to self-consciousness: it invents nations where they do not exist.'[21] This can be most clearly seen in the aftermath of decolonisation. No one supposes that the Malaysian or Indonesian nations, for instance, already existed in 1945. The later 'Indonesians' lived on numerous islands and spoke several languages. The nation had to be invented. A sense of communal unity, of community, came after the idea.

The establishment of national emblems, a flag, of patriotic celebrations, flag-raising and flag-waving, must be considered. It seems, however, that there has been less public display of national feeling in New Zealand than in, say, South Africa or the USA. In comparison with the great mixture of people in the USA, the European New Zealanders were sufficiently homogeneous English-speakers not to need much official propagandising. However, repeated attempts have been made to conjure up a completely united nation of Pakeha and Maoris. As Governor Hobson said at Waitangi, 'He iwi tahi tatou.' 'We are all one people.' Not all Maoris have been convinced by this assertion. Given the wars and the land confiscations of the early 1860s, it would be surprising if this were not so.

In the terms of 'colonial nationalism' the Maoris pose a problem, for they have had the distinct language and culture, long history and traditions which might have led them to become a nation in a European sense. But they did not. The Maori King movement of the mid-nineteenth century has been interpreted as an attempt to rise above tribalism to Maori nationalism, but it did not succeed in uniting most of the tribes.[22] So a question is: have the Maoris chosen to join the predominantly Pakeha nation? That question will be discussed rather than positively answered.

Chapter Two

PROPHECIES

Many Americans had expected, well before their revolution, that they would eventually become independent, simply on the analogy of children growing up and leaving their parents.[1] The settlers in New Zealand were well aware that, in many ways, they were following American precedents. In 1854 one of the founding settlers in Canterbury, Thomas Cholmondley (who had already returned to Great Britain), wrote that 'In New Zealand, as it stands at present, we are permitted to behold the earliest beginnings of a new national life . . . .' He believed that the experience of colonising a new country had encouraged certain traits in Americans – for instance, quickness and energy.

The American is essentially a colonist, and his ways and doings express a habit of life, rough and ready, free and daring, generous but dangerous, of infinite suppleness, dexterity, and resource. He cannot be equalled for contrivance; and the boundless field opened for national aggrandisements and private speculation, inspires him with a most ambitious temper.

New Zealand, he thought, would follow the American example:

Now, while I am convinced that society in such a colony as New Zealand must daily Americanise, I am also persuaded that the New Zealander will retain more of the Briton, than any other colonist, for the following reasons. We have no other colony which so much resembles England in climate, size, and position.[2]

Cholmondley sometimes wrote as though the New Zealanders were already a nation. Much more commonly it was supposed that they would eventually become one. In England the same assumption was 'tacitly accepted by all' about the colonies of settlement, for no one any longer proposed to keep them within the Empire by force.[3]

In Europe nationalists held that the only legitimate government must be a national government: political boundaries must correspond with ethnic boundaries. Each nation should have its own government. In New Zealand (at the antipodes), however, this doctrine was reversed. The British had, in 1840, placed a government in a country where there was no nation. In that case it was held that a government should have its own nation.

There were numerous prophecies of ultimate nationality. Governor Sir George Grey was notably given to foretelling. In 1853, at Otaki, in his reply to the farewell speeches of Ngatitoa, Ngatiraukawa and Atiawa chiefs, he said:

Hereafter a great nation will occupy these Islands, and with wonder and gladness they will look back upon the works of those men who assisted in founding their country; and when the children in those times ask their parents who were the men who founded so great a country, they will answer them, the men who did these things in the olden time were our ancestors. Yes, those things were done, not by our European ancestors alone, but partly also by our ancestors who were the original native inhabitants of these Islands, and then they will tell them many names, and amongst them those of my friends.[4]

Often these visions of nationhood were imperialistic, for it was repetitively suggested throughout the nineteenth century that New Zealand would become 'the Britain of the South'. It would take civilisation to the peoples of Polynesia and have an empire of its own. However, Australia was sometimes a rival claimant to the role of an antipodean Britain. From this point of view, a great nation was one which had an empire.

The most intense discussion of the issue of nationalism in the nineteenth century took place during the 1860s. It arose from events in New Zealand and opinions in Great Britain. This was a time when relations between the British and New Zealand governments became more antagonistic than at any time in the nineteenth century and probably in the twentieth. In this circumstance the colonists were almost forced to consider their destiny.

At first there was talk of independence, but at a theoretical, not a political level. In its first year, 1863, the *Southern Monthly Magazine*, the first journal of literature and opinion to last any time, announced that it regarded 'a future political separation between Britain and her colonies, as an event neither improbable nor undesirable'.[5]

The Professor of Modern History at Oxford, Goldwin Smith, had criticised the imperial connection in a series of letters to the *Daily News*, later published as a book, *The Empire* (London, 1863). He recommended that Great Britain should emancipate her colonies. Like Adam Smith before him, he considered that, while colonies might have been of value under a system of economic protection, they were useless to a free trading country, as Great Britain now was. Indeed, they were an 'expensive and perilous connexion'.

Goldwin Smith thought that many causes of war were in decline. He believed that England should establish 'a purely defensive force of citizens, incapable of acting out of their own country'. The existence of the Empire perpetuated the maintenance of an expensive defence establishment in numerous colonies. Moreover, the colonies were sources of war. Only recently there had been a danger of war with the USA in defence of Canada. In New Zealand there had been a costly and humiliating war against the Maoris.

In Smith's eyes the colonists were simply acquiring Maori land at the expense of the British taxpayer. However, his arguments were not purely financial. He thought that the colonies should become independent nations. In a chapter on New Zealand he urged that 'To give a nation a Parliament of its own is to give it independence.'[6] He argued that Britain could not make institutions for the colonies: 'constitutions are not made, but grow . . . they must be developed by a nation itself out of the elements of its own character and circumstances not imposed on it, however benevolently, from without.' He thought that, once the colonies were nations, some form of Anglo-Saxon federation might arise, linked not by British possession but by mutual affection.[7]

The *Southern Monthly Magazine* agreed with him that, like the ancient Greek colonies, the British colonies should become free and independent states. Its statement deserves to be quoted at some length.

[I]t seems scarcely in the nature of things that countries of such vast extent and such natural resources as the British colonies will, when they arrive at the maturity of their powers, consent to be presided over by an officer sent out by a minister in Downing street, London; that they will be willing to submit all their legislative acts to the judgment of an authority resident on the other side of the globe; that they will acquiesce in having no policy or relations with foreign powers but such as the English Parliament shall choose; that they will allow themselves to be plunged into a state of war, to be denied the use of some important article, a customary source perhaps of wealth and comfort; that they will permit their ports to be blockaded and their commerce harassed, in obedience to a policy which has been dictated at a distance, and in which they have had no voice or participation. A prima facie *view of the matter would thus seem to represent separation as ultimately almost inevitable, and as being only a question of time . . . .*

Ever since the time when America resented the too exacting notions of her parent concerning the filial duties due to her from her offspring, the dealings of England with her colonies have shown a steady progress in the career of emancipation. It seems scarcely likely that when the political bonds which unite

THE FIRST TARANAKI WAR.

PROCLAMATION.

The inhabitants will in future be required to have a candle or lamp at their front windows at night ready to light in case of alarm, and are desired to secure their doors and lower windows. The Police to see to this.

C. E. GOLD,
Colonel Commanding the Forces
New Zealand.

New Plymouth, 20th April, 1860.

us with the parent state are reduced to the maintenance of a Governor with the veto, and the denial of a foreign policy, these solitary and attenuated threads will display such a power of cohesive resistance as to defy the forces which have swept away every other impediment to the free action of the colonies.

The magazine concluded that 'the ultimate destiny of each British colony is a distinct and independent nationality.'

This was a troubled time in New Zealand. The word 'separation' meant possible independence, but it could also have meant the dismemberment of the colony. There was a heated dispute about moving the capital from Auckland to Wellington. There had been a movement in Auckland to become a separate colony and there was, in the South Island, a movement to separate from the war-torn North Island. The *Southern Monthly Magazine*, an Auckland journal, advocated separation in the first sense and opposed that in the second.

The magazine had raised the question of independence partly because of the increasing bitterness of the relations between the British and New Zealand Governments. In 1863 the New Zealand Government had passed the New Zealand Settlements Act, authorising the confiscation of the land of hostile Maoris, and also the Suppression of Rebellion Act which approved the trial and punishment of suspected rebels by summary court-martial with no right of appeal. These Acts received a very bad reception in England, both in official circles and in the press.

The Governor, Sir George Grey, became involved in a series of embittered disputes both with the British general in New Zealand, Duncan Cameron, and with his ministers. He wrote in a despatch in August 1864 that the ministers were trying to get control over 'the Naval and Military forces and the Naval and Military Expenditures of Great Britain'.[8] This was an opinion widely believed in England. New Zealand settlers were not to be trusted.

The constitutional situation in New Zealand was extremely complicated. In 1856 Governor Thomas Gore Browne had retained imperial control of Maori policy, when responsible (that is, cabinet) government was introduced. Grey had transferred this responsibility to the ministers, but when the Anglo-Maori wars broke out again in 1863, very difficult questions arose. Who was to control the imperial regiments in the country? Obviously not the ministers. And who was to pay for the war? The colonists said that it was an imperial war since the Governor had controlled Maori policy when the war began; the British authorities had other views.[9]

The Gladstone Government did not propose, like Goldwin Smith, to discard the colonies, but it was committed to a policy, approved by the House of Commons, of withdrawing British troops from the self-governing colonies, which were to accept the responsibility for their own internal security. The long periods of service abroad were discouraging enlistment in the British armed forces. In 1862 Grey had been warned to expect a speedy reduction in the British forces in New Zealand. But when the British Government began to insist on withdrawal, in the next few years, the colonists protested loudly that they were being left to the mercy of the Hauhau guerillas.

In 1864 Frederick Weld became Premier, with a policy of 'self-reliance': the British troops were to go and the colonists would defend themselves. Weld believed that colonial troops would be better at bush and guerilla warfare, an opinion which was to have a long history in New Zealand.[10] Grey agreed to very large confiscations of Maori land and the Government began to employ imperial troops to subjugate southern Taranaki. General Cameron regarded the Government's policy with great suspicion, indeed as a war of conquest for profit.

It is doubtful whether anyone believed that 'self-reliance' would work. James Macandrew, a leading Otago politician, wrote that the policy 'has never really taken root in the minds of the Colonists. It depends upon the assumption that there exists in New Zealand a Colonial nationality to some extent distinct from the nationality of the Empire, – such a feeling exists only in the minds of a few sentimentalists. The Colonists, for the most part, regard themselves as British Colonists, just as much entitled in case of need to the aid of the Military power as do the inhabitants of any town in Great Britain . . . .'[11]

In 1865 Grey ignored instructions to return the troops and the war continued. In 1868 a Maori leader, Te Kooti, who had been wrongfully transported to the Chatham Islands without trial, escaped and, with his guerilla band, fell upon the outsettlers at Matawhero. Thirty-three Europeans were killed as well as thirty-seven 'friendly' Maoris. The new Premier, William Fox, wrote that the settlers were now in 'imminent peril'; he dreaded 'very serious disasters' if the imperial troops were withdrawn, but the British authorities were unmoved. The Minister of War wrote to the Colonial Secretary that Te Kooti's attack was just what he had expected. He had feared that the Maoris ejected from confiscated land would become 'a desperate banditti'. By seizing fertile lands far in advance of European occupation the Government was exposing the settlers to Maori vengeance.[12]

Grey's appointment was terminated. The remaining imperial troops were withdrawn. At the same time the British Government was refusing to guarantee a New Zealand loan of £1.5 million which might enable the settlers to pay for their own internal security.

These events have been the subject of intense scrutiny by historians of the British Empire. They have been held to mark the climax of free trade anti-imperialism, and to have led to the beginning of a revival of imperialism which characterised the late nineteenth century.[13] Some modern scholars have poured scorn on these ideas. But at least it is conceded that there was a 'crisis of opinion'.[14] There certainly was much criticism of the self-governing colonies, notably Canada and New Zealand, in British government circles.[15]

For New Zealanders the events of 1868–70 were traumatic. Many were convinced that the British were trying to drive them out of the Empire, as the Premier, William Fox, wrote.[16] Sir George Grey and four prominent New Zealand politicians, Sir Charles Clifford, Henry Sewell, H. A. Atkinson and John Logan Campbell, who were all in London, wrote to *The Times* that the actions of the British Government were likely 'to create a bitter feeling of hostility on the part of the colonists' which might 'become a national tradition'.[17] Harry Atkinson wrote in a letter home that the English Government and people 'don't believe in us, nor in what we say, but seem to hold in a loose general

'The return of a war party', watercolour attributed to Gustavus von Tempsky. *National Museum*

way that we have somehow or other wrongfully got the land from the Maoris, and are now crying out wolf in order to live at the expense of the English people.'[18]

The Government sent Isaac Featherston and Francis Dillon Bell to London as commissioners. Atkinson met Featherston several times and wrote: 'He is in a horrible state of savageness and disgust with the Home Government and has come to much the same conclusion as that which Sewell and I arrived some months ago.' Featherston said that when he left Wellington he was opposed to separation but 'he is now of opinion that we have no other course open to us – this is pretty strong . . . .' In one interview Robert Lowe, the Chancellor of the Exchequer, said to Featherston that if the colonists were as weak as he had said, they had no business being in New Zealand. Featherston said the same remark could apply to the English in Ireland. 'Well, said Featherston, you really mean then by your despatches to drive us out of the Empire. No no, said [Lord] Granville [the Colonial Secretary], that is not what we mean – is it Rogers [Sir Frederic Rogers]? Well my Lord (said Rogers in reply) I think that is what we mean . . . .'[19]

Featherston and Bell went to see Gladstone. Bell wrote to Fox: 'As soon as I saw this Prime Minister, and knew that with his eyes intently watching us he was still sternly resolved not to yield, I gave up the ghost as far as the regiment is concerned . . . .' He continued:

You shadow out, yourselves, the possible cutting of the painter as the consequence of Lord Granville's course; and I see that many of the newspapers are agitating that way. Now for my own individual part I cannot have anything to do with seceding from England, though I admit we should be justified in going. Sir George Grey is here every day, preaching Separation & Independence with great eloquence & pertinacity, and I don't sometimes know how to answer him, except that I am resolved to have nothing to do with them . . . . I look upon New Zealand's independence as Moonshine; not mere nonsense but really very dangerous to us . . . . I believe . . . that if the question of Independence were raised now in the Colony (I don't mean as a newspaper talk but as something serious where men wd have to face the Supreme Court and make sacrifices), it would be dissipated into thin air in a moment.[20]

Relatively few people advocated independence, but there was talk in the New Zealand newspapers of the possibility of the annexation of the country by the USA, as Governor Bowen reported to the Colonial Secretary. It was believed that the American army might help against the Maoris. This possibility was raised in the New Zealand Parliament.[21]

The colonists were furious with the Colonial Secretary, Lord Granville, and the British Government, and they were frightened. Te Kooti and another brilliant and brutal Hauhau leader, Titokowaru, were winning a string of successes in guerilla actions. During the Address in Reply debate in 1870 many Members of Parliament made strong and emotional speeches, denouncing the British Government.[22] One speaker after another said that 'there must be ultimate separation'. One after another thought that New Zealand was being pushed by the British into separation, into a declaration of independence. One Member said that the colonists might ask what benefits they derived from the imperial connection. Another thought that if New Zealand had to rely on itself it should not be subject to any misfortunes brought on by the imperial connection – in short, expected to assist in imperial wars. Others thought that New Zealand must prepare for independence in case the Empire broke up. G. M. Waterhouse felt that it would be to the mutual advantage of both the United Kingdom and New Zealand to separate. A former premier, Alfred Domett, believed that the British Government wanted to get rid of the colonies. Fitzherbert said, what was certainly true, that only a small minority of settlers actually wanted separation.

Left Premier E. W. Stafford noted New Zealand's growing sense of identity in the 1870s. *Turnbull*

Right Sir George Grey (*c.* 1854): 'a great nation will occupy these Islands'.

The most interesting speech was that of E. W. Stafford, a man largely ignored in New Zealand histories, yet who was premier for about twelve years, from time to time, longer than anyone else in the nineteenth century. He said that

in the future we shall have to be guided . . . by the principle of self-reliance, some of us by preference, some perforce. I would do it by preference. I do not believe that a community of our numbers, possessing such a magnificent estate as is New Zealand, could be in a better position than that of being obliged to carve out its destiny alone and unaided. I believe it will harden us into becoming a national community, which we have never yet been. But before we talk of casting off the mother country . . . it behoves us to set our house in order, and to consider whether, with all the local jealousies and provincial suspicions which exist in New Zealand, we are in a position to become an independent state. I think we are not, and I think that we ought to pause before we take any step which might possibly result in our becoming an independent nation.

He did, however, believe that New Zealand was drifting towards independence. 'Little by little, national responsibilities are being cast upon us which we had better recognize and work up to . . . .' He went on to argue that the colonies should have treaty-making powers.[23] Nationalism was a favourite theme. Two years earlier he had said that 'we are approaching to a condition of nationality – faster, I believe, than some of us are aware.'[24]

A newspaper editor and future premier, John Ballance, strongly supported Stafford's views. He wrote, in August 1870:

A strong feeling of patriotism is growing up in the colony .... The plain fact is that some change is coming over the minds of the colonists with regard to the relations between the mother country and the colony .... Between the lofty proud spirit of self-reliance tinged with independence, *of Mr Stafford and the truckling begging solicitations of Mr Fox we have no hesitation in deciding. We know not a single advantage ... in maintaining a political connexion with the mother country.*

Two months later he wrote:

The interests of the colony point to independence .... This country, if an independent state, would command the moral support of every nation in the world .... The energy that is implanted by noble aspirations would enable the nation to triumph over internal difficulties, and to treat lightly those sacrifices which it would have to make before attaining the goal of unity and peace. Independence will come to us sooner or later. Is the time not opportune?[25]

By the time of the 1870 debate the British Government had already moved to defuse the situation by agreeing to guarantee a loan of £1 million. This would enable the New Zealand Government to borrow in London on advantageous terms. At the same time Julius Vogel presented his financial statement which proposed borrowing £6 million over ten years to spend on 'development' – roads, bridges, railways. In fact £18.5 million was borrowed on the London money market within a decade. Economic prosperity returned after the depression of the late 1860s. Moreover, by 1872 the New Zealand wars were at an end. The colonists could turn again to their old god, Progress.

Vogel's policy greatly strengthened the colony's ties with Great Britain. The loans were golden links. Moreover, thousands of British migrants were brought out in the 1870s to labour on public works projects. But, in the long run, the new communications were to establish a stronger basis for local nationalism than existed in the isolated settlements of the 1860s.

Prophecies of ultimate nationality or independence continued to be made from time to time when circumstances led to introspection. Sir George Grey, for instance, remained bitterly hostile to the Colonial Office and the British Government. He sought to have the position of governor made elective – perhaps because he was very likely to be elected himself. In the debate on Grey's Election of Governor Bill in 1887 H. S. Fish supported Grey. He said:

I left England at ten years of age; but, with all the reverence I have for the great and glorious traditions of the Mother-country, what do I care, except sentimentally, for it? When my children grow up, what will they care for England except in the same way as I do, and that more indefinitely than I do now? The true policy of all New-Zealanders should be to make a nation of New Zealand, and we should train up our children to think that they are members of a great nation, ruled and governed by themselves and in themselves.

He saw little merit in having English governors:

I wish to speak with no disrespect to the present Governor, but very often we have foisted on us men who are utterly unsuited to the position, who are utterly out of joint with the aspirations of the people. We have seen it in this country. I do not wish to mention names, but I could mention a name if I thought fit. We should resist in the strongest manner being made the nursing-grounds of the impecunious younger sons of peers, or of needy peers themselves.

Not everyone agreed with Fish; indeed Harry Atkinson made a striking opposing statement:

It has been said by some honourable gentlemen that they are proud of New Zealand: and so am I. They say they hope New Zealand is going to rise to be a great nation. I have no such hope; but I hope and believe that we are going to be an important part of a great nation. That is the difference. I am proud of being an Englishman as well as a New-Zealander but, if I had to choose between the two, I should choose to be an Englishman rather than a New-Zealander.[26]

There were to be frequent references to New Zealand's destiny after the South African war, in the years leading up to 1907 when New Zealand became a Dominion. For instance, in 1904, a radical Legislative Councillor, John Rigg, denounced suggestions of setting up an Imperial Council of Defence. He produced what he called an 'instalment of anti-Imperialism'. He asked of his opponents:

Do they wish this country, which should grow into a great nation to stand on equal terms with other countries in a great international federation, to become a mere appendage of Great Britain, to be ruled probably in the interests of money, and not in the interests of the people?

Rigg was accused of disloyalty.[27] Sometimes he was called a republican.

In 1905 an editorial in the *New Zealand Herald* reported that the bones of John Paul Jones, the American naval hero, were being transferred from Paris to the United States. It used the occasion to discuss President Theodore Roosevelt's encouragement of national sentiment and the importance of national heroes.

A new nation must sooner or later, become the occupier of each new country – linked, it may be, by ties more or less elastic to the Motherland and to each other, but each possessed of an individuality of its own, and animated by a sentiment which is New Zealand or Australian first and foremost. For the expression of this individuality, and the development of this sentiment, we shall need to cultivate an appreciation of our own history and of the great men who take a leading part in forming it. We may hope, indeed, that these experiences and services may be of a very different kind from those of the sailor's whose memory is about to be honoured in America; but we may also hope they will be as well worthy of remembrance.[28]

A few weeks later the *Herald* published a review of Richard Jebb's book, *Studies in Colonial Nationalism*. It quite accepted his view that the four self-governing colonies 'were travelling the same road – the road from the colonial to the national status'.[29]

The term was by now familiar even to the Governor. Lord Plunket wrote to the Secretary of State, Alfred Lyttelton, 'But Colonial Nationalism, the creed of Sir Wilfred Laurier, finds few supporters here, or perhaps I should be more correct in saying has not been brought before the people by any person of influence.'

He was wrong, for Sir George Grey had promoted the idea. Moreover, Plunket did not quite grasp what colonial nationalism was. In this despatch Plunket was discussing colonial subsidies to the Royal Navy and the colonial cry, 'no increased subsidy without representation'; the idea that if the colony contributed more it should be consulted. He went on to say that the Premier, R. J. Seddon, gave Babington, the British commander of the New Zealand army, very little support, and considered 'that a British officer is not at all a sure guide, while he (Mr Seddon) with his local knowledge is at least as good a judge of Colonial military requirements.'[30]

The bombastic imperialist, Seddon, was not a colonial-born nationalist, but he took a great pleasure in New Zealand achievements. He boosted New Zealand pride and pride was a source of nationalism. By this time many New Zealanders felt that they were already a nation, or fast becoming one.

II

Failures and Foundations

Communications reach outlying areas. *Jones Collection, Turnbull*

Chapter Three

THE RISE AND FALL OF THE NEW ZEALAND NATIVES ASSOCIATION

By about 1890 many people in New Zealand became aware that the generation of pioneers, the early settlers, the founding fathers, was passing away. Though many 'old colonists' remained to assist the next generation with 'their wisdom and experience', it was clear that the fortunes of the country must increasingly 'depend more directly on her own sons'.[1]

The census of 1886 revealed that, for the first time, the native-born (that is, New Zealand-born) Europeans outnumbered the immigrants. Out of a European population of 578 840, over 300 000 had been born in the colony. There arose among these New Zealand-born the first signs of what the British visitor, Richard Jebb, was later to call an 'immature' national consciousness.[2] This sense of identity was a new example of the creole nationalisms which had arisen in America; that is, nationalisms arising among locally-born Europeans.[3] It also resembled, and was influenced by, Australian nationalism.

Australian national sentiment had been organised – and tapped – by the Australian Natives Associations, first formed in Victoria in 1871. Many New Zealanders were aware of the existence and importance of the Australian Natives Associations. They had become large benefit societies. More important, they were playing a major role in organising support for the federation of the Australian colonies.

Some New Zealanders wished to follow their example. In January 1890 a Wellingtonian, 'Ekini' wrote to *Zealandia* urging that this should be done. He thought it a reproach that so few New Zealanders had entered Parliament and wanted New Zealanders, in that Jubilee year, to 'draw together in a national confederation, and assert our right to a part in moulding the destiny of our fair country.'[4]

The first known attempt to start a New Zealand Natives Association (that is, of 'Young New Zealanders') was made at a meeting in Westport in 1890. One of its members wrote confidently to the ANA in Victoria that he thought that the movement would quickly spread all over New Zealand.[5] Its aims were to form a benefit society (like the ANA), to establish a library and a debating society and to form a political association. An editorial in the *Lyttelton Times* discussed these proposals.[6] This was almost certainly written by its editor, William Pember Reeves, a Member of the House of Representatives (MHR), soon to become a leading cabinet minister. He was also a local poet and, a few years later, the colony's first historian of note.

The writer considered that the benefit society was a worthwhile objective because, owing to the youth of the native-born members, it should be able to offer exceptionally easy terms. He also approved of the second aim, for young New Zealanders should practise the neglected art of elocution, despite the fact that 'colonial lads' were generally shy of literature. The political association sounded more 'ticklish' and likely to lead to dissension within the ranks. But could the association eschew faction and party and be 'broadly patriotic'? It could perhaps avoid discord if it concentrated on New Zealand's relations with the outside world, but this was unlikely to be useful. The editorial 'we' preferred that the rising generation should interest itself more in the colony's internal affairs, in which case a Natives Association might not have good prospects, for it would be likely to be partisan.

When Reeves had first been elected to Parliament in 1887, he and a few other locally-born MHRs had been labelled the 'Young New Zealand Party'.[7] But they had not formed a 'party'; rather they differed in their opinions on party political lines. The editorial writer, apparently speaking from experience, went on to say that the materials for a Young New Zealand Party were lacking. There was no common ground, no shared political creed or objects or grievances. Attempts to weld together such a party in the House of Representatives would be hopeless. Nevertheless, it was good that the young New Zealanders were conscious of their own separate character. The writer had touched on some of the main problems of the New Zealand Natives Associations which were soon to arise throughout the country.

In Auckland patriotic feeling was aroused by the approach of the jubilee of the arrival of the first Scottish settlers in the ships, the *Duchess of Argyle* and the *Jane Gifford*, in 1842. Auckland had been established as the capital of the new colony in 1840, and the first settlers had drifted down from Kororareka and elsewhere in the north, or had come across the Tasman. In 1892 it was decided to celebrate the arrival of the first immigrant ships. It was also proposed to form a young New Zealand Society on the lines of the ANA which would foster a love of their native land among the young colonials, and inculcate a national and patriotic feeling. The proposed society was also referred to as the Old Colonists and New Zealand Natives Association. The *New Zealand Herald* reported that the oldest native-born colonists in

Left Dr W. A. Chapple, first President of the NZNA in Wellington and later MHR for Tuapeka. *Turnbull*

Right City councillor F. E. Baume was an Auckland leader of the NZNA. *Turnbull*

Auckland were John Wheeler King, a missionary's son, aged seventy-six and Mrs Letheridge, who was a year younger, having been born in 1817. Old colonists from various parts of the country wrote in, saying that they would like to join the association.[8]

The first New Zealand Natives Association was formed in Auckland in May 1894 at a well-attended meeting in the YMCA.[9] Among the committee members were some prominent local citizens such as F. E. Baume, a city councillor who was related to the wealthy brewers, the Ehrenfrieds. He was a university graduate and a lawyer.

An NZNA was formed in Wellington in May 1896.[10] The first President of the Board of Directors was Dr W. A. Chapple, a leading physician and surgeon. The vice-president and next president was Dr J. G. Findlay, a lawyer and later a prominent cabinet minister. He was to be the author of an important book on the nature of the imperial constitution. The Wellington NZNA proposed that, as well as being the home of the Wellington branch, that city should also be the headquarters of the national association. Auckland and the as yet unformed Christchurch and Dunedin Associations were to become branches and appoint one vice-president each.[11]

Unlike the Auckland branch, the Wellingtonians drew up a fairly elaborate set of rules. As well as ordinary members, who had to be native-born citizens of either sex, aged sixteen and over (the Auckland NZNA was exclusively male), there were also 'benefit' members. These had to be aged sixteen to forty and of sound health. They could receive medical fees and sickness compensation. Although this attempt to emulate the benefit society precedents set by Australian Natives Associations became part of the rules, it was not put into practice. In addition there were honorary members, who could be husbands or wives of members, or British subjects who had been in New Zealand for at least five years. The most notable of these was the Premier, R. J. Seddon. One of the important rules was that political or religious subjects were not to be discussed at NZNA meetings.[12] This was to be accepted by all the NZNA branches.

Unlike the Auckland Association, the Wellington group was launched in an acrimonious atmosphere. The Premier, cabinet ministers, the mayor, the judges and leaders of many important local organisations such as the Trades Council and the (conservative) National Association were asked to the inaugural meeting, some of them to speak. Since the Premier, Seddon, the chief Justice, Sir Robert Stout, and other political leaders were not 'natives', this led to much criticism. The Women's Social and Political League refused to accept the invitation because it thought that the NZNA would be too exclusive and would become 'a mere election machine'.[13]

But the main reason why the NZNA ran into trouble was because of the identity of its leading founder and first secretary, A. H. Logan. Logan, who was perhaps the country's first dedicated nationalist, and certainly the most active member of the NZNA, was a sharebroker and estate and insurance agent. He was the brother of Lady Stout, a New Zealander who was a leading feminist and social reformer. Her husband, Robert Stout, was a former premier and a leading Liberal. Logan's connection with Stout aroused suspicions in the local newspapers, none of which were then Liberal. The *New Zealand Times* refused to publish Logan's letters on the grounds that he wished to turn the NZNA into a Liberal political association and that he spoke of 'government of New Zealanders, by New Zealanders, for New Zealanders' and regarded the 'Outlander' (that is, an 'Uitlander', a British immigrant in the Boer republics) as wicked.[14] A *Times* columnist wrote a series of attacks on the NZNA, claiming that it was exclusive (in favour of the native-born), narrow-minded and dog-in-the-manger. He likened Logan to the three tailors of Tooley Street

Anna Stout, a vigorous advocate of nationalism, photographed with her husband Robert in 1924. *Turnbull*

who made themselves immortal by claiming to speak for the British people.[15] Logan published a denial that Stout had either originated or controlled the NZNA.[16] Lady Stout was for a time a vice-president, but she resigned her office and membership.

The NZNA never resolved the problem of whether an immigrant could ever *become* a New Zealander; of how young an immigrant needed to be on arrival to become or be seen as a real New Zealander. The parents of William Pember Reeves had arrived in New Zealand three weeks before he was born: it is difficult to believe that he would have been less a New Zealander had they arrived six weeks later. In other words, it is where one grows up, not where one is born, that determines one's feeling of identity.

The NZNA in Canterbury was started in December 1897, on the initiative of the Wellington branch, by one of its members who had moved to Christchurch.[17] At its inaugural public meeting, in May 1898, which was attended by over 800 people, the President, William Reece, a prominent businessman and later mayor, quoted a verse by the best-known Irish New Zealand bard, Thomas Bracken:

We greet you, stranger, to this land.
Where slaves have never trod,
The breeze which sweeps our mountains,
Is the wreath of freedom's God.
If you've a hand to keep us,
In the work we've got to do –
The building of a nation grand,
Then, friend, we welcome you.

As in Wellington, but for the opposite reason, the Canterbury NZNA was launched amidst some acrimony. The President, William Reece, was by no means a supporter of the Liberals. In his inaugural address the *Lyttelton Times* immediately detected tendencies towards conservative political objectives. A correspondent wrote that the NZNA looked like a branch of the Tory English Primrose League. A member of the NZNA promptly denied that it was 'a twig from the National Association' – the conservative political organisation of the day.[18]

In January 1898 another branch was established at One Tree Point in Southland under the leadership of a local MHR, Michael Gilfedder.[19] In February over 500 people attended a meeting to form a branch in Invercargill, which already possessed a Pioneer Settlers Association.[20] Its founders were an MHR, Robert McNab, who was later a cabinet minister and an historian, and J. A. Hanan, who was soon elected to Parliament too.

A. H. Logan went from Wellington down to Dunedin to help start a branch there at a meeting on 29 April 1898. An Otago Early Settlers Association was formed at the same time.[21] The President was a Dunedin barrister. As in Auckland, the Dunedin NZNA admitted only males, but it agreed to the strange exception that women who were early settlers could join. By contrast, Christchurch, like Wellington, had invited women to join.

A branch was formed in Hawera and another in Masterton. Branches were also planned, but perhaps not established, in Timaru and Featherston. In 1897 or 1898 the Auckland branch helped to start a branch in Gisborne.[22] By April 1898 there were about 1200 members of the NZNA in Auckland, 800 in Wellington, 150 in Christchurch and also in Invercargill. This was when the Dunedin branch was being formed.[23]

It was claimed of the NZNA in Auckland that it had 'achieved considerable success in removing social distinction and "breaking down

The managing committee of the NZNA at a picnic at Lake Takapuna, Auckland, 9 Jan. 1897. NZ Graphic

the barriers of *caste* and *class*." In this connection the annual picnic of the Association has been particularly successful.'[24] A picnic might not seem very convincing evidence on this point. No membership lists of the NZNA have been found, but the lists of committee members in each centre, published in the newspapers, are overwhelmingly of professional and 'establishment' people, in short, of members of 'society'. No names of well-known trade unionists have been found among lists of members. The subscription, generally £1, may have been a deterrent. But some workingmen presumably did join in order to enlist in the rifle corps.

The aims of the NZNA, adopted in various forms in the several centres, were simple. The Gisborne constitution expressed the principal objectives: 'to stimulate patriotism and national sentiment; to provide for social intercourse; and to unite all worthy sons of New Zealand in one harmonious body throughout the Colony.' As the Auckland branch put it, the object was 'to create a feeling of patriotism and nationality; in fact, to form a young New Zealand party in the widest and best sense.'[25]

Two of the NZNA branches regarded one of their aims as being 'the obliteration of local and provincial jealousies'. 'The whole of New Zealand should be as one throb – they should feel and move as one nation and they would then make their mark in the world.' Robert McNab said, in a striking speech: 'The New Zealanders were the most clannish race that had been created and they wanted every district to bind together to preach New Zealand for the New Zealanders and everybody else too, who suffered by the fact that he was not a New Zealander.'[26] The NZNA aims were not, as their Wellington critics had alleged, narrowly exclusive. J. A. Hanan said that the pioneers had 'laid the foundation of a great British nation'.[27] He implied, in other words, that there could be several nations British in their origins.

In all of the NZNA branches, 'improvement' was a major goal. They hoped for 'intellectual, artistic and social improvement'. To that end, libraries, literary clubs and the like were to be established.[28] In several of the branches, when speakers referred to the work of the pioneers in founding a nation, emphasis was placed upon 'searching out' the early local history.[29]

All of these aims expressed a pride in the people's achievements and ambition for the future. J. A. Hanan said that 'They were bound to Zealandia, which was the dearest, brightest and fairest on the earth.' They had no ruins, castles or palaces, but they had their lakes, hills and resources that made a nation great and prosperous. They had the grandest country ever thrown open to the occupation of mankind and they enjoyed its produce, riches and privileges. 'They also had a people of physical power, mental ability and great industry, and they were not divided by religion or civil disabilities, class prejudices or class differences.' Hanan, like other NZNA members, rejoiced in the 'magical changes' brought by sixty years of civilisation.[30]

A correspondent, 'New Zealander', wrote in to the *Southland Times*:

We love our land even as Scotchmen do theirs, and are only waiting for occasion to show our affection. We have not, it is true, traditions, literature, nor race characteristics such as theirs, but in this fact lies that need of a natives' association. It will be part of the duty of the society to record the history of our country, to encourage our poets, novelists, historians, scholars, soldiers, and all who reflect credit on their native land, and to hold as examples to the rising generation those of the community whose names are honoured for great and noble deeds. By this means a strong and healthy national sentiment will obtain and New Zealand will become a powerful nation.[31]

It was one thing to feel New Zealand natives and to announce it to the people. But what did New Zealanders actually do, to express their New Zealandishness? It was in not finding a psychologically satisfying answer to this question that the failure of the NZNA ultimately lay.

Certain activities were implied in the objectives. 'Fellowship' could be cultivated in the rooms of the Association in the several towns. The Auckland branch acquired a billiard table. Some of the most keen members were amateur historians, one of them, Robert McNab, later a very successful one. The Canterbury NZNA was especially interested in the historical origins of the nation. In 1856 one of the founding mothers, Mrs Godley, had erected a stone cross by a spring near the famous (and infamous) 'bridle track' linking Christchurch to its port at Lyttelton. It had been destroyed by a landslide. In 1898, on the anniversary of the arrival of the *Charlotte Jane*, the first of the first four ships bringing settlers to Canterbury in 1850, the NZNA unveiled a Greek cross of white stone, on a pedestal of grey marble, standing upon the original grey pedestal.[32]

In 1900, to mark the jubilee of the settlement of Canterbury, the local NZNA published a book, *Canterbury Old and New 1850–1900*. It consisted of reminiscences written by some of the pioneers as well as an account of Maori life and some botanical and zoological information.

The link between history and nationality was understood in all of the branches. At an early meeting in Auckland, for instance, the president read extracts from John Logan Campbell's *Poenamo*, a fascinating chronicle of early Auckland, Maori and Pakeha.[33] Very often lectures on early New Zealand history were delivered to NZNA meetings.

Other NZNA activities were in a broad sense patriotic. The Association took much interest in national symbols. Its own emblem, originally adopted in Auckland, was a silver fern leaf badge with the letters NZNA inscribed on it. Silver fern leaves were used as decorations, for instance, at NZNA balls. Occasionally the New Zealand blue ensign, with the union jack and four stars symbolising the Southern Cross, was hoisted at NZNA meetings.[34] It was generally called the 'New Zealand flag' although it was not officially adopted until 1902. A woman wrote in to the *Evening Post* when the Wellington NZNA was formed, urging that New Zealand schools should teach children to honour the flag.[35] And the custom of hoisting and saluting the flag in schools was frequently practised by the late 1890s. Sometimes the Union Jack was used, sometimes the New Zealand ensign.

One of the principal activities of the NZNA was to promote the volunteer movement. In Auckland the NZNA started three companies of New Zealand Native Rifles. All the officers and men were natives. The captain of one company was F. E. Baume.[36] In Wellington the Zealandia Rifle Volunteers was formed – not without discord, for the commanding officer was not a native.[37] These troops all wore a silver fern badge. Christchurch followed these examples and formed a Natives' Rifle Corps. The Government supported these initiatives. It decided to increase the number of volunteers from 5000 to 7000 and to provide 5000 .303 rifles and 1000 carbines.[38] Some of these young men were soon off to fight the Boers.

In Wellington the NZNA followed the example of the Australian Natives Association and put on a sports carnival, with running, cycling and other events. This was said to be the best endowed athletics meeting in the country. In 1898 4000 attended, a very large crowd for those days.[39]

The most frequent NZNA activity was organising evening lectures, concerts and other such entertainments. And it was here that the relative cultural poverty of an incipient New Zealand nationalism was most exposed. There were so very few New Zealand cultural items which could be sung, shown, or recited, at national concerts. The Wellington branch did put on a 'first class programme' including the song 'My Dearest Heart', by Hone Heke, MHR.[40]

The NZNA arranged for Mr H. Rossiter to compose a special song, which was sometimes sung at the concerts, 'All Hail Zealandia'.[41] No copy has been found, but possibly it was a version of his Recitatif and Aria, 'Zealandia', published at about the time. It concludes,

New Zealand for New Zealanders from sea to sea,
Stand shoulder to shoulder let this your watch-word be,
Our dear home, our free home New Zealand.

One programme, an NZNA 'elocutionary contest' in Wellington, included a Tennyson poem, 'Banjo' Paterson's 'The Story of Conroy's Gap', an American piece, 'The Bridgekeeper's Story', and a temperance poem, 'The Old Gardener'.[42] A Dunedin NZNA concert included Alfred Austin's 'Anglo-American Alliance', 'The Man from Snowy River' and a negro minstrel song, recently introduced by an American vocalist, 'Ma curly headed babby'.[43]

More typically, the programmes included the popular songs of the day, including songs from opera, and light opera, notably Gilbert and Sullivan. In each town there were numerous amateur singers and musicians, some of them very accomplished and eager to perform. In

Britannia and her subjects: a popular theme for *tableaux vivants*. *Turnbull*

Christchurch an NZNA Operatic Society was formed. Its members performed 'Dorothy' in 1898. In Wellington an NZNA Philharmonic Society was formed in the same year to contribute to the concerts. Some of the concerts were performed entirely by 'natives'.

Various other entertainments were offered: 'illustrations by oxy-hydrogen light' and a 'zoophone entertainment' in Wellington; a 'fire fly club exhibition' and a mysterious 'New Zealand myriorama' in Christchurch.[44] A popular feature were the *tableaux vivants* which featured in many concerts. Some of these displayed scenes from British history, but more commonly scenes supposedly representative of New Zealand and its history, such as the landing of Captain Cook. Sometimes Britannia and Zealandia were figured. Zealandia was generally portrayed as a young girl dressed in white. Some baby girls were named Zealandia at this time. In one *tableau* Britannia was accompanied by a Maori chieftainess.[45] A Wellington tableau in 1897 was fairly typical. It was called 'Maoriland' and displayed a Maori whare, ferns, cabbage trees, flax and about thirty 'Maori' figures – 'some very highly coloured natives took part'.[46]

When the NZNA sought to include 'native' cultural items in its programmes, almost the only possibilities were Maori. In Christchurch, parties of Maoris from Kaiapoi and Raupaki put on a haka or poi dances, canoe songs or powhiri, a greeting or welcome.

The formation of the NZNA was an affirmation that the Maoris were not the only native New Zealanders, but it could not be denied that they were 'native'. The NZNA failed to give any serious thought to the relations between white natives and Maoris. Partly this was because it was believed that the Maoris were dying out – their numbers were not recorded as increasing until the census of 1901. This 'grand race' was fast dying out, it was proclaimed in Dunedin, and the NZNA must help the Maoris and protect them against unscrupulous Pakeha.[47] In Southland it was felt that the NZNA should collect Maori traditions:

That there are romantic and poetic legends connected with many stretches of country, and with lonely lake and mountain side, is not doubtful for a moment. Wherever the Maori built his pah, his superstition soon clothed his surrounds with mystery and awe, and the conservation of such remnants of native folklore as remain would be one of the tasks of the historians. Antiquarianism is one of the most delightful of pastimes, and surely there are some young men with a natural bent in that direction.[48]

It does not seem that there were any Maori members of the original NZNA, and it was said, on one occasion, that they were not eligible for membership.[49] When the Wellington rules were being drawn up it was moved that Maoris could join, but no vote was taken on the proposal.[50] When the Wellington NZNA was revived in 1915 Sir James Carroll, whose mother was a Maori, was a vice-president.[51]

Some other NZNA activities and causes deserve summary mention. One of the features of native-born national movements, indeed one of their sources, was the fact that in making appointments the authorities (generally imperial) favoured men from the imperial centre.[52] Occasionally resentment about favouring the British-born surfaced in New Zealand. In 1908 a speaker at an NZNA meeting in Wellington said that New Zealanders were being driven out of their own country: '"I am a New Zealander" was not a passport to a billet – rather otherwise'.[53]

Various other more-or-less patriotic causes, such as forest conservation and native bird protection were advocated by NZNA speakers. The most active NZNA reformer was Dr W. A. Chapple of

Wellington. He was an advocate of eugenics, about which he later wrote a book.[54] He also wrote a pamphlet, *Physical Education in our State Schools* (1894), and another on alcoholism. He advocated the publication of a school journal or weekly newspaper: 'Interest in current events would be engendered and a national spirit of patriotism would follow.'[55]

Dr Chapple constantly urged reforms in municipal affairs – several years before the bubonic plague scare of 1897 and the Public Health Act of 1900. For instance, he urged that abattoirs and dairies should be inspected, as a precaution against the spread of tuberculosis. He used NZNA meetings to promote his advocacy of the municipal control of tramways, gas-works and abattoirs. He spoke in favour of better city sanitation, including controls on factory smoke, aiming at pure air and pure water.[56] Possibly inspired by Chapple, the NZNA agitated for a crematorium in Wellington. The *New Zealand Graphic* claimed that the native-born were less attached to their bodies than immigrants, who had a stronger attachment to the churchyard.[57]

In 1897 the Auckland branch raised the question of whether the Wellington branch should affiliate with it.[58] Eventually Auckland convened a conference in Wellington of all the branches. The Wellington secretary performed most of the secretarial work – a division of labour which was to lead to friction. A Wellington member, M. Myers, visited Melbourne and contacted the ANA, who offered to send delegates to the Wellington meeting to discuss the formation of an Australasian Natives Association.[59] In the event they did not come.

The conference was held in August 1898. There were representatives from six branches, with 2500 members. There was dissension even before the conference met. The Wellington president was H. D. Bell but Dr Chapple had, so he told Baume, been elected the national president. Baume said that Auckland was the parent body, as well as being much the largest branch, and threatened to go home unless Auckland's claims were acknowledged.[60]

Baume was elected to the chair and the Auckland secretary, F. Lühning, as conference secretary. There followed much wrangling over various constitutional points. The Wellingtonians wanted the national conferences to be held in the capital, the Aucklanders (who won) wanted them to circulate round the four main towns. Baume voted twice on some issues, claiming to represent Thames (where, as far as is known, no branch existed) as well as Auckland. When the voting was even he also used the chairman's casting vote.

In the end it was agreed to establish a national NZNA and branches; any native could belong, leaving it to the branches to decide whether to admit women. Dunedin alone opposed female membership. The issue of adopting a benefit system was left open. Baume beat Chapple in the election of the first national president.

The conference ended with a 'social' and a dance, but it left some ill-feeling. The *Evening Post* published a report, 'Soreness about a Recent Conference'. The Wellington members considered that their representatives had let them down. Baume reported critically to the Auckland branch about Chapple's attitude.[61] This was to be not only the first but the last national meeting of the NZNA.

By 1901 there was complaint in the Christchurch NZNA about apathy: the 'spirit of patriotism was lacking in their midst.'[62] In Wellington the atmosphere had from the first been marked by contention. Lady Stout, her brother, A. H. Logan, and J. G. Findlay all resigned very early. The branch was dissolved in 1905. For some reason not known, the Victorian ANA decided to treat it as one of its own branches and paid off its debts of £8.10.0. It was revived at a meeting in 1908 and again at a meeting in 1914.[63]

In 1915 the NZNA band put on a concert to raise funds for the NZNA Ladies' Guild fund for sick and wounded soldiers.[64] It then ran into serious trouble. It tried to raise funds for a war memorial hall, which would include some NZNA rooms, an appeal in direct competition with one by the Returned Soldiers' Clubhouse Appeal. This led to public criticism and the sensible comment in the *Evening Post* that the proposals for memorials should be coordinated and not mutually destructive. In 1918 the NZNA promoted an Easter Egg lottery as part of its fund-raising, but the War Funds Office refused a permit.[65] The NZNA was criticised in the ex-servicemen's journal, *Quick March*, which claimed that the NZNA had donated its memorial hall funds to help settlers in Raetihi who had suffered in a big bush fire.[66] At that time the committee included most of the Wellington 'establishment', but it seems to have rapidly declined.

The Auckland branch also lapsed and was revived, much later, in 1926, as a 'booster' organisation for tourism. It was very conservative and opposed to political parties – calling, instead, for national unity. Its last known act was to write to the City Council complaining about the high level of the transport tax.[67] The NZNA not only faded away, it was almost completely forgotten.[68]

Why was the NZNA a failure? Why did it fail to play a significant part in New Zealand's history, as the ANA did in Australia? In part, it is clear, the NZNA found no useful role in society. In Australia the ANA took up the task of pushing for federation, the major nationalist goal, and helped to achieve it.

One of the main reasons for the success of the ANA was that it was a large benefit society. Obviously, when it was started in 1871, a need was felt for such a body. But the New Zealanders were very wary of moving into this area of activity. Both Sir Robert Stout in Wellington and Baume in Auckland said that the NZNA did not want to compete with existing benefit societies.[69]

However, there was a more fundamental reason for the failure of the NZNA: the fact was that there were very few adult European natives. In 1896, out of a European population of 703 360, 441 660 were New Zealand born, that is, 62.8 per cent. However, of these, 330 032 were under twenty-one. There were only 111 628 natives over twenty. Since some of the NZNA branches excluded women, they had a very small electorate.

Any social organisation like the NZNA faced a further problem. Less than half of the population lived in the boroughs; less than 200 000 in the four cities. It was very difficult to organise regular meetings of any association of citizens. Presumably over half of the native New Zealanders lived in the country, often far from meeting halls. That scattered distribution of natives further reduced the size of the electorate.

A final suggestion may be made. The NZNA became simply a social organisation, like the Savage Clubs and others. Their concerts were not likely to stir the nationalist breast. But within a short time of the foundation of most of the NZNA branches, the Anglo-Boer war created a wave of patriotic feeling which required no middle-class entertainment to organise it. The new patriotism gripped all sections of the community, and especially the young and native-born. In short, the NZNA was swept aside by events.

Chapter Four

THE EMPTY LAND: LITERARY NATIONALISM

There was another variety of premature nationalism, that is, literary nationalism. It was constantly asserted that a nation must inevitably produce a national literature and that New Zealand would do so. A national literature would express and interpret the qualities of the growing nation. In other words a literature would be both a consequence of and an encouragement to nationalism. In Europe it was thought that a unique culture, including a literature, was a cause of nationalism, but in the New World literature was expected to be a product. Language as such was not an issue for New Zealand nationalists any more than for the Americans, but the emphasis on a national literature – and sometimes art – was shared with most aspiring nations. The discussions on the subject were prolonged, repetitive, and, certainly in the 1890s, earnest, heart-felt.

Nineteenth-century magazines like the *New Zealand Graphic and Ladies Journal* (1890–1913) aimed 'to foster and assist the cause of Colonial Literature'.[1] The *Southern Monthly Magazine*, for instance, in 1864 published a long review of some of the verse published in the colony.[2] It held that 'the first literary efforts of nations have generally been poetical.' Not everyone agreed. A professor at the new Victoria University College said, in an interview in the journal *Atea* in 1899, that literature was 'generally a late development in a nation's history'.[3] But he was in a decided minority. Hutchinson's *New Zealand Pioneer of General Literature and Colonial Progress* (1866) maintained that the pioneers had completed 'the rough work', or nearly so. It was now the duty of the New Zealand-born generation to combine the beautiful with the useful, to think of art, science and literature.[4]

Some early journals, like *The New Zealand Magazine* (1876) professed to be 'national' in the sense of 'colony-wide', rather than local.[5] But a number were launched to the sound of nationalist manifestos. The first of these was *Zealandia, A Monthly Magazine of New Zealand Literature, by New Zealand Authors*, which appeared in 1889. Its editor was William Freeman, the author of a novel, *He Who Digged a Pit*. The first editorial announced:

Colony though it may be, New Zealand is a nation – not yet beyond its embryonic form, but still a nation; and to the realisation of this truth is due the fact that Zealandia *has been established as a distinctively national literary magazine. Its contributors will be all New Zealanders, and no subject will be dwelt upon in its pages that is not of interest, directly or indirectly, primarily to New Zealanders.*

The editor recalled that in 1847 Charles Dickens had written; 'Inimitable very mouldy and dull .... Disposed to go to New Zealand and start a magazine.'[6]

Some verses by Robert Roden entitled 'The Work We Have to Do' proclaimed:

We've got to build a Nation, boys,
The greatest earth has seen.

A few months later Roden was celebrating 'How fast our infant Nation grew.'[7] But, like many of these literary journals, *Zealandia* was very short-lived and did not survive to publish the national literature it promised. 'Insufficient capital' and other problems forced its closure.[8]

In 1899 a New Zealand Literary and Historical Association was founded, with 150 members. They included many leading citizens, such as the historian and economist, James Hight, Apirana Ngata and F. E. Baume, the founder of the New Zealand Natives Association, which promised to support *Zealandia.* Several writers, such as Isabel Maud Peacocke and Jessie Mackay, also belonged. The Association launched the *New Zealand Illustrated Magazine.* The editor was the secretary of the Association, Thomas Cottle, a minor novelist. Its manifesto, written by the English-born Professor of Classics at Auckland, H. A. Talbot-Tubbs, asserted: 'We stand in the parting of the ways. The young scion of New Zealand national life has begun to awake to a knowledge of itself. Already, for some time past, the self-consciousness of the nation has asserted itself in the political sphere.' A national literature would follow.[9] This journal lasted only until 1905, when its editor confessed that it could not compete with the flood of English and American magazines which reached New Zealand.

There were numerous less well-known journals, such as William Satchell's *The Maorilander*, written mostly by himself, a weekly which lasted only seven issues. It aimed 'to reflect . . . the life and colouring of the land of our birth and adoption.' Another with a nationalist manifesto was *The Huia* (1903) which appeared only once. There was *The Pioneer* (1905), *The Citizen* (1909) and several more.

Journals making similar appeals continued to be published early in the twentieth century. *Quick March*, the ex-servicemen's journal, was possibly more nationalistic than any of its precursors. In 1921 in an article on 'New Zealand Nationality. Does it exist yet?', 'Dionysius' wrote that New Zealand industry and politics were still in the hands of immigrants. This was correct – seventy-nine per cent of people over fifty-five had been born in the United Kingdom or elsewhere outside New Zealand.[10] He realised that it was only among the young of the second or third generation 'that a distinctive New Zealand nationalism begins'. He thought that nationalism was much less vehement than in Australia:

What I want is to see the ordinary New Zealander more confident of the ability of his country and his countrymen to give expression to a genuine pride in New Zealand as a nation.

Pre-eminence in Rugby football and dairy products is not enough. I want to see our scientists, our artists, our writers (when discovered), encouraged so that they may put New Zealand's name on the map as a country which produces ideas as well as butter-fat, as a nation that has spirit as well as population and area.[11]

Another writer, C. Godfrey Turner, deplored the notion that New Zealanders must strive after a nationality of their own – they should be British all the time. But he agreed that:

New Zealanders are not content to have earned a place in an Empire of age, worth, and tradition. They want to be intensely themselves, being already satisfied with themselves. They want to write – perhaps in argot – something which will be distinct; and they believe it will be distinctly better. They want to sing new songs in a new pattern. To paint with new paints, and be as definitely of New Zealand as the artists who sculped [sic] all their figures with three fingers only.

To this the editor replied that it was not a question of New Zealanders deliberately setting out to be different: the difference was happening naturally as English, Irish, Scots and other 'races' intermarried.[12] Correspondents and writers in this journal quite frequently lamented the lack of 'a vital national spirit in connection with arts and crafts' and contrasted this with the more dynamic nationalism in Australia.[13]

Sometimes these journals tried actively to encourage the growth of a New Zealand literature by conducting poetry or story competitions, like the *New Zealand Graphic*'s juvenile Christmas story contest. The New Zealand Literary and Historical Association offered the Premier's Prize for New Zealand stories and a Governor's Prize for essays.[14] More generally, however, it was believed that certain circumstances were creating the pre-conditions for a literature: the journals would provide a medium for publication when it arrived.

Talbot-Tubbs had thought that isolation would be the main factor: New Zealand's 'insular position must assist in the development of a national type – in character first and then in ... artistic creativeness ....'[15] The most frequent emphasis, however, in discussions about the formation of a national literature, as with the so-called 'national type', was on the environment in general and climate. There was much talk about the influence of the local scenery on the native mind, and the likely influence of the land itself upon future poetry. Now that the strenuous work of colonisation was nearly done, 'we may hope to get poetry, "filled full of the smell and colour of the land," fired with the beauty and bloom of the native bush and ... the cluck of weka and kiwi and the harsher note of the kakariki and kaka ....'[16]

Sometimes it was thought that climate could be a direct cause of artistic expression. Arthur Adams argued in his novel, *Tussock Land*, that:

> *The Australian will be an artistic people. Under the brilliance of that sky, under the germinating influence of that heat, he will reach heights of artistic expression impossible to his more sturdy cousin in Maoriland. The New Zealander dwells in a mountainous country; and it is not the Himalayas nor the Alps that produce the great poets, the masters of painting and of music. It is the sleepy, level, fat lands, the wide and monotonous plains, the smallnesses of a quiet countryside, or the sordid dreariness of the city that rear genius.*

He went on:

> *The Shakespeare of Australia will come slouching down to the feverish life of Sydney from some drear, sun-baked, God-forgotten backblocks township, made superbly articulate by the endless and enigmatical silence of the bush. The New Zealand race, meantime, at ease in a paradise of majestic scenery, will rest content with that. No stimulus, save the great stimulus of patriotism, will call them from their lotus-land.*

The 'clarion that would awake them from their dangerous content' was war.[17]

Basically, it was believed, a native literature would arise from and be inspired by the same process that was creating the new nation, that is, the experience of life in New Zealand. One aspect of it was the attempt, possibly without contemporary parallel in the other British settlement colonies, to base an English literature on Maori culture. Maori legends, such as that of Hinemoa and Tutanekai, were regarded as *New Zealand*,

Film poster at Stratford Theatre, 1913. *McAllister Collection, Turnbull*

not just Maori stories. The best known of these attempts was Alfred Domett's ramshackle epic, *Ranolf and Amohia* (London, 1872). Of his work, the *New Zealand Illustrated Magazine* said that 'here in New Zealand we have infinite advantages over Australia in the way of material for ... a national literature. Our country has a history; Australia has none – at any rate none that can equal our own in all those stirring elements which invest the past with a halo of romance, and make food for the poet, the painter, and the novelist.'[18]

Innumerable poems were written poeticising Maori traditions. This literary attempt to ransack Maori culture continued certainly up to the 1940s. The story of Tinirau and Tawhiri was, for instance, recounted in some student verse as late as 1941.[19] The attempt failed.

The local market was too small to sustain a national journal for any length of time. A high proportion of New Zealand verse and fiction appeared in the Sydney *Bulletin*. In the 1890s about ten per cent of the *Bulletin*'s stories, for instance, came from New Zealand.[20] One attraction was that the *Bulletin* paid – in 1904 in New Zealand *The Voice* and the *New Zealand Magazine* paid contributors,[21] but that was unusual.

The *Bulletin* was widely read in New Zealand,[22] but some writers were jealous of its influence and of Australian cultural dominance in general. In launching a new magazine, *The Critic*, to publish New Zealand writing, Joseph Spence Evison wrote in 1899: 'There is no good reason why New Zealanders should depend solely, as at present, upon Australia for their literary market.' The *Bulletin* he thought all 'claptrap and sexual problems'.[23] On the other hand, there was frequent lamentation in the New Zealand newspapers and journals that

New Zealanders neglected, indeed ignored, local writers. In a long article on 'Literary Taste in New Zealand' a journalist, Frank Morton, claimed that New Zealand writers were better known and held in higher regard in Australia than at home.[24]

Although numerous New Zealand authors published in the *Bulletin*, there was a striking distinction between New Zealand writing and the writings of the *Bulletin* school. The *Bulletin* was 'rude, slangy, smart, happily vulgar . . . .' Its ballad-writers wrote from a working-class point of view, wrote for the uneducated.[25] Some New Zealanders, like Irish-born David McKee Wright and English-born Claude Jewell, also wrote *Bulletin*-style ballads, but the ballad never became popular among New Zealand writers. They mostly wrote for more educated readers and from an educated vantage, even when writing about the ordinary workers. One Australian writer in the *Bulletin* complained that New Zealand writers were 'usually tame and uninspiring' because New Zealand was 'a curiously "educated" country'.[26] One should hasten to add, however, that the *Bulletin* should not be equated with Australian literature. Henry Handel Richardson was educated and far removed from lower-class attitudes.

The literary nationalists foretold the appearance of great writers who would contribute to the materialist colony a literary culture, presumably interpreting the lives of New Zealanders. But local writers wrote little work of distinction until the 1910s when Katherine Mansfield's writing first appeared, and the 1920s when R. A. K. Mason as well as Frank Anthony and Jane Mander began to publish. Of these, only Mason was not an expatriate and his poems rarely refer to New Zealand. The others did, however, write about New Zealand.

The literary nationalism of the 1890s made little headway partly because so many of the writers left the country. David McKee Wright, one of the few balladists, went to Sydney. The New Zealand-born Arthur Adams left to write the 'Red Page' of the *Bulletin*. William Pember Reeves went to London, as did Frank Anthony and A. B. Marriott-Watson. Katherine Mansfield and the painter Frances Hodgkins followed them. Jane Mander lived abroad for many years. A complete roll-call of absent writers and artists would be long. Those who remained often lamented the fact that 'the "Pig Islander" is a rolling stone . . . .'[27]

Expatriatism became a major theme in New Zealand literature. In Arthur Adams's novel, *Tussock Land*, the hero departs for Sydney, regretting that he could not become an artist in New Zealand.[28] In

Alexander and Currie's anthology, *New Zealand Verse* (London, [1906]), in itself a nationalist affirmation, we find not only the desolation of the migrants leaving England for New Zealand, but also verses written 'in the bitterness of exile', by Adams in Australia and Dora Wilcox in London.[29]

Many New Zealand writers – almost all in the early days – were expatriate British in New Zealand. Some of these, like Blanche Baughan and William Satchell, made significant contributions to New Zealand literature. Many of them adopted New Zealand as their country with great enthusiasm. The anthologist, W. F. Alexander, asked the University of London graduate, Blanche Baughan, whether she regarded herself as a New Zealand writer and she replied: 'I wish I had been born in New Zealand, so you can imagine if I am willing to be called a N. Z. writer!'[30]

Nevertheless, it was the local-born people who wrote in nationalist terms. In the preface to *The Spirit of the Rangatira* (Melbourne, 1889), Jessie Mackay wrote: 'I am convinced that the heart of young New Zealand, in these days, beats with the free, untrammelled pulsation of enterprise; and, side by side with this aspiration after culture goes the dawning of a national spirit . . . .' In Reeves's poem, 'A Colonist in His Garden', the Colonist reads a letter from an English friend calling upon him to leave his lonely islands:

Isles nigh as empty as their deep,
Where men but talk of gold and sheep
And think of sheep and gold.

The Colonist replies, in a fine statement in defence of the pioneering life:

'No art?' Who serve an art more great
Than we, rough architects of State
With the old Earth at strife?
'No colour?' On the silent waste
In pigments not to be effaced,
We paint the hues of life.

In real life the poet had already gone to London, though then intending to return to New Zealand.

As we have seen, Edith Searle Grossmann made nationalist affirmations. So, too, did Arthur Adams. In his *Tussock Land* he writes of the heroine, Aroha Grey, whose mother was a Maori: 'Between her generation and that of her father there was a great barrier. For she had

Writer Jessie Mackay was commenting late last century on the 'dawning of a national spirit'. *Turnbull*

been born in New Zealand.' Her father was 'outlawed from civilisation, set in a land that was not even finished.' 'She was a New Zealander. This land and she were kin . . . she belonged to a newer people, a nation that had no past.'[31]

It was often acknowledged by New Zealand politicians and journalists that nationalism was much stronger in Australia. Nevertheless, the New Zealand-born writers recognised this characteristic in one another's work; Mary Colborne-Veel wrote to Archibald Currie that Adams's novel showed a 'fine infusion of national spirit, both in the N.Z. & Sydney chapters'. She thought that you could see his 'Maoriland poems in his prose'.[32]

By 1900, New Zealand had a quite extensive published literature for such a recent settlement. About eighty New Zealand novels had been published and some 150 volumes of verse. A large number of short stories had appeared in the *Graphic* and other journals – including 150 in the *Bulletin*.

It has been suggested that no major writer appeared until the 1920s, and no modern student of nineteenth and early twentieth century New Zealand literature has disagreed with this judgment. But that is not to say that the New Zealand writers did not have valuable achievements.

The aim of the writers was perfectly clear: to take literary possession of the New Zealand experience and the environment. Alexander and Currie wrote in 1906 that as a 'result of natural influences only, New Zealand landscape-writing is surely a class of poetry by itself, and if there is a "school" of poetry here it is certainly a school of landscape.' They went on to say that this was only to be expected, since the country was perhaps unequalled for the variety and grandeur of its natural scenery.[33] The partial success of the poets in expressing visions of the land in rhymed verses set a tone or pattern in New Zealand poetry which was to persist (with a decreasing number of rhymes) until well after the Second World War. In the 1950s Louis Johnson and James K. Baxter could be heard berating their elders, especially Allen Curnow, for perpetuating a landscape school. They proposed to populate the landscape with neurotic suburban housewives and tortured Catholic bodgies and widgies.

What impressed many writers about 1900 was the emptiness of landscape – in the South Island the lack of people; everywhere the lack of monuments. In 'The Dwellings of Our Dead' Arthur Adams wrote of the pioneers;

No insolence of stone is o'er them builded;
By mockery of monuments unshielded . . . .

Their 'throne' was the 'nation of their making'.[34]

Arnold Wall, an English-born Canterbury poet, wrote of the country before the Polynesians came: 'The land lies empty, nameless and unknown.'[35] The poetic point was that this was still true. In one of Blanche Baughan's poems, fancy leads her to suppose that the country had, not only no monuments, but no graves:

Here at the end of the earth, in the first of the Future,
  Thou standest, a country to come!
Thou art not defiled with the dust of the Dead . . . .[36]

Equally fanciful, an idea not a fact, was Edward Tregear's

> *All still, all silent, 'tis a songless land*
> *That hears no music of the nightingale,*
> *Nor sound of waters falling lone and grand.*[37]

His deafness was purely literary.

Observations similar to these are also to be found in prose. We have no 'history running back into past ages', the Rev. W. Rowse wrote in 1899. The Maoris left no cities or monuments, 'not even a carved stone temple'.[38] The 'untrodden', the inhuman, the unpeopled land dominated the imagination of New Zealand poets for decades. The same aspect of the country had a comparable hegemony over the minds of authors of prose fiction. A Canadian scholar, Bruce Nesbitt, first observed that the 'man alone', the archetypal male in New Zealand fiction, appeared in the New Zealand novel nearly fifty years before the publication of John Mulgan's *Man Alone* in 1939. In George Chamier's novel, *Philosopher Dick*, the New Zealand shepherd, Dick Raleigh, lives alone in a remote boundary walker's hut, philosophising at length about the value of solitude and communing (as he said) with nature. The 'glaring newness of everything' in the 'mushroom townships' simply distressed him.[39] He preferred his 'hermitage' on Mount Vulcan. The short stories and novels of the late nineteenth and early twentieth centuries are full of solitary swaggers, rabbiters, outback farmers.[40]

Many of these stories are melodramatic, and sometimes preposterous in plot and weak in characterisation. But if they are examined for their subject-matter rather than their literary merit, a quite different judgment emerges. In numerous stories there are accounts or descriptions of scenes in colonial life. The poets often aimed at an inspired romanticism; seeking the sublime, they often fell flat on their faces. Most prose writers aimed at realism, tried to use local colour, in a kind of reportage of the colonial experience. Their accounts of local activities are often vigorous; collectively they give a broad and interesting survey of New Zealand social life eighty or a hundred years ago.

The *New Zealand Graphic* in the 1890s provides stories about the Anglo-Maori wars, the Tarawera eruption, cooking in the bush, getting lost in the bush. There is the Maori princess and the 'new chum' meeting a beautiful half-caste girl. There are Maori and Pakeha heroes in the New Zealand wars. There are gold-miners and saw-millers. People go to a race meeting. There is pig-sticking and some boozing.

Often, as in 'The Ghost of Blind Gully', the rough life of stockmen and shepherds is well portrayed.[41]

Certain themes became symbolic of the colonial experience. One was life in the bush, as in J. M. Thomson's story, *The Bush Boys of New Zealand: or Dinkums and Mac* (London, 1905), a lively story of life in a bush clearing in Taranaki. It would be difficult for people who have not seen New Zealand 'bush' to imagine what life was like in that environment as the stupendous trees of mixed podocarp rain forest, enormously bigger than European trees, were felled or burned.

On occasions the fictions make a political point. Jane Mander tells us that 'New Zealand, even more than any other part of the world, seethed with the atmosphere of social and moral experiments', though they did not extend to sexual experimentation.[42] In *Zealandia* W. P. Reeves wrote a clumsy story about sheep-farmers, a polemic against the run-holders.[43] The struggle of the 'cockatoos' (later 'cockies' and 'cow cockies') against the climate, the land, the rich and general adversity became a perennial theme, explicitly discussed in George Chamier's novel *A South Sea Siren* (London, 1895).

Social comment often went well beyond simple description. In many stories the 'new chum', invariably a British immigrant, is a figure of fun, awkward at adapting to the colonial environment, while boosting the colonial ego. The rivalry of the immigrant and the native-born male for the hand of a local girl was a useful topic to bring in the conflict between the ancestral British 'Home' and the actual colonial home. In 'A Summer Romance' by 'Dum Spiro, Spero', Madge prefers Colonial Dick to the Englishman, Arthur.[44] Edith Searle Grossmann contrasts New Zealand and genteel English behaviour. Adelaide, a colonial returning to New Zealand after education in England, meets the New Zealand farm worker, Dennis MacDiarmid, and wonders 'However ought one to treat inferiors here?' Inferiors acted as though they were equal: 'His manner was not even insolent, it was quiet and unaffected.' That was a New Zealand ideal. Class, we learn, was an English phenomenon. When her father tells her that the Englishman, Horace, is a gentleman, she replies, 'Dennis is a man, Father, and that is more.' She had come, in short, to choose the New Zealander. 'His patriotism was local and narrow, but it was intense. . . . Here he had been born, and here . . . he would have been content . . . to die and be buried.'[45]

In Jane Mander's *The Story of a New Zealand River*, too, we are told that 'there are no class distinctions here.' In a gang of forestry workers individual eccentricities were 'lightly taken': 'The one thing the motley group would not stand, individually or collectively, was "side", and any man who arrived with affectations soon had them . . . knocked out of him . . . .'[46]

The literary landscape was almost entirely rural. Arnold Wall wrote some pallid sonnets about the main towns,[47] but most writers preferred the country. In Jane Mander's novel, *The Story of a New Zealand River*, Auckland, with its 'sort of fifth-rate Bloomsbury atmosphere', was thought of as 'Demoralising!'[48] In this bucolic aspect, of course, the literature faithfully reflected the society: in 1900 the biggest towns held only about 50 000 inhabitants each. The set scene for New Zealand fiction became rural areas remote from towns, like North Auckland in Jane Mander's *River* or in William Satchell's *Land of the Lost* (London, 1902). Often the protagonist is a bachelor; living alone and stumping and draining his property, like Frank Anthony's heroes in *Follow the Call*, published in the *Weekly Press* in 1924 and *Me and Gus*, published in the 1920s.[49] They are inarticulate, clumsy males, not successful with women. Gus says, 'I'm not what you'd call a ladies' man at all. Far from it! I'm the sort the fellow you often see in the back-blocks.'[50] By the 1920s themes first explored by writers in the late nineteenth century had become the substance of New Zealand fiction. It should be added that Anthony's 'cultural heroes' talk in New Zealand vernacular. These 'men alone' are not inventions, legends, or myths. They represent an aspect of reality which struck the writers as characteristic of New Zealand life, since so many men were living alone, or 'baching'.

Reeves had called New Zealand 'a land without a past'. That it had no history was a commonplace of New Zealand literature. Nor was that thought to matter. Arthur Adams wrote:

Here, aloof, I take my stand –
Alien, iconoclast –
Poet of a newer land,
Confident, aggressive, lonely,
Product of the present only,
Thinking nothing of the past.[51]

Reeves, however, set out to provide his countrymen with a history. He fulfilled the prophecy of the Canterbury pioneer, Thomas Cholmondley, who wrote in 1854 that any history worthy of the name would be written 'by a New Zealander, and not by an Englishman; by a born citizen of the new nation, and not by a colonist'.[52]

W. P. Reeves's *The Long White Cloud. Ao Tea Roa* (London, 1898),

Writer and politician William Pember Reeves gave New Zealanders a 'useable past' in his history *The Long White Cloud. Ao Tea Roa* (1898). *Turnbull*

was an outstanding example of the short history of a country or people. It was well written, scholarly but not pedantic. Reeves wrote it in England and it was aimed at the educated British reader. The New

Zealand market was too small a commercial target. Nevertheless, it provided New Zealanders with a 'useable past'. Reeves's account became the traditional interpretation of the country's history. The book remained on sale into the 1950s.

It starts from a slightly sentimental yet genuine respect for the Maori people. Interestingly enough, though Reeves believed the Polynesians could navigate, there is no Kupe, no Toi, and no Maori 'fleet'; these ingredients were added to the story as it developed, and they are now largely discounted. Reeves merely remarks: 'It will be safe to say that the Maori colonists landed at different points and at widely different dates.'

Secondly, an exaggerated importance was given to Edward Gibbon Wakefield and the New Zealand Company as the authors both of annexation and settlement. Like much else in Reeves's book, this emphasis may be related to his own experience. He grew up in Canterbury – a 'Wakefield' settlement – and knew some of the first settlers. More significantly, he was much impressed by Edward Jerningham Wakefield's *Adventure in New Zealand* (London, 1845), from which New Zealand Company propaganda passed into our historical writing. For instance, he condemns Hobson's choice of Auckland for the capital, while ignoring the reasons for it, notably the importance for relations with the Maoris.

Ancestor worship, and the accompanying assumption that imperial expansion was meritorious, were scarcely compatible with sympathy for the Maoris. Reeves achieves this reconciliation by blaming Governor Thomas Gore Browne for the Anglo-Maori wars: he sees the Waitara purchase as 'a blunder worse than a crime'. But he scarcely sees the land conflict and wars as arising from colonisation itself. In attacking government policy leading to the wars, he echoes the view of the *Lyttelton Times*, which his father owned and he edited for a time. The Vogel borrowing policy is defended (Reeves's father was in Vogel's cabinet). The 'continuous ministry' (Reeves's political opponents) are treated with respect but labelled 'conservative', while the radical legislation of the 1890s, which Reeves helped to pass, is praised and emphasised. Reeves was more fair-minded than might be expected of a politician fresh from battle, less partial, indeed, than this summary may suggest. But the important thing is that he provided an intelligent and intelligible, a coherent and widely acceptable, view of the colony's history.

Reeves was not the only historian of the time. Another, younger man was T. L. Buick, another journalist-historian from Canterbury.

His most important historical work was *The Treaty of Waitangi* (Wellington 1914). Many settlers and other citizens were very aware of the contribution historians might make to the process of self-definition. Ellinor Hunter Brown wrote to her children: 'We are launched into "The Treaty of Waitangi", by Buick – which all New Zealanders ought to read – perhaps I will send each of you a copy for Christmas.' A few months later, after she had done so, she wrote to her 'chicks' that she hoped they would all find time to read it: 'it is so unique to say nothing of its being an important part of the history of their native land.'[53]

E. H. McCormick wrote that 'the literary movement petered out in frustration and indifference.'[54] Certainly, apart from Reeves and Jessie Mackay, the writers of about 1900 were soon forgotten. Greater literary success came to their immediate successors, Mansfield and Mason. There was less nationalism to be heard in literary circles after the First World War, but more of it to be heard outside, notably among ex-servicemen and the less educated native-born.

Chapter Five

CENTRALISATION AND SOCIAL REFORM

Despite the ignominious collapse of the New Zealand Natives Associations there was, in the late nineteenth and early twentieth centuries, a perceptible strengthening and extension of both the foundations and the structure of nationalism. This was largely a result of the creation of networks of communications which had been lacking in the provincial period of the country's history. It should be noted that railways and telegraphs were being established in many other countries at the same time. In other words, although New Zealand was often called 'a new country' or 'a young country', some of the preconditions for nationalism were laid down here at about the same time as in 'older' countries, in America as well as in Europe.

Julius Vogel, in the 1870s, and the Liberal cabinet minister, J. G. Ward, somewhat later, were equally enthusiastic promoters of communications systems. Vogel's motive, in proposing a great borrowing programme in 1870, was simple. The 'Maori wars' (*te riri pakeha*) were more-or-less over. The settler economy could not grow, settlement could not expand, without roads, bridges and railways to link up the towns and districts, the country with the ports. Moreover, much more immigration was needed if the settlements and the economy were to grow, especially in order to build the railroads and clear the North Island bush.

The New Zealand settlements were extremely isolated, separated by mountain ranges, dangerous rivers, heavy bush and, in places, by hostile Maori tribes. Almost all travel was by coastal shipping between the large number of small ports. The movement of people, freight, or mail from one settlement to another could take weeks or months, waiting for a coastal vessel and then sailing. Given the nature of New Zealand physical geography, the important thing for communications was to replace sea by land transport.

In the nineteenth century drowning, in sea or rivers, was called 'the New Zealand death'. Not until 1928 did traffic accidents pass drowning as the most common form of accidental death. During the previous fifty years, rail transport, which was much safer, was more important than road transport. Most roads, even city streets, were only 'metalled'; they were not 'sealed' until well into the twentieth century. Many roads and streets consisted of deep mud in the winter.

Cobb & Co. coach crossing the Waimakariri, from the *Illustrated NZ Herald*, 1875. 'The ferryman with a lifebelt is showing the way, as the fords shift in every flood.' *Turnbull*

Under Vogel's scheme railway construction, especially in the South Island, was pushed ahead rapidly. By 1879 Lyttelton (the port for Christchurch), was linked with Dunedin, Invercargill and Bluff by rail. The line south from Auckland had reached Te Awamutu, and the 'King Country', where supporters of the Maori King, some of whose tribal lands had been confiscated, remained implacably hostile to Europeans. The Auckland to Wellington line was not completed until 1908. In the early twentieth century Aucklanders had to travel by sea to New Plymouth and then by train to Wellington.

Quite as important as travel were messages – both being kinds of communication. In 1860 there were only 107 post offices, and mails were subject to endless delays; by 1880 there were 856; 1700 by 1900. J. G. Ward, the Postmaster-General 1891–96 and 1899–1906, was a tireless crusader for a universal penny postage. New Zealand adopted the penny postage in 1901, halving the cost of posting a letter. In 1906 Ward advocated the penny postage at a World Postal Conference.[1]

An electric telegraph was first installed between Lyttelton and Christchurch in 1862. By 1866 Wellington was linked to the South Island. By 1872 there was a telegraph line between Auckland and Wellington, constructed via Napier to by-pass the King Country.

Postal service, Paranui to Mangonui. *Northwood Collection, Turnbull*

Telephones were also introduced. By 1896 there were 5000 installations; 12 000 by 1904.

This new technology enormously increased the ability of people to communicate with one another. In 1900 the Post Office handled about 70 million postal articles, 3.5 million telegrams and 250 000 telephone toll calls. The population was about 750 000. The importance of post and telegraph communications in causing progress was widely appreciated. Professor Frank Parsons published, in Philadelphia in 1904, some 'Tables of Civilization'. He thought that 'the postal statistics tell the story of civilization with great emphasis.' The number of pieces handled annually by the post offices in the USA and New Zealand was ninety-six per head of population, far more than in Europe or anywhere else. Moreover, in New Zealand every hundred inhabitants sent 500 telegrams each year; in Australia 242; in the USA 98.[2]

New Zealanders were perfectly aware of what was happening, of the acceleration of change. Blanche Baughan, who came to New Zealand in 1900, wrote in the preface to her book of sketches, *Brown Bread from a Colonial Oven* (London, 1912):

The reason why I want to put into book form efforts so fugitive and meagre is, that, with all their faults, they do yet seem to me honestly to delineate in some degree a phase of New Zealand life that is already passing, and that, so far at least as I have been able to gather, lacks not only an abler chronicler, but any chronicler at all. Young things alter very quickly, the lapse of five years, even, can render unrecognisable one of our Bush settlements; and, what with roading and bridging, telephones and motor-cars, movable wash-tubs, and acetylene gas, the rate of our up-country progress is becoming in these days so rapid that it is quite doubtful whether in another twenty years there will be left so much as one Colonial oven for a batch of brown bread to come out of.

In the mid-century the idea of New Zealand as a centre of allegiance scarcely existed. The colonists were loyal to Great Britain and to their own province. But by about 1900 it became possible to feel a New Zealander instead of, say, a Wellingtonian. As communications broke down the isolation of the settlements and conquered distance, it became possible to think and act on a national basis. The fact that Vogel abolished the provincial governments in 1876 greatly encouraged this trend.

Until the late nineteenth century it was widely recognised that politics and opinion were localised. The *New Zealand Magazine*, for instance, argued in 1876 that there were no common labourers' or trade union organisations because they had as yet 'no common political purposes to achieve. Their interests and industries are almost wholly circumscribed by particular localities . . . .' The author thought that because of 'the constant rivalries between different districts, on the only occasions when these were gathered into a focus [in Parliament] . . . the formation of any national public opinion has been infinitely retarded.'[3]

That the people were beginning to think in national terms is illustrated by the very large number of colony-wide, or national, organisations which were established in the late nineteenth and early twentieth centuries. Such organisations as had been created earlier in the century had often collapsed. For instance, the New Zealand Law Society, formed in 1869, had effectively separated into district law societies by 1878. The Royal Society, originally the New Zealand Institute (1867), however, survived. With some of these organisations the label 'New Zealand' was a false advertisement. For instance, the New Zealand Academy of Fine Arts, founded in 1889, seems to have been the Wellington Art Society renamed.

The first nation-wide political organisations date from the late nineteenth century. Seddon's Liberal–Labour Federation was established in 1899. An earlier attempt by John Ballance to establish a

National Liberal Federation in 1891 had failed, though some branches survived. From 1892 the Conservatives had their National Political Associations. These organisations were short-lived, but were followed by Labour and Reform parties. The trade unions began to organise nationally at the same time. In 1885 the Trades and Labour Councils held their first Congress. The Trade Union Council was formed in 1887. The Knights of Labour organised a national assembly in 1895.

The trades and professions formed 'colonial' organisations at about this time. The New Zealand Educational Institute was inaugurated in 1881. The doctors, manufacturers, accountants, public servants, railway officers, coachmakers, journalists and ship-masters all organised nationally in the 1890s. In 1894 the seamen reorganised after the failure of the 1890 strike.

Many of the national sporting bodies were formed in the late 1880s and 1890s. They include those for athletics, mountaineering, bowling, golf, horse racing, cricket, soccer, rowing, swimming and tennis. The New Zealand Rugby Union was formed in 1892, though the southern rugby unions remained aloof for a few years. Hockey and boxing supporters formed national organisations shortly after 1900. The National Rifle Association had existed since the 1860s, but it held its first national meeting in 1902. There was a New Zealand Gun Club in 1899.

The Farmers' Union dates from 1899; the Horticultural Trades Association was formed in 1904. The New Zealand Poultry, Pigeon and Canary Association, established in 1892, claimed that it would 'bring together from various parts of the Colony, men engaged in a common pursuit that will enable them to compare notes and compete in friendly rivalry, substituting a spirit of healthy emulation for narrow minded jealousy, and overweening conceit born of ignorance of the merits of others.'[4]

The St John's Ambulance Association was organised nationally in the 1890s; so, too, the Foundation for the Blind, the Society for the Protection of Women and Children, and the Society for the Prevention of Cruelty to Animals. The Women's Christian Temperance Union was formed in 1885 when an American woman activist came and established branches. A number of organisations owed their origins to overseas missionaries, such as Australian trade unionists. The New Zealand Alliance for the Suppression of the Liquor Traffic was formed in 1886, the National Council of Women in 1896, the Royal Humane Society in 1898.

Such a list, if exhaustive, would be exhausting. Suffice it to say that the list includes organisations for chess, draughts, the Philatelic Society (1888), the Polynesian Society, formed at a meeting in Wellington in 1892 with 112 members, and the New Zealand Brass Bands Association in 1889. Since modern communications were being formed over a large part of the globe, no doubt a similar enumeration could be made for many other countries.

These colonial associations were expressions of a number of phenomena. They were cooperative; they represented but also encouraged a sense of community; they were educational.

It is very significant that this was also the great age of the spread of popular education. The 1877 Education Act had made attendance at primary schools compulsory. The overwhelming majority of schools were state primary schools; secondary schools were few. However, by 1903 the government had forced the grammar and other high schools to provide 'free places'. By 1899 there were three university colleges and one university in the four main towns.

New Zealanders were not highly educated by modern standards, but they were by the standards of the time. In 1886 73.25 per cent of the population were literate, while another 4.77 per cent could read but not write. By 1901 82.78 per cent of the total population was literate. By then over 99 per cent of New Zealand-born people aged five to thirty-five were literate, and about 99 per cent up to the age of forty.[5] This is a remarkable figure for that time, closely approaching the modern position in Australia and New Zealand in which illiteracy scarcely exists. In England the situation was similar. In 1880, 86 per cent of adult males in England and Wales were literate, though illiteracy was higher among women. By 1900 most men were literate.[6] There is, however, some evidence that literacy was higher in the colony. From 1873 to 1880, 6 per cent falling to 4 per cent of marriage partners in New Zealand signed the register with a mark. In England the figures for 1870 to 1880 were 25.5 per cent falling to 16.2 per cent.[7]

The level of 'intelligence', in the old-fashioned sense of information, was also exceptionally high. The Sydney *Bulletin* noted with astonishment in 1885 that, with a population of only 500 000, New Zealand supported a hundred newspapers, of which thirty were dailies. New South Wales, with twice the population, maintained only about a dozen newspapers. Presumably that was because the population was concentrated in Sydney and not as scattered as in New Zealand. New Zealand supported four times as many daily newspapers per capita, in 1882, as Victoria and New South Wales together.[8]

The advance of education was crucial in the development of New Zealand society. The schools encouraged a sense of community, ultimately of nationalism. A high level of education enabled the people to take advantage of modern technology – for instance, the Babcock test for butterfat and other farming equipment and refrigeration. New Zealanders were helping to develop something which had never existed, an international dairy industry, exporting to a market 12 000 miles away.

The striking, complex and often subtle changes in society were associated with, and may be described in terms of, two ideas much discussed in recent sociological and historical literature – modernisation and the establishment of communities and community.

While it is true to say that the early settlements were isolated, and indeed regarded as separate colonies, this by no means expresses all that isolation meant, in terms, for instance, of loneliness. A high ratio of males to females was typical of societies of migrants, whether Chinese in nineteenth-century Malaya or British in Australasia. This was especially true during the gold-rushes to California, British Columbia, Victoria and New Zealand.

Date of New Zealand Census	*Number of Females to 100 Males*
1858	76.41
1861	62.16
1864	61.53
1867	65.75
1871	70.52
1874	75.17
1878	79.40
1881	81.72
1886	85.28
1891	88.26
1896	89.31
1901	90.33[9]

In 1864, not counting soldiers, sailors and Maoris, there were 1.63 males to every female. The proportion varied from province to province and was more equal in the towns than in the country. In 1874 in 'towns' of over 500 people, the proportion of men to each woman was 1.03, whereas in the country it was 1.43. On the goldfields at that time there were 2.87 men to each woman. Taking the population over twenty-one, in 1874 there were 1.70 men to each woman. By the 1901 census the proportions of the sexes were approaching a normal balance, 1.11 men to each woman.

The consequences of the imbalance of the sexes were numerous. One was that society was strongly male-dominated. Another was that there were a large number of people, mainly men, without kin. The historian, Miles Fairburn, has written that New Zealand society was 'atomised'. There were few local communities except, perhaps, of the rich, who dominated politics.[10] In the late nineteenth century over 40 per cent of men never married. The Old Men's Homes, were, indeed, full of old men;[11] in a modern society Retirement Villages and the like are peopled mainly by women, because they tend to live longer.

Fairburn sees society as heavily infiltrated by 'kinless individuals'. A large proportion had no family at all – whether parents, brothers, sisters, wives or children. They were unrestrained by the social ties and control which lead most people to behave in a socially acceptable fashion. Crimes of violence were very common in the mid-century. Another consequence of the imbalance of the sexes and the 'rootless condition of the colonial population' was a high degree of transience.[12] The rate of population retention has been tested in several towns and districts. Only about 40 per cent of residents remained in the same locality after ten years. This is a very well-known phenomenon. Once a person had migrated, say from Essex to Bluff, it was easy to move again, to Dunedin or Auckland, or, indeed, to Sydney or San Francisco.

By the late 1890s society was being transformed. There was 'a rise in home ownership, a fall in the proportion of single adult males, a waning in the proportion of transient employment . . . .'[13] There was a remarkable decline in crimes of violence. As we have seen, at the same time there was a strong growth in national institutions, as a more modern type of society was established to replace the colonial frontier. A new, more organised community was being formed.

A related process, or a different way of describing the same thing, is called 'modernisation'. 'Modernisation theory' is an idea often employed by sociologists and social historians, sometimes to bear intellectual loads it does not easily support.[14] Traditional society is envisaged as relatively unchanging, where people are resigned to life as it is; modern society as future-oriented, rational in making decisions aimed at greater economic efficiency. At its weakest, this theory can sound like a glorification of modern capitalism. It is partly a fiction, except over long periods of time, yet it is relevant to some changes in the Victorian world – in the USA and the self-governing colonies as well as in Great Britain.

The early immigrants to New Zealand did bring with them elements of traditional behaviour in rural, backward and pre-industrial society, as has been shown of rural protest in the new settlement of New Plymouth. But it has also been discovered that the people involved soon became land-owners; they were upwardly mobile.[15] The very act of migration was future-oriented, looking for upward mobility.

There is some evidence (suggestive rather than conclusive) that the labourers who migrated were of superior ability. Joseph Arch, the leader of the British National Agricultural Labourers' Union, said of his men who migrated to New Zealand that they were 'picked men': 'the drones of course would not go.' Evidence from the 1871 English census suggests that those who migrated were the steady workers. There was also evidence that the migrants were more literate than the stay-at-homes.[16]

To say that modernisation was Victorian is simply to say, in an old-fashioned way, that it was 'Progress', often, but not always, measured in terms of hard cash. In New Zealand a clear example of rational decision made for good economic reasons is the late nineteenth-century development of the dairy industry and the frozen meat industry, the export of high quality protein to the British population; the borrowing of British money to finance the industry; and the receipt of steadily increasing overseas earnings as a result.

An important part of modernisation was industrialisation, which is defined in terms of 'modernisation' as 'sustained economic growth'. It is rarely recognised that the growth might occur without the factory system. However, New Zealand is one of the few countries which experienced modernisation without industrialisation. The technology changed, but on the land, not in factories, a fact recognised, by a perceptive commentator on modernisation, the English scholar, E. A. Wrigley. He wrote that, 'A country which retains a large, even a predominant, agricultural sector may be described as industrialized if real incomes rise and technology changes. New Zealand is an example of this possibility . . . .' Writing in 1972, he added that by that time the proportion of the New Zealand labour force in agriculture was in fact modest.[17] But the rise in real income had occurred in the previous century, though it was not steadily sustained.

There was another aspect of industrialisation often referred to in publications on modernisation, yet typically absent in colonies of settlement. Its absence was very important for the growth of New

New Zealand's first railway, the Christchurch–Ferrymead line, was opened on 1 Dec. 1863. Engraving by R. S. Kelly. *Turnbull*

Zealand society. That was the division of labour, which maximises efficiency and productivity. In traditional societies, a man might be called upon to perform a number of different roles.[18] However, in British migrant societies, strongly marked in some ways by characteristics of modernism, almost every man, woman and child was called upon to improvise in different roles. The ability of colonials to do that was to be repetitively remarked upon in wars to come. New Zealand settlers often had a wide range of occupations. For instance, James Bodell, a Tauranga settler, was a store-keeper, photographer, a brewer, a soft drink manufacturer and piermaster. He owned a saw-mill and a couple of small coastal vessels. He owned a cattleyard. Earlier in his life he had been a soldier, a publican, and a carpenter. In 1888 he was the mayor of Tauranga.[19] This list, while remarkable, is characteristic of the occupations of energetic settlers. Such a variety of roles was not incompatible with modernisation. However, not everyone approved of the lack of specialisation. One of the leading politicians, Dr William Fitzherbert, said, 'It is impossible that the various relations of life, which are the attributes of civilization, can possibly go on where there are not means of carrying out this civilization, and where every man in the country has to do all sorts of incongruous work.'[20]

New Zealand was not, in any comparative terms, industrialised in the early twentieth century. Nevertheless, one feature of modernisation proceeded remorselessly, as technology reduced the need for rural labour and increased that for urban labour: that is, urbanisation. This, and other themes, have been explored by Erik Olssen, who wrote:

Population growth transformed the towns. In the last decade of the nineteenth century they had been walking towns, dominated by pedestrians and horses. Market gardens and livestock were common within urban boundaries,

The opening of the Gisborne–Ormond line, Coronation Day, 26 June 1901. *Gisborne Museum*

Premier 'King Dick' Seddon turns the first sod on the Hokitika–Ross railway. *NZ Collection, Canterbury Public Library*

independent boroughs proliferated, and many houses stood amid empty sections. Most people worked, played, and lived within the suburb or borough. By 1926 the cities and towns had become centralized and more densely peopled. Most of the farms and market gardens within urban boundaries had been subdivided for residential purposes and the suburbs, which expanded rapidly after the turn of the century, became more exclusively residential. The electric tram, found in all cities by 1905, facilitated suburbanization and the integration of the urban region. During the 1920s the car, the tram, and the truck became the major means of transport within the cities . . . .[21]

The processes of modernisation and centralisation had clearly begun in New Zealand by the late nineteenth century. Indeed, some overseas observers were, for a few years, astonished by the phenomenon. The American professor, Frank Parsons wrote in 1904, 'A new civilization has come. A new age has dawned. New Zealand is the birth place of the 20th Century.'[22]

These changes in New Zealand society were accompanied, especially from about 1890 onwards, by a tremendous surge of communal confidence. One cause of this was the realisation that the citizens had achieved a standard of living beyond the dreams of most people in Great Britain.

In 1865, when Weld's 'self-reliant ministry' was in power, the question of imposing an income tax became an issue. The colonists were criticised in England for trying to fight a war at the expense of the British tax-payers (who did pay income tax) instead of taxing themselves. No income tax was levied in New Zealand until 1891. However, the Government instructed a Civil Service Commission chaired by Charles Knight, the Auditor-General, to report on the possibility. In their report the Commissioners included an estimate of the national income in 1865. This estimate, possibly the first made in New Zealand, has received the approval of a modern economist.[23]

The Knight report showed that New Zealanders had probably the highest standard of living in the world at the time. The per capita income was £78, 40 per cent above that of Australia, where people had a far higher income than either in the USA or the UK. In the UK the per capita income was £25.

During the depression of the 1880s the New Zealand standard of living declined a little, up to 1893, but then there was a rapid improvement of about 3 per cent per annum. By 1900 the New Zealanders were again boasting that they had the highest standard of living in the world.[24] The newspapers did not fail to notice. According to the *New Zealand Times* in 1900, 'As soon as the cabled digest of the state of our finances reached Great Britain, the majority of the newspapers set about making complimentary references to our political and material progress.'[25] They were not alone in their belief about the country's standing. Frank Parsons' book, *The Story of New Zealand*, places New Zealand ahead of all other countries in 'net wealth', in average annual income, though second to the USA in the wages of skilled labour.[26]

Whether these statistics were perfectly accurate is irrelevant. What matters is that in New Zealand they were widely believed. The migrants could feel that migration had been a great success; their descendants that theirs was a great country to live in; in fact, as Seddon and journalists often called it, 'God's Own Country'. New Zealand (like Australia) was frequently labelled 'the workingman's paradise'.

An advertisement in a union newspaper in England in 1873 had cried:

Not a farm labourer in England but should rush from the old doomed country to such a paradise as New Zealand .... The exiled labourers will be requited for their ages of suffering as a class in the Eden of New Zealand, and avenged for all the spoliation they have suffered from the plundering landed aristocracy, and a mean, thoughtless set of farmers by leaving them ..., by taking themselves off as fast as ships and steamers will take them to the land of promise; – A GOOD LAND – ... A LAND OF OIL, OLIVES AND HONEY: – A LAND WHEREIN THOU MAY'ST EAT BREAD WITHOUT SCARCENESS: THOU SHALT NOT LACK ANYTHING IN IT.

Away, then, farm labourers, away! New Zealand is the promised land for you ....[27]

In the 1890s many of those who had migrated must have felt that it was true. The people's mood was celebratory. In 1898 a local bard wrote, in 'Hail Zealandia':

Hail thou land of plenty,
Home of the nobly free.
Long mayest thou shine as beacon
To the nations of the world![28]

New Zealand, he alleged, was Atlantis risen from the sea.

The Liberal Government, led by John Ballance and then Richard John Seddon came to power in 1891. There followed a burst of radical legislation paralleled only in some Australian colonies. New Zealand probably received more international recognition for political achievements than at any time in its history. The introduction of what was then the world's most extensive social security system occurred in 1939, the year when the Second World War began, but no book was written about that achievement for many years.[29] The legislation of the 1890s was widely publicised in books by well-known authors: *Democracy in*

New Zealand by André Siegfried; *Le Socialisme sans Doctrine* by Albert Métin; *A Country without Strikes* and *Newest England* by Henry Demarest Lloyd; and *The Long White Cloud* and *State Experiments in Australia and New Zealand* by William Pember Reeves. Sidney and Beatrice Webb and Charles Trevelyan toured the country and wrote about it. Such praise was balm for the nationalist breast, but the New Zealanders did not refrain from singing their own praises. In thinking about a nation, one question to ask is: what do its members boast about?

Newspapers and Liberal politicians boasted about all of the principal government reforms. New Zealand had been the first country to give women the vote, only preceded by two American Territories, Wyoming and Utah. One man one vote had been introduced in 1889; and one Maori male one vote as early as 1867. The female franchise, in particular, received international publicity, especially among women. New Zealanders were very proud of their democratic achievements: 'Almost every page of the statute books bears the democratic stamp . . . .' said the *New Zealand Graphic* in 1897 and asked, 'Has it ever occurred to you that the truest reflections of our national character and tendencies are to be found in our statute books . . . .'[30]

New Zealanders were especially proud of their social legislation. When New South Wales introduced an old age pension in 1900 the *Auckland Star* editorial was headed, 'FOLLOWING OUR LEAD'. It expressed 'not a little satisfaction' that the most powerful Australian state should copy 'a socio-political experiment which New Zealand had been the first country in the Empire to make.'[31] New Zealand's programme, the *New Zealand Graphic* proclaimed, was to 'abolish want' in God's Own Country.[32]

Much of the social legislation is almost forgotten. In 1896 the *Graphic*[33] quoted the Sydney *Bulletin* praising a child adoption Act, removing the effects of illegitimacy ('a deliberate slap in the face of English common law'); a Family Homes Act, which saves the home from the garnishee;* and several other New Zealand Acts. A Supreme Court judge, Mr Justice Williams, speaking in London about the Industrial Conciliation and Arbitration Act, said that New Zealand was 'a sort of political laboratory where experiments were made. New Zealand did not imitate other nations, but set them an example.'[34] It was argued that being 'spared the curse of war and of standing armies' New Zealanders had a duty 'to contribute in a peaceful way their

*One in whose hands money belonging to a debtor is attached at the suit of a creditor.

quota towards the solution of the great impending questions of society'.[35]

Politicians and journalists frequently asserted that there was no need for the colony to follow Britain; that New Zealand was 'leading the world'. Sometimes this attitude was criticised: people were only too 'fain to imagine that at least one of the axles of the world sticks out visible in New Zealand.'[36] More often, however, New Zealand's mission to lead was accepted without question. Mrs Stella Allen wrote in *United Australia* in 1900, 'We are a special people, assuredly a little superior to others and destined to guide the world in the path of social reform . . . . Our destiny is to remain isolated [from Australia].'[37]

One reason why foreign journalists and political scientists like André Siegfried were interested in Australasia was that the colonists had introduced extensive state activities to establish land, labour, social and other reforms more talked about, than acted upon in Europe or the USA. The New Zealanders were well aware that they had adopted a novel style of radical statism. In 1906 a correspondent in the *New Zealand Times* said, 'Here life to us is a whole-souled interest in the State. We teach every atom of humanity his duty thereto, and flaunt it as you may, our progressive laws are an object lesson to the world.'[38] Of course free enterprise conservatives took a different view of this reliance on the state.[39]

The role of the state received serious discussion in a book written in the 1890s, by the New Zealand politician, F. J. Moss, *Notes on Political Economy from the Colonial Point of View*, in a chapter entitled 'Nationalism'. He described how the settlers very quickly 'learned to use the State's credit and the State's financial resources for the common good'.[40] The list of state activities, in for instance, education, communications, utilities was already formidable. The most penetrating comment on what he called 'colonial governmentalism' is to be found in William Pember Reeves's *State Experiments in Australia and New Zealand*, (London, 1902). He contrasts American individualism and private enterprise with the state enterprise in New Zealand and Australia, and speculates on its origins. Certainly one important circumstance was the fact that the state was, from the first, the great landlord, selling lands purchased or, at one time, confiscated from the Maoris. So, too, was the fact that the state was more credit-worthy than any person or other institution in the colony. It could borrow in the United Kingdom more cheaply than anyone else. The colonists turned to the state to build their railways and lay the telegraph lines. Reeves believed that the colonial legislation was 'deeply tinged with socialism', or at least 'a sort of socialism'.[41]

None of the 'centralising' and 'modernising' discussed here means that 'New Zealand' was a unity or a nation by, say, 1900. Provincial sentiment persisted well into the twentieth century. Rather, the process of nation-building had effectively begun.

III

Identities

Young Moaland: 'I don't want to play in your yard.'
A comment on federation with Australia, *Critic*, 9 Sept. 1899

Chapter Six

IS THERE A NEW ZEALAND TYPE?

Since it was assumed that a new nation would arise in New Zealand, journalists, editors, authors and politicians occasionally speculated on whether the young New Zealander had yet shown distinctive characteristics. Such comments and assessments need to be treated with caution: whenever possible we need to know whose views we are reading. For instance, in 1910–11, a journalist called 'Tohunga' wrote strongly patriotic articles in the *New Zealand Herald*. New Zealanders, we learn, demand 'LOVE ME, LOVE MY LAND'. They were quite intolerant of any criticism of it. 'For love of country is, after all, only a nationalised sense of possession that has become part of every faculty and every thought.' When an American said that New Zealanders had one fault, to call Great Britain 'Home' when they should be New Zealanders and colonials first, as the Americans were Americans first, 'Tohunga' was aroused to an ecstacy of patriotism. 'In America, with all its greatness, there is not yet any instructive national ideal worthy of the name', he pronounced.

'Home' means that we have transplanted to these alien lands and seas the national ideals of the North, the racial vigour and aspirations of our sires. It means that we have tried and are trying to be true to type, to keep our blood clean and pure, to preserve our past traditions, to be worthy of our great history, to progress undeviatingly and steadily along the lines instinctively taken by the heroes and leaders of our ancestral people. In a word, we seek to make of New Zealand a Better Britain.

And he went on:

New Zealand is dear to us, her every breath is sacred to us, not because of what others see in her, but of what she is to us, because through her we attain to the highest in us, because in her soul she is akin to the manner of man we are.[1]

All of this tells us little about the feelings of New Zealanders, although some of it was perhaps accurate comment by an outsider. Its author was an Englishman, William Lane, who had migrated to Canada at the age of sixteen and then to Australia. He was a prominent radical journalist and active in the trade union movement. In 1893 he led a group of Australians to found utopian communities in Paraguay. These were failures. In 1900 he became a leader writer for the *New*

Left Sir Julius Vogel: 'I was much struck on returning to the colony, to notice what appears to me the palpably characteristic type already taken on by the colonists'. *Turnbull*

Right The New Zealand type. *Waitress:* 'What will you take to drink, Sir – Tea or Beer?' *Backblocks Bill* (scathingly): 'Now which do I look as though I'd take?' *NZ Illustrated Magazine*, Nov. 1904. *Turnbull*

Zealand Herald and eventually its editor. During the First World War he wrote perfervid patriotic editorials, both New Zealand and British, for this conservative newspaper.[2]

One of the more striking early remarks on the subject of the local type was made by Julius Vogel in the second reading of the Women's Suffrage Bill in 1887:

. . . I am convinced that the fact that the population of New Zealand has been to all intents and purposes a selected one, the circumstances and spirit which are inseparable from colonizing labours, the effects of education and of climate, and the influences of the striking scenery of the colony, all must in time combine to give to the people so distinct a type that it will not be necessary, in order to recognize a New Zealander when he travels in other parts of the world, that he should wear a piece of greenstone on his watch-chain. I was much struck on returning to the colony, to notice what appears to me the palpably characteristic type already taken on by the colonists . . . .[3]

He did not say whether speech, appearance or some other characteristic would lead to instant identification.

In 1899 a Mutual Improvement Society in Gisborne wrote to some prominent men, asking what were the leading characteristics of the young New Zealander, 'the youth of European parentage born and brought up in this country'. 'King Dick' Seddon declined to answer, since he did not think it fair that active politicians should be asked to express their views on such subjects. Sir Robert Stout, the Chief Justice, thought it too soon to classify the New Zealand type, but believed that 'our climate will evolve a different variety, and that, he will be fonder of out-of-door life and amusements.' Edward Tregear, head of the Labour Department, thought the New Zealand youth clear-headed, 'especially in matters of self-advantage', but rather 'lacking in poetical thought and imagination', he is 'hard and matter-of-fact, prosaic and Philistine'. A parson thought that 'the average young colonials offer all their sacrifice on the altar of the god sport' and were 'not over much given to intellectual activity'.[4]

The Revd Rutherford Waddell of Dunedin published at this time in

Australia an article on 'The Influence of Climate on Character', which was reported in the *New Zealand Times*.[5] Waddell believed that

New Zealand has a climate that approximates perfection so far as regards formation of character. The one fault in our climate is its variableness; and as it is held that the calm confidence of the English people is due in no small degree to the uniformity of their climatic conditions, it is concluded that the capriciousness of the New Zealand climate will 'make character more eager, inventive and resourceful. It will also tend to produce a strongly marked neurotic element in the inhabitants.' We cannot say that these characteristics are fully developed in young New Zealanders as yet, but the tendency towards them is undoubted. Dr Waddell states a palpable fact when he points to the effect of a bright and enervating climate in producing 'a strain of world-weariness of pessimism,' as expressed in literature. Many young New Zealanders are world-weary and cynical before their time; more especially is this the case in the North Island.

Dr Waddell also attributed to climatic conditions the growth of the 'secular spirit'. Church attendance was markedly lower in New Zealand than in Great Britain and less than in Australia. It was clear that British elders did not entertain lofty expectations about the emerging colonial national character.

Novelists, journalists and politicians were alike fascinated by such meteorological or geographical speculation. It especially arose in contrasting New Zealanders with Australians. Here is Captain W. R. Russell addressing the delegates to the 1890 Australian federal convention:

Mr Clark, the Attorney-General for Tasmania, remarked, when addressing the Conference to-day, that with every distinct physical environment there comes a distinct national type. With a population of 700 000 people in New Zealand, dwelling in an island where the climate is dissimilar to a very great extent from that of Australia, which has been colonized in an entirely different manner, and, speaking, colloquially, having had a very much rougher time than the colonies of Australia, we are likely to develop a very complete individuality – a distinct national type. We have had to struggle against not only a more boisterous climate than Australia, but against a dense vegetation; and we have had to carve our homes out of the wilderness, which, though marvellously prolific and fertile, nevertheless marks a country in which self-denial has had to be practised by its settlers to an extent of which the people of the Australian continent have no conception ....

Russell believed that the northern and tropical parts of Australia were destined to be settled by non-Europeans. The New Zealanders would, in a hundred years, have evolved a type of person completely different from the Australians.[6] Sir George Grey held the same opinion. He told the New Zealand Parliament in 1884 that Australia would be divided into several states and that the result would be militarism and civil war.[7] It was frequently said that the New Zealanders would be stronger and sterner types than the Australians because of the allegedly more bracing insular climate, just as in Canada and Europe it was often held that the northerners were tougher than the pleasure-loving Mediterranean types.

The one point on which there was very general agreement was that the nation would be very healthy. Dr A. K. Newman, with assistance from a statistician, F. W. Frankland, published an article in the *Transactions and Proceedings of the New Zealand Institute* in 1882, 'Is New Zealand a Healthy Country'. He said that New Zealand had the lowest death rate of any country in the world. The death rate was 11 or 12 per 1000 living: in Great Britain it was 23.[8]

It was often said that New Zealanders were very inhibited; for instance, that they did not know how to cheer. 'There is noticeable in a New Zealand crowd an unhealthy self-consciousness, a mean dread of giving expression to the nobler impulses of our nature.'[9] Sometimes this quality was said to be a survival of 'the true unbending British character'. In the late 1890s 'floral fetes', that is, carnivals of flowers, were the rage. They attracted huge crowds – 20 000 to one in Auckland in 1896. It was supposed to conclude with 'a battle of flowers' but most people ignored the invitation. Anyone who threw a flower was greeted with stony stares. The floral festival came from Italy. In discussing this fete the *New Zealand Graphic* advanced the opinion that

Probably it is one of the signs of the change that is coming over the New Zealand character and differentiating it from the original British that the floral festivals of Southern Europe should have become so quickly acclimatised here. Perhaps we should say the north New Zealand character, for it is under the semi-tropic skies of the North, with its mild winters, that a distinctively New Zealand character will, I believe, first begin to show itself. In the North the differentiating forces are peculiarly at work, and in the course of a generation or two the result will be very plainly manifest. So far as I can judge the Aucklanders of the future will approach more to the modern Italian type. They will possess the artistic temperament of the Florentines, and the love of

Floral fete, New Plymouth, 1896. *Turnbull*

pleasure which distinguishes the Neapolitans. Auckland will be the home of musicians and artists ....[10]

A national stereotype is not an idea which has a profound or permanent significance. The dreamy, philosophic Germans of British imagination could become militaristic conquerors to later generations; the militaristic French conquerors could become amorous, artistic types in a century, say between 1815 to 1914. The proud Spaniard, the chundering Aussie, the loud American, the macho Mexican – all these are common coin likely to depreciate in value. Nevertheless, what a people say about themselves is presumably self-revelatory. The problem is that opinions expressed are often contradictory. People can be several things to others and to themselves.

It is highly probable that the description of New Zealanders as what is now called 'up-tight' was fairly accurate. During the First World War in France the New Zealand troops were labelled 'the Silent Division': they did not sing, as the 'Tommies' did, when on the march.[11] They were a dour lot. Yet the opposite was sometimes said. A Sydney journalist was reported in 1908 to be 'particularly struck by the spontaneous enthusiasm shown by our crowds, which were in marked contrast to the self-contained and rather shy demeanour of New South

Wales crowds . . . .' The *Weekly Graphic* confessed that this was a great surprise for 'If there is one thing in which we imagined we were, as a people, somewhat seriously deficient, it was this very capacity to openly enthuse . . . .'[12] However, only a week earlier, a writer in the same journal had claimed that New Zealanders were not dour and puritanical, like the British, but optimists, who 'take our pleasures gaily, and have a rare faculty for enjoyment'.[13] Similarly, it was alleged by a bishop that New Zealanders were cocksure and complacent but, by a reporter, that they were too modest, and would not brag to glorify their country like Australians and Americans.[14]

There was a similar ambivalence about whether New Zealanders were conventional and conservative, or advanced and radical. When a bishop was in 1896 observed upon a bicycle the *New Zealand Graphic* exclaimed upon the 'remarkably advanced and unconventional views the colonists take in all matters'.[15] But it was often alleged that the colonial-born were politically conservative. Certainly this was what conservatives believed. The first object of the anti-Liberal National Associations was 'To create and foster a true national sentiment to promote Reforms – economic, legislative and constitutional; to protest against undue interference with the rights and liberties of the subject; and to oppose class legislation.'[16]

Sometimes newspapers published a series of letters or articles on the question 'Is There a National Type?' which obviously aroused much public interest. In 1906 in the *New Zealand Times*, a British visitor signing himself 'Outlander' wrote a long letter saying that the unique character of New Zealand legislation had led him to expect the New Zealanders to be 'a distinct racial type, with national ideals and aims of their own'. He found them purely British, content to be colonials, unlike the Canadians and Australians, who were 'adolescent nations'. In a country where the people bought more books per head than in any other, there was not enough national spirit to sustain a single national magazine. The architecture was found equally wanting. He had seen no sign of the existence of the New Zealand Natives Associations, while Yorkshire Societies and Home Rule Associations flourished. This effusion produced various reactions. Another 'Outlander' wrote that 'the Maorilander slides through the world negative, a nonentity'. 'A Young Colonial' admitted that they were devoid of polish of manner, but claimed that they possessed a freeness instead. 'Native' asked, 'what about our footballers?' Another correspondent thought that if New Zealanders could fight and make money, things were not so bad. 'An

Inside Outlander' wrote that 'we live in . . . a sphere where man is recognized as man, where ability is accepted at its true worth, and where the true, innate humanity of man gets its full fling.' 'Pakeha' wrote that most New Zealanders 'would rather live in a humpy of their own design than in a land where mildewed tradition dictated the position of the bath-room – if any . . . .' New Zealand was not a home for long-haired neurotics: axes, not oil paints were the tools of colonisation. 'The artistic temperament dies as the corns of toil harden the palm.' Art would follow generations later: 'it is based on a new and active art that has grown with the nation's growth imperceptibly, and was not imported in cases in a ship's hold.' The best contribution was perhaps two rhymed couplets:

I – know them well, from Orepuke up to Auckland town.
They like you, yes, but like you more, if they can take you down.
They boast and brag, but of their deeds there's very little known,
Except, when the Great Trumpet sounds, the trumpet of their own.[17]

In at least the first two decades of the twentieth century such speculation, not always wholly serious, was repetitive. In 1901 Frank Morton, an English-born journalist with wide experience working for newspapers in Asia, Australia and New Zealand, wrote two long articles for the *New Zealand Herald* on the subject 'Is There a New Zealand Type?' He was rather cooler and probably more objective than William Lane. He was strongly of the opinion that there was such a type which rose 'superior to all merely local differences'. He thought that the Anglo-Maori wars had 'spurred imagination'. 'New Zealanders have never been sufficiently imaginative. The New Zealand type is always somewhat smug.' Despite 'spurts of pathetic radicalism' he thought New Zealanders were 'essentially conservative'. There was, he believed, 'a sort of spiritual antipathy to new thought'. He saw New Zealanders as 'self-reliant, dogged, eager'. 'The typical New Zealander believes in himself and his star, and is perfectly confident that his star at his bidding can at any moment outshine Canopus.' The New Zealander was 'rollicking and gay, but very seldom witty'. He hated outsiders. 'When English settlers arrive, he grins disparagingly at their socks and trousers.' He held that the British were effete. The New Zealander was 'more intolerant of criticism than any other man in the world'. He was keener on developing his muscles than his mind. But he also had some good qualities; he was 'hospitable and cordial and energetic'; he was shrewd and kind. But Morton concluded that the New Zealanders had not yet formed a nation: 'you cannot make a nation of typical New Zealanders at this stage. At most, you can have an interdependent association of oddly diverse cliques and factions.'[18]

A year later the *Herald* published another long article on 'The Colonial Man' by 'Colonel Bogey'. He asked why the New Zealander had not 'evolved to a higher type'. Were the climate and the New Zealand existence too easy? New Zealanders were mere raw material. They had a limited mental radius; they were 'intelligent, but uninteresting; dependable but unoriginal'. They were conceited and self-satisfied.[19]

Similar discussions continued for years – for instance, in a lively journal, *Quick March*, published by the Returned Servicemen's Assocation. The RSA president urged all members to 'think nationally'. The RSA wanted 'the spirit of young New Zealand' to fight on the political field as it had on the battlefield.[20] But the journal sometimes wondered how far that spirit extended: 'New Zealand Nationality. Does it Exist Yet?' asked 'Dionysus' in 1921.[21] His reply was that it was as yet embryonic, found only among the young people and especially among ex-servicemen.

More considered and serious attempts to assess the national character appeared in several books. The historian, poet and politician, William Pember Reeves, gave his account of 'The New Zealanders' in two books published in 1898.[22] He asked whether 'the island race' had signs of qualities distinguishing it from Britons, Australians or North Americans and found the question hard to answer. Certainly the New Zealanders were 'British' 'in a sense which the inhabitants of the British Islands scarcely are': English, Irish, Scots and Welsh intermarried far more in the colony than in Great Britain. Moreover, the proportions of these groups varied in different colonies: New Zealand had a higher proportion of Scots than Australia and a much lower proportion of Irish.

Reeves claimed, what was often said, that the New Zealanders were more heavily built than the Australians. The New South Welshmen were called 'Cornstalks', the Victorians were 'Gum suckers'. It was sometimes said that Australians in general were more lanky.[23]

Reeves believed that New Zealand had no plutocracy and virtually no paupers: the average income was among the highest in the world. There was a relative absence of class distinction; there was a 'certain republican equality of manners', as J. A. Froude had written. He thought that his fellow countrymen were of average intelligence, generally upright and honourable, rather than witty, original, artistic or poetic. They were, however, great readers and great travellers (upon which fact many writers commented), who had seen much of the world.

When New Zealanders defined themselves and their society it was not in terms of importance and power, not in terms of ruling the waves as some great nations did. Seddon and some other leaders, as we shall see, thought in terms of acquiring a Pacific Empire, but there is no evidence that this was a popular ambition. New Zealanders defined their nation in terms of their style of life. Theirs was a caring society, where the old and the widow were looked after; where there was a decent minimum standard of living, while the people at large were relatively well-off, in an egalitarian way.

Both Reeves in 1898 and O. T. J. Alpers, writing in 1902, agreed that there was no sign of a 'national twang, drawl, or peculiar intonation'.[24] Alpers, a Dane who had come to the colony as a young man, was probably echoing Reeves. In this opinion they were much mistaken: perhaps they knew few school children.

What came to be called 'the New Zealand accent' was developed among the New Zealand-born children, as was often recognised. At a meeting of the National Council of Women in Wellington in 1898, Mrs Sievwright spoke on 'Parental Responsibility'.

One thing more, do not let your child unlearn at school the mother tongue which it has lisped at your own knee. A lady just come from England, said to me the other day 'Men and women here – parents – speak like other people, but the children! Well I really can scarcely understand a word they say.' This may seem to you a very small matter, and so it is perhaps, comparatively, but well-bred mothers like their children to speak English, and the Cockney-American-Colonial jargon, sometimes supposed to be such, is catching, and Mrs Robinson does not therefore care to let her child play with Mrs Jones's children, and so misunderstandings and bitterness arise, and these last are not little things.[25]

Ten years earlier an Australian teacher had reported on the tendency of Australian and New Zealand children to sound like Cockneys, for instance, saying 'kyow' or 'caow' for 'cow'. Throughout the 1890s complaints about the pronunciation of English in schools became a repetitive feature of inspectors' reports.[26] Politicians joined in the lamentation.[27]

New Zealand speech became a frequent topic for comment in the press and in speeches. A dialect, and that 'not a defensible one, is gradually becoming fixed in the Dominion among the children and the younger adults', the president of the Secondary Schools Assistant Teachers Association proclaimed in 1910. 'Correct English', he argued, was that 'accepted as the best by people of the best education and social standing in England'.[28]

A magazine, *The Triad*, fought a campaign for the better teaching of English pronunciation in the schools.[29] It was one of the best journals of literature, art and music the Dominion had seen. Its editor was a colourful Australian, Charles Baeyertz. Among other occupations, he was an elocutionist. The appearance of a distinctively New Zealand pronunciation seems to have been regarded by adults with hostility or resignation. Few praised it. When Seddon was asked in 1899 whether he would direct teachers to pay more attention to pronunciation in order to get rid of the 'Cockney' accent, he said that he enjoyed a diversity of dialects (he had come from Lancashire) and opposed a uniformity. However, he wrongly believed that the speech complained of was learnt in the home, not in the school.[30]

New Zealand slang also proved a rich field for reflection. Writers like Alpers, foreign visitors, poets and authors of fiction alike referred to the Maori words, Australian and American slang being incorporated into the language. Usually this side of New Zealand speech was welcomed. The best known of these comments is G. P. Williams's 'An Old Chum on the New Zealand Scenery':

> *Then there's what we call a* gully, *which of course we take to mean*
> *Just a small and narrow valley, in which bush is sometimes seen;*
> *You perchance, were you a new chum, might describe this as a dell,*
> Bushy gully *suits me better, serves my purpose just as well:*
> Bush, *too, means the native forest; you will never, I'm afraid,*
> *Hear a self-respecting bushman call a bush a leafy glade.*
> *Nor a copse, nor shady bower; ev'ry kind of native shrub*
> *Growing rank in wild profusion, he denominates as* scrub .... [31]

But there are numerous other examples. In 'The Maid's Story' by Marie Bullock, some of the bush-whackers, like 'Scobie-eye' and 'Flash Dick' work hard all the year for the 'big burst' (of boozing). A lady says that such terms will shock a young English girl, Miss Carlyon. 'Well, we are a bit slangy here', said Miss Dunmore, 'and no mistake, but Miss Carlyon'll get used to that in time, if she means to settle down in the colony.'[32]

It was recognised that most of the slang was imported; and that the words themselves were often not modern corruptions, but survivals of older forms of English dialects.[33] But there was much speculation on the origins of the 'colonial twang'. The president of the Farmers' Union, Sir James Wilson, proclaimed at the Dominion Conference in 1910 that the reasons for the children's nasal twang were 'that there was something wrong with their tonsils, or something else which required attention: adenoids were often the cause.'[34] *The Triad* believed that the poor English was a result of 'this abomination' of having the children read lessons in unison.[35] Another view, in which there was probably a great deal of truth, was that 'many New Zealanders think it affectation to speak good English.' The lady who said this, in 1931, was a representative of the British Drama League, and she attributed the characteristics of New Zealand speech to extreme isolation.[36]

It is clear that by about 1900 a recognisable dialect had been adopted by the native-born, and by schoolchildren, wherever born. It did not seem to matter where their parents had been born: 'the influence of parentage is very slight', an inspector wrote.[37] The protest against this change persisted up into the 1930s. In 1925 the Minister for Education, Sir James Parr, announced that vigilance was necessary to check 'mischievous tendencies towards the deterioration of our English speech'. A pamphlet on phonetics and voice production was prepared and published by the government that year.[38]

In the discussions about the national type, on one topic there was unanimity: it was to be white. How the Maoris would fit into the national scheme was a complex problem which is reserved for separate discussion. Ignoring the Maoris, it was assumed that New Zealanders would be of European, mainly British, descent, though with an admixture of Maori 'blood', that is, genes.

There was, from time to time, protest against almost every group of immigrants, including new British immigrants. Strong objection was made to the introduction of German and Scandinavian immigrants under Vogel's public works scheme. The latter were alleged to be drunken and unintelligent. When one newspaper suggested that the racial stock would be improved by the acquisition of 'Vikings', another newspaper said it was preaching 'a doctrine of miscegenation'.[39]

During the First World War, as in other Allied countries, there was strong anti-German feeling, and some persecution of Germans. This turned against the Dalmatian immigrants, mainly in North Auckland. They were known as 'Austrians' and some of them were treated as enemy aliens. However, two Commissioners appointed to look into the question reported that the Dalmatians were anti-Austrian and had burned the imperial Austro-Hungarian flag. The flag they flew was South Slav or Serbian.[40]

Discussion in the newspapers and in Parliament about the best way to build up a new nation referred to American experience as demonstrating the need for 'a reasonable admixture' of continental Europeans. But it was claimed too that the vital element in the growth of the USA was the quality of the early British settlers.[41]

The late nineteenth and early twentieth centuries was the period of the so-called 'Yellow Peril'. Sometimes the threat was thought to come from the Japanese and there was much criticism, in Australia and New Zealand, of the Anglo-Japanese Treaty of 1902. Seddon hinted darkly that it was 'a cloud on the horizon'. It was essential to guard 'the purity of race'.[42]

Most of the racial protest, however, was directed at the Chinese, of whom there were 3700 (including 24 women) in the colony in 1896. Their numbers had declined to 3000 by 1921. Despite such small numbers, there was a constant fear of 'celestial hordes' invading the country.

The Chinese were denounced for working for low wages, and hence threatening the standard of living of the workers. It was argued that they would drag the white workers down to their level. They were accused of debasing white women, seducing children, introducing drugs. They were thought immoral, dishonest and dangerous. They were regarded as unassimilable: they would never become true settlers. All settlers had to become, 'as early as possible, in feeling and in fact, "New Zealanders"'.[43] It was held that the British settlers would 'surely degenerate' if there were further Chinese immigration.

The most widespread New Zealand ideal in the late nineteenth and early twentieth century was that 'small men' should have access to the land – an ideal promoted by the Liberal and Reform parties alike. A real settler was thought of as a yeoman, a sturdy small farmer. The strongest political attack was on the owners of great estates, who employed armies of casual, seasonal labour. The rural ideal explains, in part, the hostility to Asian labour, for it was incompatible with a society with a pool of cheap labour. The Chinese were seen as potentially disturbing the New Zealand dream, which was originally British.

The stereotype of the Chinese was in substance imported from California and Australia, where there was similarly virulent hostility to the Chinese. Almost certainly it was brought by diggers during the great gold-rushes. It need scarcely be emphasised how irrational this

'Will It Come To This?'

A cartoon by Ellis in the *Free Lance* in 1920.

was. If the Chinese were an inferior race, why would they win? Why should they reduce the European's standard of living rather than improve their own? And how could a 'horde' reach New Zealand? Nevertheless, the fear was real.

The trade unions demanded that Chinese immigration should be prohibited. From 1881 onwards a series of anti-Chinese immigration Acts were passed, putting a poll tax on each Chinese who arrived. An Anti-Chinese League was formed in 1895. Later it became the Anti-Asiatic League, opposing the immigration of Indians (who were called 'Assyrians') as well as Chinese. They wanted the Chinese to be deported.[44]

There was a further outburst of anti-Asian agitation after the First World War. John A. Lee's first political pamphlet showed evil-looking Asian shop-keepers looking out at unemployed ex-servicemen. The RSA journal, *Quick March*, was full of protests about the immigration of Chinese and Hindus. It was urged that they should be deported. If they stayed, they should be forbidden to buy land. In Timaru there was an assault on Chinese fruiterers and their shops. In Pukekohe there was a virulent, racist White New Zealand League in the 1920s.[45]

Racism is now generally regarded as evil, but there is no point in deploring the past. Some writers on national histories place racism near the centre of their focus,[46] but that will not be done in this account. Xenophobia, or racism, did not distinguish the white Australians, New Zealanders or Americans from other people. Similar views of foreigners were to be found in China, Japan and probably in most other parts of the world. Moreover, in the nineteenth century few people felt that they should not express their racist opinions.

Chapter Seven

'HOME' AND 'HOMIES': the Empire

Pakeha New Zealanders had to decide who they were, but also who they were not. That meant considering their relationships to the British and the Australians. There was endless discussion about those two issues especially in the late nineteenth and early twentieth centuries.

It is impossible in a chapter to examine all of the complexities and subtleties of New Zealand feelings and opinions about the Motherland, the Empire, or the British Commonwealth of Nations. It must be said that those relationships were debated at least as obsessively as the idea of a new nation. The same assertion may confidently be made of Canada or Australia, despite the republican or separatist views of the 'Canada First' movement and the Sydney *Bulletin*. The debate on the relationship of New Zealanders to the British continued longer than that about the Australians. The latter, however is more likely to be resumed in the future.

Many settlers in New Zealand remained strongly attached to their birth-place. Their children, too, came to refer to Great Britain as 'Home'. The expression 'He's going home' came to mean a person leaving the land of his birth and sailing for the ancestral homeland.

For many New Zealanders 'Home' became a passion. The writer, Alan Mulgan, was born in New Zealand, of Ulster stock, in 1881. He wrote that so far as he knew he had no English blood in him, yet he took no interest in Ireland. Books had determined his sympathies. Granchester and Sussex Downs, Winchester and Westminster, had captured his imagination. He wrote that:

> *The trend of all this literature, read desultorily and with no purpose, was to fix my thoughts ever on England. Nor do I suggest for a moment that my experience was unique or even exceptional. Perhaps more powerful still was the influence of poetry. That anyone can love English poetry without loving England, I cannot conceive, for if the soul of England is anywhere it is in her poetry ....*

His book was entitled *Home. A New Zealander's Adventure.* (London, 1927). Two years later a second edition bore the sub-title, *A Colonial's Adventure.* Mulgan's verse, too, as in *The English of the Line*, celebrated his longing to find, 'on England's very ground', 'in bay and lane and field the joy my fathers found'.[1]

HOME

The cover of Alan Mulgan's *Home: A Colonial's Adventure* from the 1934 edition published in London by Longmans, Green and Co.

"HOME" is England—the Old Country as seen in the Summer by a visitor from one of the Dominions. He saw London, Devon, Oxford, Cambridge, the Wye Valley, Manchester, etc.

READ THIS BOOK
AND FOLLOW IN HIS FOOTSTEPS

Mulgan was a sentimentalist, but tougher writers have supported his testimony. E. H. McCormick wrote that 'No New Zealander who grew up in the years centred in the First World War would challenge the essential accuracy of his statement [about the effects of reading English literature] . . . . Education, reading, prevailing sentiment, economic interest – all turned the New Zealand writer's thoughts and ambitions towards England; and, given the opportunity, it was to England she or he migrated.'[2]

Sometimes people grew weary of the comparisons made or implied between the colony and England. In 1904 the young Ernest Currie, soon to be an anthologist, referred to the old world in a letter to a friend, the poet Mary Colborne-Veel, and she replied, '"We are happy, our land is beautiful; we like it better than all the lands we are always reading about!" Sing me a song, please without comparisons; a song of sheer joy that protests not – because it simply can't admit the thought of any other place – there would be the true national song.'[3]

Despite such protests, there can be little doubt that New Zealanders retained their attachment to Great Britain longer, for instance, than Australians. In 1866, 630 000 Victorians sent 1 100 000 letters to the United Kingdom; 430 000 New South Welshmen sent 550 000 letters; 220 000 New Zealanders sent 1 000 000.[4]

For this stronger attachment several reasons may be suggested. New Zealand had been settled more recently: the European inhabitants were mostly immigrants. New Zealand had a much lower proportion of Irish than Australia – about 13 per cent as compared with 25 per cent. Consequently there was less anti-English feeling. Moreover, it may be presumed that the convicts and their descendants were no more likely to idealise England than were the Irish.

There was much nonsense talked about the Britishness of New Zealand. In 1919 a cabinet minister published a book, *New Zealand Today*, in which he asserted that the population was 98.12 per cent British.[5] This remarkable figure was achieved by counting all people from Empire countries and all New Zealand-born people as 'British' irrespective of their ancestry. He went on to speak of the New Zealanders' 'intense patriotism to the Empire'.

Much of the talk about the pioneers being of 'selected stock', 'the best British' and so on implicitly referred to Australia. The New Zealanders frequently emphasised that they were not descended from convict stock. Sometimes there was a hint of superiority, but sometimes the assertion was a psychological booster to sustain the New Zealander against Australian competition.

What was unequivocal was the New Zealanders' loyalty to the Crown. Like large numbers of Canadians and Australians, the New Zealand-born retained a strong attachment to the royal family, an emotion not at all incompatible with feeling themselves to be New Zealanders. On the occasions of royal visits New Zealanders expressed a powerful sense of loyalty and affection. When the Duke and Duchess of Cornwall and York, the future King George V and Queen Mary, toured New Zealand in 1901, there were endless scenes of enthusiasm, Maori as well as Pakeha. The *New Zealand Illustrated Magazine* welcomed the event with a fervent mixture of imperialism and local pride: pride in being part of a great Empire and 'heart-felt pride' in the achievements of the pioneers and their descendants.[6]

In books on British imperial history New Zealand has often been portrayed as clinging to the skirts of the mother country, while Canadians and Australians sought to grow up, to strengthen and extend

Coronation Day, 1901, outside the new Gisborne Post Office. *Gisborne Museum*

Proclamation of King George V, Stratford, 1910. *McAllister Collection, Turnbull*

their independence. Many imperialist statements by New Zealand politicians can be cited to support this view. The most striking evidence, often quoted, was that one New Zealand politician after another spoke up in favour of imperial federation. That was seen by its opponents as a new super-imperialism. When Seddon supported Joseph Chamberlain's proposal for 'a great council of the Empire to which the Colonies would send representative plenipotentiaries – not mere delegates', C. C. Kingston of South Australia said that there was no demand at all in Australia for 'the creation of fresh political bonds'.[7]

It was possible to view imperial federation in such a light. One of the earliest advocates of imperial federation was Julius Vogel, who was arguing, in the mid-1860s, that colonies should have no right to secede from the Empire; Britain should establish the most powerful federation ever known. He was aware of the strong forces opposing that possibility but regarded imperial federation as a way of containing colonial nationalism within an imperial framework. Twenty-five years later his aim had not changed but he doubted whether federation was possible, the movement towards nationalism seemed too strong.[8]

However, most New Zealand (and many other) supporters of imperial federation saw it not as a way of limiting colonial autonomy and nationalism but as a consequence of colonial nationalism. As long ago as 1854 Thomas Cholmondley had foreseen that the British Empire would become a 'vast federation of States governed by one sovereign'; the 'New Zealand nation' would be one member.[9] This vision was not far removed from that of the Canadian, Wilfred Laurier, late in the century. He called the self-governing colonies 'a galaxy of free nations', a remark then regarded as expressing a strong colonial nationalism: however, they were, after all, still British.

Cholmondley's views were often repeated. For instance, in 1905 an editorial in the *New Zealand Herald* said that the colonies had become 'populous and self-governing States that promise ere long to attain to the proportions of nations'. What was now needed was 'imperial consolidation' such as that proposed by Chamberlain.[10]

Imperial federation, which was repeatedly discussed in Great Britain and the self-governing colonies from mid-nineteenth century until about the First World War, was a term with no single meaning. There were numerous federal schemes. For instance, colonial representatives could have been elected to the imperial parliament. Generally it was thought that Great Britain and the settlement colonies would remain self-governing and that some sort of imperial council representing them all would be set up in London to control 'imperial' subjects such as foreign policy, defence, perhaps trade policy. W. P. Reeves took part in formulating one such proposal.[11] Sometimes it was urged that local parliaments should be set up in the United Kingdom, so that Ireland, Scotland and perhaps Wales would have Home Rule, rather as the self-governing colonies did. The imperial parliament would be in London.[12]

The support given by New Zealand politicians to these plans was so strong as to seem very convincing evidence about New Zealand public opinion. Every premier of the colony from 1883 to 1912 may be quoted in favour of imperial federation. At the Colonial Conferences of 1897–1907 and at the first Imperial Conference in 1911, the most distant colony was the only one consistently to advocate closer union. One of the most persistent and enthusiastic imperialists was Joseph Ward. In 1906, in Cambridge, England, he spoke about the fact that the creation of an Imperial Council was on the agenda for the Imperial Conference in 1907. He thought that a council should, at least, advise the British government on imperial concerns.[13] At the conference, the Australian Prime Minister Alfred Deakin, supported by Ward, took the lead in pressing for the council, but without success. The Canadians objected to the term 'council' because it suggested a more formal body than 'conference', and this might come to be seen as encroachment on colonial autonomy.

The best-known New Zealand effort to secure a federation was Ward's speech at the 1911 Imperial Conference. Before the Conference the New Zealand Government forwarded to London a resolution once more favouring an advisory imperial council. The *Round Table* correspondent remarked that this resolution suggested 'aspirations on the part of the Government and people of New Zealand for which there is not the slightest foundation in fact'. There was, the *Round Table* alleged, 'a conspiracy of silence' on this subject. Ward had made no attempt to educate public or parliament – indeed, he excused himself by saying that too much prior publicity might embarrass the other premiers at the forthcoming Conference. Consequently in New Zealand his proposals were treated with 'utter indifference'. The press, however, was rather more sympathetic. In his speeches at a series of farewell dinners, Ward uttered vague sentiments of loyalty and unity and was rewarded with editorial praise for avoiding any 'cut and dried schemes of Imperial consolidation'. As soon as he reached Sydney, however, he made a speech to the New Zealand Association there in which he urged that Great Britain could not maintain the two-power naval standard without the aid of the Empire and advocated the creation of 'an Imperial Council of Defence or an Empire Parliament of Defence'. He thought that the time might not be ripe, but that ultimately there must be a Parliament elected on a population basis. This time his press was less favourable. The *New Zealand Times* in Wellington thought such a parliament 'inconceivable'; the Christchurch *Press* agreed; and in Auckland the *New Zealand Herald* ignored his proposals except for reporting his speech.

Ward had told the 1907 Conference that New Zealand public opinion would not tolerate any executive or legislative function in the proposed Imperial Council. Now he had jumped into the extreme federal camp.

There was at this time in England and elsewhere in the Empire a new organisation, the Round Table, pressing the cause of federation. The Round Table groups were discussing a memorandum on the subject. About the time he sailed for Sydney a copy of this memorandum was given to Ward, probably by Sir John Findlay, the Minister of Justice and Attorney-General. Some of Ward's proposals clearly derived from the memorandum.[14]

At the Imperial Conference Ward delivered a very long, rambling and incoherent speech in the course of which he referred to an imperial assembly. He referred to it variously as an advisory 'Imperial Council of State', an 'Imperial Parliament of Defence', a 'Council of State or Parliament', an 'Imperial Council of Defence', and an 'Imperial House of Representatives.' This was the last occasion on which imperial federation was discussed at an Imperial Conference.

After the Conference, Findlay wrote a book, *The Imperial Conference of 1911 from Within* (London, 1912), which expressed in a more articulate fashion than had the Prime Minister some New Zealand opinions. The British Prime Minister, H. H. Asquith, had spoken of the autonomy of the Dominions as 'absolute, unfettered and complete'. An Australian editor had announced, 'Colonialism is dead'. Findlay regarded such assertions as nonsense. He would not join them 'to gloss in glowing rhetorical periods' the hard facts of constitutional law of the Empire. 'Free nations', he thought, was merely a figure of speech, 'voluntary association' a polite term for bondage. An imperial statute could override any inconsistent colonial law, though the self-governing colonies had no voice in the Government which decided whether this imperial veto should apply. In the case of New Zealand, eighteen bills had been reserved by the Governor for royal assent since 1885 – one as recently as 1910 – and several had not been sanctioned. The British Parliament had sovereign power over the Dominion and could at will destroy its rights of self-government so that, Findlay felt, 'we are masters in our own household only so long as our master permits.'[15]

There is no doubt that Findlay's analysis of imperial bonds was substantially correct. Few people in the Dominions understood the position so clearly. He did not, however, foresee the future as clearly as the Canadian or Australian leaders, a future of independence and free association, not federation.

Almost all the New Zealand politicians who argued in favour of federation saw it as a means of extending New Zealand's powers, not of restricting them. A Dominion was simply a colony writ large; it had no say in foreign policy; it had no international existence. The New Zealand leaders hoped that, through some sort of imperial council, they would be able to influence British policy, notably in the Pacific.

New Zealand imperialism was not, as some writers have supposed, evidence of an absence of nationalism. Seddon was in some ways the first national political leader. Reeves and Ward entered Parliament in 1887 as members of the 'Young New Zealand party'. Findlay was, like Reeves, New Zealand-born. Ward was an Australian who crossed the Tasman as a small child. Imperialism was an expression of an emergent nationalism. A similar conclusion has been reached about Canada.[16]

There was a surprising aspect of New Zealand support for imperial federation. In New Zealand alone of the self-governing colonies there was no imperial federation movement, a fact which reflects negatively upon the idea that New Zealanders were extremely imperialistic. The Imperial Federation League was very active in Canada, eastern Australia and South Africa. In New Zealand a branch was started in Christchurch. After the inaugural meeting it met only once, to receive a letter from the Canadian branch. Two historians R. F. Irvine and O. T. J. Alpers, said that the people, while imperialist to a man, cared nothing for federation in the political sense.[17]

Perhaps as a consequence of public indifference, the political leaders very rarely referred to federation in their New Zealand speeches. The subject was not for local consumption. On imperial occasions abroad, they had to have something to say. In this respect, the Colonial and Imperial Conferences inspired the imperialist sentiments expressed by politicians. The fact that they made no effort to rouse support among New Zealand voters is a fitting comment on the depth of their feeling about federation. Probably they knew that it was not politically feasible. Nowhere in the Empire did it become an important electoral issue.

In practice the Empire was to evolve, not towards federation, but

'The Evolution of a New Zealander', *NZ Artists' Annual*, Dec. 1926.

independence for the Dominions and free association with the United Kingdom. To this process New Zealand contributed very little. Canada and South Africa took the lead in ensuring that the Dominions were not subordinate; Australia and New Zealand lagged behind.

New Zealand leaders deplored the Balfour Report of 1926 which defined 'dominion status', declaring Great Britain and the Dominions equal in status not subordinate to one another either in domestic or external affairs, though united by a common allegiance to the Crown and freely associated as members of the British Commonwealth of Nations. One minister felt that there was 'a certain degree of danger in searching minutely into the advantages and disadvantages of the existing commonwealth association'. In 1931 the Government shrank from contact with the Statute of Westminster, which removed the last vestiges of inequality in the status of the Dominions.

The governments of the 1920s thought that New Zealand already had enough independence. Although there were differences with British Governments (for instance, with Ramsay MacDonald over fortifying the Singapore naval base) in general the New Zealand Government acquiesced in British foreign policy. New Zealand already had the power to follow independent policies. It could make treaties, appoint diplomatic representatives, express its own views in the League of Nations. But it did not do so. Only in the years 1936–39 was the first Labour Government to seize with enthusiasm the opportunities for independent initiatives.

In New Zealand the achievement of political independence was not an emotional issue. Self-government had been progressively gained in the 1850s and later in the nineteenth century. The British had never sought to encroach on the colony's powers. In this respect the New Zealanders' experience was very different from the Americans'.

The remaining restrictions upon dominion autonomy were not such as to arouse a clarion call for national independence. Those restrictions were defined in the Balfour Report and removed by declaration and by the Statute of Westminster. Extra-territoriality, the power (no longer used) of disallowance, the consequences of the Colonial Laws Validity Act of 1865 – these and other legal matters meant nothing to the public. They were of academic interest. In 1944 J. C. Beaglehole edited a group of lectures by historians, a lawyer and a political scientist, *New Zealand & the Statute of Westminster*, urging that New Zealand should adopt the Statute. In 1947 New Zealand did pass the Statute and thus became fully independent in the same year as India. It ceased to use the title 'Dominion' and became plain 'New Zealand'.

At the end of the nineteenth century the people were probably willing to regard themselves, as John Ballance said, as 'New Zealanders and Britons'.[18] But he was British-born. It certainly was not true that the native-born regarded themselves as British in the sense of being English or Scottish or Irish. In the late nineteenth century the 'new chum' was

'Taking a Rise Out of a New Chum'. *Cocky:* 'What would you be scared of, mate? She's as quiet as a lamb!' *Tommy:* 'Good on you, Dad! My eyes, can't he scoot!' *NZ Illustrated Magazine*, Oct. 1904.

regarded with good-natured contempt by the old settler or colonial. He was criticised for having too much 'side'.[19] During the 1920s large numbers of British immigrants, averaging from 8000 to 15 000 a year, came to New Zealand under an Empire Settlement Act or on their own initiative. New Zealanders no longer needed to travel to meet English people. There was now a large English-born minority alongside a New Zealand-born population. Many of the immigrants spoke in northern English dialects very different from local speech. There was, during the 1920s and 1930s, a good deal of resentment expressed towards the immigrants, who were generally known as 'Homies', that is, as having come from 'Home'. It was felt that, like the post-war Chinese and Indian immigrants, they were getting jobs while many ex-servicemen were unemployed. In the journal '*N.Z.*' some verses entitled 'The Homie' conceded that 'Homies' had been the pioneers, but concluded:

Yet you can hear it far and near
Asked, over foaming pots of beer;
Whythehelldoeshecomeouthere,
The Homie?

This was followed up a month later:

THE HOMIE *(another version)*

Who is it comes from overseas,
In numbers growing by degrees
And with a too apparent ease?
The Homie

Who thinks that our employers ought
To find him work of any sort,
No matter if our men go short?
The Homie

Who moans and always has a grouse,
But never seems to have the nouse
To know five bob won't rent a house?
The Homie . . . . [20]

There was frequent criticism of the custom of recruiting staff in Great Britain, and over-looking 'local talent'. At an Auckland Grammar School reunion in 1912 the headmaster, J. W. Tibbs, deplored the practice of importing English teachers to fill higher educational positions.[21] It was held that the custom of looking abroad when filling important positions was one reason for New Zealanders leaving the country.[22] In 1898 at a meeting of the Wellington New Zealand Natives Association there was complaint that the Petone Borough Council was advertising a position outside the colony. Men just as competent as outsiders could be found within the colony: 'New Zealand for the New Zealanders' was the speaker's theme. As late as 1947 the Lecturers Association at the Auckland University College protested that an Englishman appointed to a chair did not seem better qualified than two local applicants.[23]

However, Homies were sometimes said to be unemployed because of prejudice against them. In a short story by Alice Kenny, 'A Friend . . . a "Home" Girl on her Last Shilling', an English girl is sitting disconsolate on a park seat. She had lost her job, her money and her confidence, 'but she had not yet lost her North Country accent and her unmistakable "Homie" look . . . .' When she had applied for a job she was asked, 'You're a "Homie", aren't you?' A young New Zealand couple make fun of her. The New Zealand girl says: 'I want to sketch this priceless girl. A most perfect type of "Homie." Do look at her –

'A "Home" Girl on her Last Shilling', 'N.Z.', 1 Aug. 1925. *Auckland Public Library*

clumsy, florid, and cocksure – and her clothes!' They agree that 'A certain thickness, you note, is characteristic', especially of the ankles, face and figure. The girl comes and speaks to them and they realise they have been blind and heartless.[24]

The word 'Homie' was the New Zealand equivalent of the Australian name 'Pom' or 'Pommy'. It was pejorative, but not more so than the word 'colonial' in England. The shrewd French observer, André Siegfried, wrote:

> *One must hear the Englishman speak with his air of condescending patronage of the colonial, to realise that all the imperialistic ideas in the world will not prevent the citizen of the mother country from regarding the other citizens of the Empire as, in spite of everything, a slightly inferior class: unintellectual, think the cultured; rather rough, thinks the snob. One must hear the colonial speak in his turn of the 'old country,' to realise that with his filial affection, real and touching as it is, is mingled a contemptuous pity for those conservative and prejudiced Europeans, who are afraid of their own shadows when there is any question, as some philosopher has said, 'of stirring something in the great reservoirs of the future.'*[25]

Criticism of the British was far more common in New Zealand than one is led to expect by the historical and other literature of the time. It could even appear in a children's story. A fantail and a tui are talking to a fairy. The fantail asks the tui what she is saying. 'I think she is English,' answered the tui gravely. 'At all events she talks very fast and very badly; I cannot understand what she says.' 'She looks English,' said the fantail. 'She is shy and stupid, not like the New Zealanders at all.'[26]

Sometimes British immigrants were called 'foreigners'. The *New Zealand Graphic* published a joke in which a native-born boy, young O'Donovan, says to his father, 'Don't yer go deceiving yerself by thinking I'm a cryin' 'cause yer licked me, for I ain't. I'm all upset at being struck by a furriner, an' not bein' able to strike back!'[27]

Sometimes the British hit back at their critics. Correspondents wrote in the English *Nursing Mirror* warning nurses not to go to New Zealand, where 'English folk were not liked'. 'Ship's Surgeon' alleged that 'the local feeling is New Zealand for the New Zealanders, first, last, and all the time.' An 'old "Barts" man' wrote to the New Zealand nurses' journal, *Kai Tiaki*, denying such allegations and saying that he had never felt handicapped because he was not a native-born New Zealander.[28]

Criticism of the British can be found from time to time after the settlers arrived, but it seems to have become much more common after the First World War. New Zealanders still had feelings of loyalty to the Crown; many felt a loyalty to the British Empire and later British Commonwealth. They were still British subjects as well as citizens of New Zealand. However, there is no doubt that, by the 1920s most New Zealanders were very clear that they were New Zealanders and not English, Irish or Scots.

It would be difficult to prove but it does seem that a sentimental attitude towards 'Home' was most likely to be found among the better educated and most widely read, among people like Alan Mulgan. Such people would almost certainly not have talked about 'Homies', a term which was definitely popular, if not working class. This class distinction helps to explain how such different attitudes could coexist in one community.

What was occurring seems very clear. A new nationalism was rising strongly among the New Zealand-born. This sentiment was, in the long run, bound to predominate. But earlier British and imperial attitudes persisted and, indeed, in some ways were being reinforced. In the nineteenth century trade with the Australian colonies had been important to the colony. With the development of refrigerated shipping in the later nineteenth century, New Zealand began to export ever-increasing quantities of protein to Great Britain. The Australian market became of little significance. By the 1930s over 80 per cent of New Zealand exports went to Great Britain.

Almost all of the country's overseas loans came from Great Britain. The Pakeha culture derived from Great Britain. Most of the immigrants still came from the same place. In other words, the direction of trade and migration strengthened the imperial bonds. Politicians could rarely be heard criticising the Empire or the British.

The position of New Zealanders resembled that of Canadians rather than that of Australians or Americans. The two latter people had to decide, 'are we British?'. They had to break away from Europe. But, in asking that question, Canadians were acutely aware of their aggressive American neighbour. Similarly New Zealanders faced two ways, towards England and across the Tasman. In Canada and New Zealand being British was a counter weight against a more powerful neighbour. New Zealand's neighbour, however, was less dominant than Canada's.

Chapter Eight

THE 'AUSSIES': Australian Federation

The term 'Australasia' was invented in the eighteenth century by a Frenchman, Charles de Brosses, for the land *au sud de l'Asie*, including New Guinea. In its narrower sense, as applied to the seven British colonies in Australia and New Zealand, it had a very real meaning in the nineteenth century. Many authors of books with such titles as *A Vacation Tour at the Antipodes* by B. A. Heywood (London, 1863) remarked on the strong family resemblances between the colonies there. Almost every visitor was struck by the Englishness of the towns: Melbourne was thought to resemble Wimbledon, Auckland was likened to an English seaside place – the author failed to notice the mangrove swamps.

Antipodean drinking habits were a frequent cause for comment. Colonial men did not, it was alleged, greet one another with 'How do you do?' but 'What do you drink?' It was considered that the colonists were noted for 'blowing', that is, boasting. In the 1880s New Zealanders claimed to have the biggest water-wheel, the biggest trout, the biggest wooden building and the highest wooden bridge in the world.

Travellers did of course notice differences – especially in the race relations. C. W. Dilke wrote that 'nothing would persuade the rougher class of Queensland settlers that the "black-fellow" and his "jin" were human.' By contrast, in New Zealand the settlers never 'affect to think [the Maoris] less than human'. But travellers did not regard Australia and New Zealand as distinct. They often thought that Tasmania was as different from the continent as was New Zealand.[1]

Despite the distances between them, the seven colonies formed a community in many different ways. There was a constant exchange of population. In 1891 23 800 New Zealanders were living in Australia; in the same year there were 16 000 Australians in New Zealand, a number rising rapidly to 21 600 in 1896. Many British people also moved from one side of the Tasman to the other, and no doubt many people crossed that sea more than once.

Some of the early trade unions had Australian connections.[2] They included the unions of miners, shearers, seamen, wharf labourers and the Maritime Council of 1889–90. The churches had similar connections. The Australasian Wesleyan Methodist Church had Australasian conferences from 1875 until 1913, when the New Zealanders went their separate way.

In addition to Australasian associations of citizens there was also a good deal of cooperation, or efforts at cooperation, between governments. In the years 1865–83 there were a number of Australasian intercolonial conferences, in which New Zealand fully participated, to endeavour to organise ocean mail services and cable services. They also negotiated over inter-colonial tariffs and tariff preferences, and other very important matters.[3]

In the 1880s the question of Australasian federation arose. At a meeting in Sydney in 1883 it was decided to set up a Federal Council to deal with common problems and to 'accustom the public mind to federal ideas' as a step towards federation. Upon returning home, both the New Zealand delegates, Harry Atkinson and Sir Frederick Whitaker, spoke in favour of New Zealand becoming a member, though Atkinson admitted that the idea was not received with much favour. The House of Representatives did not support New Zealand joining. New South Wales also stayed out.

In 1890 there was another conference to discuss federation in Melbourne, and in 1891 in Sydney. New Zealand was represented at the first by Sir John Hall and W. R. Russell; Russell, Atkinson and Grey were the delegates in 1891. Once again there was little support in New Zealand for federation with Australia. A former cabinet minister, John Bryce, said that there was 'universal astonishment' when he referred to federation in a speech: 'It is not a subject that is much spoken of in the colony or in which much interest is taken and I believe that that arises from the fact that it is instinctively felt that we should be making a very great mistake if we abandoned our independence and joined in federation with colonies so very distant from our own.'[4]

In 1890 nineteen MHRs (out of seventy-two) had opposed sending any New Zealand delegates at all. A year later, the Liberal minister, W. P. Reeves, said that the Government decided to 'cease to play with the question' of federation. The Premier, John Ballance, said that 'We might supply Australia with a few oats, but we should lose our freedom.' This was a reference to the anticipated Australian tariff, which might exclude New Zealand produce. After 1891 New Zealand was not represented at the federal conferences. This was in some respects a decisive absence, since during a crucial period the issue dropped out of sight, but most New Zealanders had in fact already made up their minds. The general feeling was that 'our destiny lies apart'.[5]

There is no doubt that this opinion was common. The views of journalists and politicians were overwhelmingly against federation. So was general public opinion, as expressed in the submissions of 186 citizens and organisations to a Royal Commission on the question in 1901.

In the 1880s the issue was widely discussed, in pamphlets as well as in editorials. J. M. Dargaville, MHR, published a very hostile pamphlet in which he urged New Zealanders, who had governed themselves for nearly thirty years, not to become 'subject to the people of Australia and Tasmania'.[6] A year later, in 1885, J. C. Crawford published a pamphlet, *Australasian Federation: Federation of the Empire and Colonial Defence*.[7] Dr A. K. Newman, another politician, published an article in 1891 arguing that if New Zealand did not join it would soon be faced with a hostile federal tariff.[8] In 1899 a school teacher, H. J. del Monte Mahon, published an article in favour of federating. In the same year G. M. Newton wrote an article on the Australian federal constitution, a subject about which most New Zealanders knew almost nothing, except that the Maoris would probably lose the vote which Maori men had possessed since 1867.[9] This was a feature of federation much criticised.

Federation was canvassed in the press, especially in 1883–85, in 1890–91 and in 1899. Only a single newspaper, the *Evening Post* in the late 1890s, campaigned for federation. Most of the newspapers in the main towns were indifferent or hostile. There was no public campaign for federation until the last moment. There was no organisation fighting for federation. Some of the Australian leaders realised this.

In 1889 the New Zealand and South Seas Exhibition was held in Dunedin. The large exhibits of pioneering life, Maori culture, kauri gum, local minerals, agriculture and fishing were, it was claimed, better displayed than those at the Melbourne Exhibition of 1888.[10] The Exhibition was, in itself, an assertion of national pride – a year before the Jubilee of the colony. Several Australian leaders, guests at the Exhibition, took the opportunity to preach the evangel of Australasian federation. One of them was Alfred Deakin, soon to be the Australian Prime Minister, who urged the people of Dunedin to 'carry a fiery cross throughout this land' until New Zealand took its proper place in the Federal Council.[11] They did not take up the challenge.

In various parliamentary debates speakers referred to federation. The majority spoke in opposition. Of the political leaders, Atkinson and Whitaker (in 1883) spoke in favour of federation. Grey and Stout at times sounded favourable. J. G. Ward, who was to become prominent during the 1890s, was in favour. He was born in Victoria and lived in Southland, a district whose farmers exported oats to Australia. Vogel, Ballance, William Montgomery, W. R. Russell, James Macandrew, William Rolleston and Reeves were all opposed. Seddon, in 1900, pretended to be unwilling to give his opinion, but his speech in the House in 1899 was critical of the idea of federating.[12]

Speakers in the General Assembly who referred to Federation

	Pro	*Anti*	*Non-committal*
1884	3	11	6
1885	1	4	1
1890	7	26	3
1899		1	1
1900*	1	1	
	12	43	11

*In this debate only two speakers, Herries and Wilkes, pronounced on the main issue of federation.

The most vigorous agitation in favour of joining Australia occurred in 1899. There is no doubt that the Liberal Government was surprised. Reeves said there was more support than he had thought possible.[13]

The federal movement in New Zealand was sparked off by the decision of the Australian colonies to federate. The Australian constitution, drawn up at several Conventions from which New Zealand was absent, had to be submitted in referenda to the voters in each colony. In 1898 the constitution was approved in several colonies, but rejected in New South Wales. In June 1899 the New South Welshmen voted in favour of federation. It was now certain that the Australian colonies would federate. The *New Zealand Herald* said that now New Zealand would have to decide whether to join. It published reports and letters every few days on the topic. On 24 June a meeting of gentlemen resolved that New Zealand should join Australia. The leading activist was J. Kennedy Brown, a manufacturer's representative about whom almost nothing else is known except that he was an ebullient nonentity; at the public meeting on 12 July at which an Australasian Federation League was formed, he shouted out 'This is slavery!' and other nonsense, when not getting his way at one point.[14] A hundred and fifty people attended this meeting. The 'Provisional Council' and main speakers at these meetings were lawyers, a timber merchant, other merchants (including some of the largest, one of them the President of the Chamber of Commerce), a doctor, a chemist and other city men. Several of them were Australians by birth or residence.

The previous president of the Chamber of Commerce and some other citizens opposed the League, both at meetings and in letters to the press. The League resolved to educate the public. Some meetings were held in the suburbs and one or two branches formed. A pamphlet was published and circulated to municipal and other local body organisations.

The only Federation League was in Auckland. In Wellington the *Evening Post* campaigned in favour of federation for a few months, and said it had long tried to arouse public interest in federation: 'New Zealand's sleep has been unduly prolonged.'[15] Another Wellington paper, the *New Zealand Times*, conducted an amateurish newspaper poll of politicians' opinions. Its reporters interviewed most of the Members of the House of Representatives. From late August to mid-September their opinions were reported every day or two. According to a leading article, some seventy members were interviewed. Some twenty Members, including Seddon and one or two ministers, as well as the four Maoris, declined to comment. Of those who did, thirty favoured joining Australia, twenty were opposed. The newspaper had expected the majority to be hostile 'to a proposal so revolutionary and so far-reaching in its ultimate consequences'.[16]

This 'poll' was widely reported in Australia and New Zealand. It led Australians, notably Edmund Barton, the first Prime Minister, to believe that most New Zealanders favoured federation.[17] As a guide to political or public opinion, however, it was exceedingly defective. The newspaper reported interviews with the Members as they took place, on one occasion in a group. The opinions of sixty-four Members – not seventy – were reported. Twenty favoured joining Australia and nineteen were against, while twenty-five were neutral or expressed no opinion. Most of them said that careful inquiry was needed.

Other newspapers, like the *Lyttelton Times* gave considerable publicity to the issue, without supporting federation. The Chamber of Commerce in Christchurch set up a committee which recommended arranging a treaty with Australia with some free trade clauses (thus anticipating NAFTA by sixty-six years). The issue was discussed by the Farmers' Cooperative Association and at meetings in Kaiapoi and Invercargill. It was discussed at meetings of various local councils and trades and labour councils. A public meeting in Dargaville declined to discuss the issue. Several newspapers published long special articles on

'How We See It'. *The Ogre:* 'Come Into These Arms.' *New Zealand:* 'Nay, sir, those arms bear chains.' *NZ Graphic*, 1900.

federation. The League invited Edmund Barton to come over from New South Wales to speak to the public, but he was too busy.[18] There was, in short, a three months' flurry of interest. By early October federation had almost disappeared from the news.

The referenda in Australia suddenly confronted New Zealanders with a hard choice. Previously it had not been clear that the Australian colonies would in fact federate. Now New Zealanders had to confront their destiny.

There is no doubt that Seddon adopted an attitude of 'passive resistance' to federation.[19] He said it should not become an election issue. The Opposition announced, as one of its 'planks', that there should be a referendum on federation, but there was no Opposition political organisation, and on election day the Opposition was reduced to a pathetic handful. In Wellington one man who campaigned for federation was defeated,[20] but federation never became an issue.

After the election Seddon appointed a Royal Commission to look into the whole question. The Government was sufficiently uncertain that it proposed several amendments to the Australian Commonwealth Bill, which was about to be debated in the British Parliament. The only one which need concern us was that New Zealand should preserve the right to join the Australian Commonwealth on the same terms as the original states.

The Agent-General, W. P. Reeves, wrote to the Secretary of State for the Colonies, Joseph Chamberlain, about the Bill on 30 March 1900.[21] He had already been interviewed by a reporter from the *St James's Gazette*, who quoted him as saying that the Bill might need to be referred again to the people.[22] Since they had already waited twelve years, he was quoted as saying, there was no reason why they should not wait another twelve months. The Australians had already had nine federal referenda since March 1898 and certainly wanted no more. Besides, it had been a close shave in New South Wales and the 'Billites' were not going to risk it again. Next day Reeves denied making this statement, but the damage was done.

Delegates from the Australian colonies were already in London for discussions with Chamberlain. Reeves's relations with the New South Wales delegate, Edmund Barton, became very strained. Explanations were called for.[23] Reeves was called to a conference with the Australian delegates and the Secretary of State. He spoke and answered questions. Among other points, he suggested that New Zealand should have the right of entry on the original terms for seven years. He was not permitted to stay to hear their discussion.[24] The delegates unanimously refused to agree to the amendments requested by New Zealand. They believed that the constitution already made adequate provision for admitting new states, though not necessarily on the original terms. Chamberlain gave way almost completely, Reeves wrote, to the Australian delegates.[25]

Reeves thought that the Australians were 'very short-sighted not to grant the "open door" amendment because it would strengthen the hands of the Federal Party in New Zealand . . . whereas their rather overbearing and ungracious refusal should, I think, tend to get up New Zealand's back.' Seddon replied that Chamberlain had 'proved a regular jelly fish'. The episode had 'settled matters as far as New Zealand is concerned for many years to come'.[26] Certainly these events produced some ill-will on both sides of the Tasman. New Zealand received a 'bad press' in Australia. The Australians felt that New Zealand had stood aside from their labours and now demanded what they could have requested before. The New Zealanders felt that it was only now that the Commonwealth Bill had been approved in Australia and was submitted to the British Parliament that they knew what was in the Constitution and that there was someone to negotiate with.[27]

The voluminous evidence presented to the Royal Commission in 1901 was published. It enables us to estimate the opinions of various sections of the community. Some of those who gave evidence represented quite large constituencies. The following table divides up the witnesses by occupation and according to their opinions on federation. Sixty-eight per cent of the manufacturers and 52 per cent of merchants were opposed to federating, businessmen of all sorts were 62 per cent opposed; professional people were 55 per cent opposed; trade unionists were 90 per cent opposed. The only fairly 'pro' group was the farmers (other than fruit-growers), 46 per cent of whom favoured federation. Of the 186 witnesses, 61 per cent opposed and 26 per cent favoured federation.

The leaders of the Trades and Labour Councils in the main towns represented thousands of trade unionists – 2500 in Christchurch, 2000 in Wellington, and ten unions with 500 members in Auckland. They had passed resolutions against federation after holding meetings. In Wellington there had been one pro vote among sixty-two delegates and there was only one dissenter in Dunedin. The unionists in Auckland said they feared competition with coloured labour in Australia. The unionists in general believed that New Zealand wages, working conditions and social legislation would be set back ten years. It was characteristic that the unions had *debated* the issue. In the absence of any political struggle over federation, public debates had been arranged – the issue was debated, for instance, in a theatre in Invercargill.

Of the farmers, one man spoke for the Waikato Farmers Associa-

	Pro	*Anti*	*Non-committal*	*Total*
Manufacturers	12	34	4	50
Merchants	13	21	6	40
Businessmen (including retail)	2	7	1	10
	27	62	11	100
Farmers	6	5	2	13
Fruit growers		3	1	4
	6	8	3	17
Professions	12	18	6	36
Politicians		4		4
Public Servants		2	1	3
	12	24	7	43
Trade Unionists	1	9		10
Craftsmen	1	10	2	13
	2	19	2	23
Miscellaneous	2	1		3
	49	114	23	186[28]

tion, which had 400 members. They had held a meeting at which nineteen out of the twenty present favoured federation. The President and the Secretary of the Auckland Agricultural Pastoral Association were in favour. It had 542 members. The other agricultural interest favouring federation was grain merchants and millers in Southland. No farmer from that region gave evidence. Farmers and grain merchants said that they feared exclusion from the Australian market by a federal tariff. The General Manager of the New Zealand Dairy Association (who was personally opposed) said that New Zealand needed access to the Australian market because it was 'open' at a different time from the British market. The fruit growers belonged to two Auckland associations which had 400 and 125 members. The latter had held a meeting which unanimously opposed federation. The fruit growers said that they could not compete with Australian growers, for instance, of grapes.

There were far more witnesses who feared Australian competition than those who welcomed it. In particular, most manufacturers said that the scattered, small New Zealand industries could not compete with the more centralised Australian ones. Some of the manufacturers spoke on behalf of industrial associations. Some said that their industries would be wiped out if New Zealand federated. Among the merchants and manufacturers who favoured federation, no clear pattern emerged. Most of them said that they wanted access to the larger Australasian market, but few of them actually exported to Australia. A few did export drugs, agricultural machinery and preserved meat as well as grain.

Both press reports and the evidence to the Royal Commission indicate that the federal movement in New Zealand in 1899 was fuelled by a sudden fear that the Commonwealth would adopt a hostile tariff. This argument was considered by the Commission to be unconvincing. In 1900 New Zealand exported £470 000 worth of goods to the 'protected' Australian colonies and only £623 000 to free trade New South Wales.[29] Since New Zealand products could pass the Victorian barrier, there seemed no good reason for supposing that they would be stopped by a federal one, which was likely to be a compromise between the policies of New South Wales and Victoria.

From the evidence, considered as a whole, it seems reasonable to conclude that most New Zealanders did not want to become Australians. This is not to say that they felt secure in their own identity by 1899. Basically, however, in that year New Zealanders suffered from a brief attack of nerves at being isolated in the Pacific, rather than from a traumatic identity crisis.

Why was it that the New Zealanders did not want to federate? The most common reason given was simply geography. As Sir John Hall put it, the 1200 miles of ocean separating the two countries were 1200 arguments against federation.

It was frequently said that there was no strong community of interest between Australia and New Zealand. For instance, it was asserted that the defence of Australia was primarily a military matter, while the defence of New Zealand was a naval matter, with which Australia could offer little help.

New Zealand was already, in some ways, distinct from the group of Australian colonies.

New Zealand was much less dependent upon the Australasian market for its exports than were the other six colonies. In 1890 New Zealand sent only 16.7% of the value of its total exports to its sister colonies: by comparison

Western Australia sent 28.4%, Victoria 35.1%, SouthAustralia 40.2%, New South Wales 52.8%, Queensland 71.7%, and Tasmania 82.5%. From this situation it follows that compared with the other colonies New Zealand would have had fewer – and less highly motivated – pressure groups with vested interests in the Australasian market capable of driving its public men to resolve the federation question.[30]

The Australian and New Zealand markets were not complementary but competitive; they produced the same exports. Australia was not a principal export market for New Zealand except for oats and timber (New Zealand exported soft timber to Australia and imported hard wood). Australia was not an important market in comparison with Great Britain. New Zealand exported £10.2 million of goods to the United Kingdom in 1900 and only £1.7 million to Australia.

Another relevant economic circumstance was that the Tasman economies did not always run in parallel. During New Zealand's long depression of the 1880s thousands of people crossed to Melbourne, which was enjoying a great building boom. But by 1893 the flow of migration was reversed; that boom burst just as New Zealand's economy was beginning to recover.

However, the argument most frequently advanced against federating was not economic but political: that New Zealand would lose its right to speak directly to the imperial government; would lose its political identity, its independence, its right to nationhood. Few people said that the New Zealanders were already a nation. If there was a consensus it was that of the Royal Commission: that New Zealand could support 'a population which might at no distant date be worthily styled a nation'. One MHR spoke for many others, in a speech confused and far from precise but plain in its intent: 'We have been an individualised nation, and we should keep up our identity and nationality. I think we ought to have a nationality, and that New Zealand should be a country for New-Zealanders. With the wings of Great Britain over us we need look to no other country or colony for protection .... We are here the pioneers of a great nation, and shall, no doubt, have a glorious history ....'[31]

What was happening is clear: two nations were separating out of the British Australasian population – not yet distinct, but beginning to become so. No New Zealander felt herself or himself to be an Australian; many New Zealanders felt superior to Australians. On rare occasions, as in Dargaville's pamphlet, opposition to Australians was strongly expressed. It must be added, however, that New Zealanders generally were not hostile towards Australia; rather, there was a wry blend of rivalry and inferiority as well as compensatory superiority, strongly sibling. A notable example of jocular, irreverent, ambivalent, yet serious assertion of rejection was expressed in some verses by Eugene Paul Foveaux (possibly a pseudonym) published in 1899 in a journal, *The Critic*:

I swear I am beginning to see things!
For I had a vision,
Or, to be more correct and explicit, I had a nightmare.
A land overrun with larrikins, bookies, spielers, medical quacks, yesnoes, Chows, and the Japanese-what-d' ye-caller?
Lepers, uncaged gallow's birds, sundowners, and others afflicted with delicate health and chronic fatigue, active, however, in all the different shades of iniquity: a land afflicted with hot and debilitating winds, bush fires and droughts.
These are not the Othersiders' faults, but their historical, climatic, and geographical misfortunes,
With which some propose to federate.
But there is a natural gulf fixed between here and there,
And on such occasions as this we should pray that it be made more so than otherwise.
The native-born animal of this country is as superior to the native-born animal of the other country,
As the Maori to the blackfellow,
As our oats to their oats.
I sing not skiteingly, because I sing of ordinary facts (whitmanesque and whitmanese, you'll perceive)
And, apart from the exciting question of the price of oats, there is such a thing as nationality.
What is this mild hankering after the flesh-pots and the birth-stains of the Otherside?

He went on to urge that New Zealand should not become the tail of Australia: was it not 'preferable to federate with the infernal regions. direct? Instead of indirectly?'[32]

New Zealand visitors to Australia often remarked that nationalism was much stronger there.[33] Sometimes it went too far. When in 1900 Australians suggested changing the name of the Tasman to the Australian sea there was loud protest.[34]

After 1900 the Australian Commonwealth was frequently perceived as hostile in New Zealand. The *New Zealand Illustrated Magazine*, for instance, alleged in 1901 that the new federal tariff showed 'a spirit of hostility' to New Zealand for not having joined the federation.[35] In 1906 Seddon visited Australia and, with Deakin, drew up a preferential tariff agreement, but Seddon died and the New Zealand Parliament refused to ratify it.[36]

In 1912 when the Australian Prime Minister, Andrew Fisher, claimed that New Zealanders favoured federation, the *New Zealand Herald* said that New Zealand was, because of its climate, 'destined to display a different national temperament', and already possessed 'a national character, national aspirations and national peculiarities'. It said that 'To New Zealanders the question of federation with Australia is dead.'[37] Fisher's statement aroused quite strong criticism in New Zealand.

After Gallipoli relations between the two countries became more cordial: there was 'a more brotherly feeling towards the people of Australia'.[38] This did not, however, prevent a Member of Parliament asking that the use of the term 'Australasia' be discontinued in the schools as it had a detrimental effect on business negotiations with the United Kingdom: it gave people the impression that New Zealand was part of Australia.[39] From this time onwards, few New Zealanders would accept the use of the names 'Australasia' or 'Maoriland'. Between the two world wars the friendly relations between the two countries were constantly marred by feuding over tariff matters.[40]

There was one aspect of New Zealand's reaction to Australian federation which will not be rehearsed here at length, as it has been much discussed in earlier books – that is, New Zealand's efforts to acquire a Pacific empire. From early colonial times, successive governments laid claim to various island groups. Though there is little evidence of public interest in this aspiration, at least at the official level it was important in the search for a New Zealand identity. It could be discussed in relation to the imperial connection but it was equally relevant to the colony's relations with Australia.

The idea that the colony should acquire an island empire went back to New Zealand Company propaganda about it becoming the 'Britain of the southern hemisphere'. Australia aspired to the same role. By the later nineteenth century the Australasian colonies were all fearful of French, German and other intrusions into what they saw as a British ocean. They demanded that Great Britain, to protect them, should annex most of Polynesia and Melanesia. In 1883 Queensland attempted to annex part of New Guinea. Shortly afterwards the New Zealand Premier, Robert Stout, sought to annex Samoa, but was snubbed by the British Government. Instead, the Germans tightened their grip on Western Samoa. It was, Stout said, New Zealand's Alsace.[41]

In the 1880s fear of foreign powers led the Australasian colonies to collaborate in pressing their views upon the British Government. It was often advanced, as a reason why New Zealand should join federation, that if Australasia spoke with one voice it might have a greater influence upon British foreign policy. However, that was not the only federation foreshadowed. Stout talked of the possibility of New Zealand forming a federation with Samoa, Tonga or Fiji.[42] In 1900 Seddon took up this ambition quite explicitly to establish, as the *New Zealand Times* put it, a 'counterpoise and complement' to the Australian Commonwealth. This newspaper had been founded by the Liberal Government. It argued that Seddon had sought the right of late entry into the Commonwealth and had been rebuffed. New Zealand now had no choice but to acquire fresh outlets for trade in the Pacific. Otherwise New Zealand would be at the mercy of the Commonwealth in trading matters and might be forced into federation 'with all the consequences therein to our national life'. New Zealand must establish a new federation, 'the Dominion of Oceania'.[43]

Seddon said of the Australians, 'They will think more of us as a nation in years to come, with islands of our own . . . .'[44] In a speech in 1902 Ward went so far as to argue that New Zealand must be 'the central and controlling power' among all the islands of the Pacific except New Guinea. He claimed that then New Zealand would 'be able to decide its own terms as regarded the tariff that should prevail between the Commonwealth and New Zealand'.[45]

The way in which imperial and federal themes were interwoven with national ambitions is well illustrated in this speech. He advocated the establishment of an imperial *zollverein*, a customs union with internal free trade. The New Zealand Agent-General was to occupy a seat in the House of Commons. The *Evening Post* said that his speech was 'an effort to inculcate a feeling of nationality in the people of New Zealand'. New Zealand's 'sub-imperialism' resulted only in the acquisition of the Cook Islands in 1900 and of Western Samoa during the First World War.

IV

The World of Men

The First World War strengthened feelings of national identity. *Australian War Memorial*

Chapter Nine

NEW ZEALAND VOICES FROM SOUTH AFRICA, 1899–1902

When the short-lived Australasian federation movement was at its peak in New Zealand in 1899 Richard Jebb, the author of *Studies in Colonial Nationalism*, was visiting New Zealand. He was struck by the absence of 'a distinctive national sentiment' and wrote, 'nationalism is not spontaneous when the soil is too new . . . .' However, he was still there when the first troops left to fight in the war in South Africa, the 'Boer war'. He believed that the war was 'the really decisive factor which determined the national destiny of New Zealand':

Suddenly the people of the colony had seized the idea that they were indeed an island race apart, to their future glory rather than to their present misfortune; no longer 'Britons of the South', nor Australasians, but Maorilanders first. In those thrilling days scant respect would have been paid to the suggestion that the most vigorous national individuality of the southern hemisphere should forego its splendid prospect of independent evolution. Nevertheless the nationalism of New Zealand is recent and immature.[1]

No good book has yet been written about the New Zealand troops in South Africa, it is said because their letters, diaries and other documents, collected in Wellington, were destroyed in a fire. Certainly the effect of the South African war upon New Zealand opinion has been underestimated, and obscured by the greater influence of the First World War. Jebb was right in stressing the importance of that war in stimulating national feelings. From that day to this very little has been heard, in New Zealand, about becoming an Australian state.

The war in South Africa was a major stimulus to nationalism among Canadians and Australians as well as New Zealanders, and – for different reasons – among the Afrikaners. For the first time troops from the colonies of settlement fought alongside British troops. They fought for the Empire, but in doing so they came to feel great pride in their own achievements. They became aware of differences between men from Great Britain and from the several colonies. They came to consider their identity self-consciously. The difference between their own unit and other units, especially foreign ones, is always a frequent subject of conversation among servicemen at war. Thus the war stimulated divisive forces within the Empire, separate nationalisms. We may occasionally hear an individual New Zealand voice from before 1899, but the first unmistakable New Zealand voices which we can hear as a group come to us from the soldiers in South Africa.

When war seemed imminent some people spoke out against the evils of imperialism. Even a newspaper which said, 'We in the colonies are all Imperialists', could deprecate 'the "jingoistic" impulse' and refer to 'the "seamy side" of imperialism'.[2] The Canterbury Women's Institute and the Auckland Peace Society opposed the idea of a war.[3] Two MHRs, T. E. Taylor and George Hutchison, opposed sending troops.

It would be difficult in the late twentieth century to regard the war as just. The links between the 'gold bugs', the Rand millionaires who controlled the richest goldmines in the world, and some of the British authorities, notably Sir Alfred Milner, the British High Commissioner, and through him with the Secretary of State for the Colonies, Joseph Chamberlain, amounted to a conspiracy. In particular, Chamberlain had prior knowledge of the dangerous and absurd 'Jamieson raid' into the Transvaal which helped to precipitate the war.[4] The war was an attack by the greatest imperial power the world had known against two small Afrikaner republics which challenged British dominance in southern Africa – and hence British control of 'the route to the east', to India, the greatest jewel in the imperial crown.

Once New Zealand troops went to the war there was a strong backlash against its critics. The *Otago Daily Times* denounced the 'croaking Quaker or denaturalised British Boer'. The New Zealand Agent-General in London, William Pember Reeves, was denounced as 'pro-Boer' when some of his cables about the war seemed insufficiently optimistic. T. E. Taylor was on one occasion chased home by a mob throwing rocks. He confronted them at his gate and invited their leaders in for a cup of tea and a chat.[5] There were few men of such courage, but even in 1902 an incautious Dunedin MHR was reported to have said that the Empire was concentrating 'on killing a few farmers and grabbing some goldmines in South Africa for the benefit of a few unscrupulous and avaricious gold bugs'.[6]

To most New Zealanders criticism of the war seemed close to treachery or sedition. It belittled the sacrifices of the troops and potentially undermined their confidence. Wars often produce a terrifying but unifying, almost religious, fervour.

Moreover, many New Zealanders felt some sympathy for the Uitlanders, British immigrants in the Transvaal who were denied full civil rights. Many of them were colonials. Seddon himself expressed this point of view.[7]

The Boers had beaten the British in 1881 at Majuba, after the latter had annexed the Transvaal. Gladstone had then come to power in Britain and recognised the independence of the Boer republic, subject to British control of its foreign policy. Now the British sought once again to take over the republics – and their goldmines. The largest overseas expedition in British history up until then was mounted. The usual Boer guerilla tactics would be useless, the *New Zealand Times* proclaimed, against a fully-equipped army corps.[8] Within a month the Boers had beaten 'the cream of the British army' in open warfare. Over 2000 British troops had surrendered; over 700 were dead and 3000 wounded. The British authorities turned increasingly to using, not regular army infantry or cavalry, but volunteer irregulars, Mounted Infantry or M. I. The Imperial Yeomanry were recruited in Great Britain. In addition, 29 000 white troops were brought to South Africa from the self-governing colonies.[9]

Seddon had offered to send a contingent of mounted rifles two weeks before the war began. At that time there was some doubt about whether the British army wanted volunteers, but the offer was immediately accepted. Queensland had already offered troops, but Seddon was able to boast (at every opportunity) that New Zealand's offer was the first to be approved by a colonial parliament. The enthusiasm of the House of Representatives was so great that the Members stood up and sang 'God Save the Queen', an event it was believed without precedent.[10] The New Zealanders were the first colonial contingent to reach South Africa.

Altogether New Zealand sent ten contingents, totalling 6495 men, to the war. The casualties were not great, by the standards of later wars: 70 men were killed in action or died of wounds; 158 died of disease or were accidentally killed; 166 were wounded.[11]

No statistics are available for the birth-places of the contingents as a whole, but 62 per cent of the first contingent were New Zealand-born,[12] which is what would be expected of men of military age. It is likely that a good proportion of the remainder had grown up in New Zealand. The late 1880s and early 1890s had been years of depression marked by emigration to Australia rather than by a strong flow of immigrants.

The New Zealand troops were big men by the standard of the day.

The first contingent leaving Karori, Wellington, for the South African war, October 1899. *'Making NZ' Collection, Turnbull*

The first contingent averaged five feet nine inches in height and eleven stone six pounds. According to the *Cape Times* they were 'a contingent of sharp-shooters'.[13]

The New Zealand contingents were known as the New Zealand Mounted Rifles (NZMR), but sometimes they were nicknamed the New Zealand Independents. It was suggested that the third contingent should be called the 'Bushmen' but Seddon disapproved because they would be confused with the New South Wales 'Bushmen' or, worse, the South African Bushmen. They became the 'Rough Riders' (and sailed in the *Knight Templar*). The fourth contingent was given the same name.[14]

Sometimes the troops were referred to, at least in newspapers, as 'Maorilanders', though there was protest about this because the name had allegedly been coined by the Sydney *Bulletin*.[15] In fact, it had occasionally been used before the days of the *Bulletin*. There was apparently no general nickname for the New Zealanders like the later names in the First World War: 'Fernleaf', 'digger' or 'Kiwi'. The troops wore a badge bearing the letters 'NZ'. Soldiers from the New

Zealand Native Rifles and other volunteer companies wore a fernleaf. Returned servicemen also wore a fernleaf badge.[16]

The Governor warned the Colonial Office that there was much jealousy between New Zealand and Australia. A joint contingent had been proposed, but Seddon rejected the idea.[17] His attitude was probably widely supported. One newspaper said, 'If we were federated with Australia there would be no New Zealand contingent it would simply be Australian. Federal defence, Imperial and colonial is a good thing . . . . It should, however, be such that national patriotism and the pride of each country in her own sons should not be impaired.'[18]

Seddon had hoped that the New Zealanders could fight as a unit. It would have been small, as there were usually only two or three contingents in South Africa at a time. However, despite the New Zealand Government's protests, the contingents were often divided up among British units. This received a bad press in New Zealand. The *New Zealand Times* complained about 'our contingents losing their distinctive character' as New Zealand soldiers. 'As New Zealanders they have gained a great reputation.' The complaint was made that other units were getting the credit for New Zealand successes. The *New Zealand Illustrated Magazine* complained that because the contingents were divided up and not allowed 'a free hand to work together, much of their efficiency was wasted . . . whenever they were allowed their heads, free of restriction, they rendered excellent account of themselves . . . .'[19] The fact was that British generals made no concessions to the national feelings of colonials. The New Zealand Government was to have the same problem in the Middle East during the Second World War.[20]

Because they were generally divided up in small parties, the New Zealanders fought in few actions as units. However, some of these received widespread publicity and big headlines in the New Zealand newspapers. In the first action the first contingent occupied a farm called Jasfontein and held on under artillery and musketry fire until the British artillery, which had been left behind, was brought up. One trooper wrote, 'The General said to Major Robin [the New Zealand commander] that the men who held the koppie [sic] were a credit to the British Army so what do you think of that for New Zealanders.'[21] They suffered their first casualty. One man died of wounds after being taken prisoner.

In January 1900 there was another action when the Boers attacked a *kopje* near the camp at Slingersfontein. The hill was defended by about thirty Yorkshiremen and seventy New Zealanders commanded by

'Plucky Deeds by New Zealanders': impressions of the South African war, *NZ Collection, Canterbury Public Library*

Captain W. R. N. Madocks. Although this was scarcely ever mentioned, he was an English RA officer who had come to New Zealand as a staff officer and was to return to England in 1901. His name was appropriated by New Zealand nationalism.

The Boers attacked the Yorkshiremen, killing or wounding some of them. The New Zealanders counter-attacked with a bayonet charge, killing many of the enemy. Two New Zealanders were killed in this action. The *kopje* was henceforth called 'New Zealand hill', a fact often mentioned in New Zealand newspapers.[22]

The worst New Zealand casualties were suffered in an action early in 1902 when General De Wet broke through a 'drive' carried out by Kitchener's best MI forces, including the New Zealand seventh contingent, in an action in the Orange Free State, sometimes called Bothasberg. The New Zealanders lost twenty-four dead while forty-one were wounded out of about eighty men. These and other actions, famous in New Zealand, were reported by the newspapers' 'Special Correspondents' at the front, some – and perhaps most – of them soldiers themselves. (Sometimes they were named with the reports.)

The New Zealand troops, including a party of Maoris, had already earned high praise in Great Britain for the fine appearance and performance of the contingent which went to London for the celebration of Queen Victoria's diamond jubilee in 1897. Their commander then was Major Robin.[23] Now the British generals were effusive in their praise of the New Zealanders and of the colonial troops in general. There is no doubt that this praise greatly boosted the self-confidence of the troops. 'Overseasure', the need for success and praise from abroad, is a colonial condition, one which survived even in the United States into the twentieth century. 'We have been complimented on several occasions by the general, so that we are doing some good for our colony, Queen and country', Private Fred Wood, who fought on 'New Zealand hill', wrote to his family.[24] British generals praised the New Zealanders in addresses to the troops, in press interviews and other public statements and on occasion in letters to Seddon, as well as in despatches. There are numerous press reports of General French's praise of the troops after the action at Slingersfontein. Roberts, Kitchener, Hutton and other British generals were equally complimentary. General Sir Ian Hamilton wrote, 'I have soldiered a long time now but I have never in my life met men I would sooner soldier with than the New Zealanders.' Similar praise was repeated after the war. The *Times* history of the war said that the New Zealanders were, 'by general consent, regarded as on average the best mounted troops in South Africa'.[25] Similar praise was also lavished on the other colonial troops.

Probably more influential on New Zealand opinion than the observations of generals were the remarks made by the troops themselves. They were often interviewed on returning home (most of the contingents signed on for a year). More important, the newspapers frequently published the letters that the soldiers wrote to their relatives and friends. Sometimes these letters were republished in other newspapers. This practice, which would have seemed strange during later and more security-conscious wars, was also adopted in Australia. There is no doubt about the authenticity of the letters – often the recipient as well as the writer was named.

Sometimes the soldiers reported what the generals had said to them. One said, 'We have become our General's favourites, and are called, in camp, "the General's white-haired boys."'[26] Another reported that General French had said, 'Major Robin, officers and men of the New Zealand contingent, – words cannot express the admiration and esteem in which I hold you. Your courage and coolness under fire, etc. etc. This bit of jam did not cost him much, and pleases some of us.'[27] Another wrote that 'General French has taken a great fancy to the New

Zealand Contingent, and shows it by sending us all over the place.'[28] Not everyone found this fact to their liking. An Otago trooper observed that 'The General thinks too much of the New Zealand crowd for my fancy, for he will expect too much of us.'[29]

One trooper wrote home, 'General French has complimented us on many occasions for our coolness under fire and our horsemanship. He said we could gallop across country where English cavalry could only walk.'[30] While holding the general's horse one trooper overheard some of his off-the-cuff remarks about the contingent: 'They are the most independent crowd of men I have met. I spoke to them once about so much chattering and swearing at each other in their ranks. They take no notice; it still goes on, yet they never lose their place in the ranks, and take good care that they are not left behind. As for gallopers, damn me if ever I saw anyone like them.'[31]

On 24 January 1900 the *Otago Daily Times* published a letter from Sergeant Gourley. By this time the sergeant had been killed on 'New Zealand hill'. He told his brother that

The New Zealanders compare most favourably with the regulars. In fact, I must own I am greatly disappointed with them, and the majority are not up to much as riders. We can beat them bad, and the authorities reckon us the very best at reconnoitring and patroling. It is very rare that a party of us go out without bringing something home. One paper here called us the 'white-haired boys of the British Army,' and said that we never thought of getting home without a prisoner, or something of the sort.

The meaning of the last phrase was explained in a letter from Trumpeter Johnstone who reported General French as saying that the New Zealanders 'never go out but what they bring something in. If it isn't cattle, it is prisoners.'[32] After only five days in one camp a trooper reported that the New Zealanders had taken about 2000 sheep, 50 cattle and some horses.[33]

Not everyone approved of the tone of these letters. One trooper said that he bitterly resented 'the irresponsible and disparaging comments' about Australian and British troops in some of the letters.[34]

Some of the troopers expressed much scepticism, especially about the praise from the generals. One trooper wrote that 'The reading of troopers' letters published in the New Zealand papers . . . constituted one of the chief sources of amusement in camps, so full were they of false and ridiculous statements.' A letter to the *Press* suggested that the letters were so swollen-headed and stuffed with 'fulsome rot' that they should be edited. One such letter, describing a charge on what proved to be an unoccupied farmhouse said that General French 'considered Balaclava was a mere nothing' by comparison. The editor thought that the troopers expressed themselves with 'delightful frankness and unreserve', with 'a commendable absence of colonial "blow"'.[35]

It could not accurately be said that there was no 'colonial blow'. Nevertheless, from these often naive and not always very literate letters, and from Special Correspondents' reports, a portrait of the New Zealand trooper emerges, partly fact, partly doubtless fiction, but as he saw himself and wished to be seen. Like members of almost all nations, they prided themselves on their courage.

Trooper Hearn wrote that one of the 6th Dragoons had said to him, 'Well, you are about the coolest, and yet the wildest men I ever saw.' 'Why?' I asked. 'Well', he replied, 'if the 6th Dragoons were in your place with the lead flying about us, as it was you, we would not have walked coolly away, nor yet have faced the bullets, as you did at the farmhouse.'[36]

A typical letter recounts an action at Ottoshoop, in which New Zealand troops attack Boers on a *kopje*:

After exchanging a few shots our No. 3 troop was ordered to take the hill. They went on foot along with some of the South Islanders, and had to cross a 100-yard flat to reach it. Not a shot was fired at them while they were crossing that flat or climbing the hill, but when they reached the top a terrible fire was poured into them. Captain Harvey was shot dead, and a sergeant and several troopers were wounded. They were in a terrible fix when we (No. 2 troop) were ordered to charge the hill. We were mounted, Bob Collins in command, and went down the hillside, over rocks, through trees, and across the flat at full gallop. As soon as the Boers saw us coming they turned their fire on to us, and the bullets fell like hail around us. We raised the cry 'Come on New Zealand.' and rode like the very devil. We were lucky enough to reach the foot of the hill without a man or a horse being struck. Arriving there, we dismounted and climbed the hill; the Boers retreated about 200 yards to a ridge, and the firing was fast and furious on both sides. Shortly after this, about 5 p.m. Bob Collins was shot through the wrist.[37]

The New Zealanders were often used as scouts. They took great pride in their ability at this work, and at not getting lost, which it was easy to do on the veldt. They found hunting or spotting 'Joeys' or 'Jackies', as they called the Boers, exciting work. It was said that they had only one fault as scouts, that they were too eager and got too far ahead of their units![38]

They felt that they were very resourceful and had great initiative. A

New Zealand colonel said that 'the New Zealand soldiers were allowed "a wide latitude" in doing their work. It was of such a nature that the chief officer had to depend much upon his captains and subalterns, they upon the N.C.Os, and they in turn upon the troopers. The latter largely went on their own, exercising their own judgment to a great extent. Fortunately they had been successful because the work they were asked to do was admirably suited to New Zealanders, whether from bush or plain.'[39]

It was often said that the New Zealanders, like the Australians, disliked ordinary army discipline and were very egalitarian. One trooper rephrased the old colonial adage that Jack is as good as his master: 'If you want the straight bally truth, there's as good officers among the men as there are men among the officers.' And Corporal Frank Twistleton wrote, comparing New Zealand with British troops, that many New Zealand soldiers were the social equal of their officers.[40]

It was frequently said that colonial troops disliked saluting.[41] Certainly there is evidence that, while generally friendly with their officers (a point which will recur) they were not over-respectful. One trooper, Joseph Linklater, recorded in a small book that, on one occasion the 'Silent Sixth' squadron put on a 'general strike' as a protest at not getting more clothing, their own being in rags. The Colonel 'admitted his oversight, and promised to get us all the garments we required in three days if we would, like good New Zealanders, saddle up and get on trek. This we considered satisfactory, and moved out soon after.' He also recorded another protest, similarly against the Queen's 'regs':

December 23rd.—Newcastle. Paraded before Lieutenant in a body, and threatened to go to the Commandant if he did not get us our pay. He promised us £3, so we had to be satisfied. He told us parading was against all military rules. We knew nothing about military rules, but thought it a very effective style.[42]

Commenting on the strict discipline imposed on the 'Tommies', Corporal Twistleton wrote that 'We will obey an order right enough, but we will not knuckle down to any military red tape.' Twistleton also wrote a book on the war.[43]

Above all, the New Zealanders claimed that they excelled at riding and shooting, and many commentators agreed. The *New Zealand Mail* claimed that the New Zealand Rough Riders and the New South Wales Bushmen were said to be 'the best riders in the world, the cowboys of the plains not excepted. Their horses are as hardy as themselves . . . .'[44] The New Zealanders were said to upset the Boers by using their own guerilla tactics against them.[45]

Some of the praise and self-praise was justified. The colonials were used to galloping about in open country, to camping out, to roughing it, and this was often recognised. Kipling wrote in 'The Islanders', that the British had had to fawn 'on the Younger Nations for men who could shoot and ride'. He also wrote that the colonials had 'learned us how to camp and cook an' steal a horse and scout'.

To the great pleasure of many New Zealanders, a poet equally well-known to them. 'Banjo' Paterson, who was an Australian war correspondent, more than once reported that the New Zealanders were 'probably the best troops in South Africa'; 'superior to other colonial contingents in South Africa'.[46]

There was a vast amount of boasting. The New Zealanders were said to be the best troops in swamps; the only troops to complete the ride all the way from the Orange River to Kimberley, and without losing a horse. The greatest boaster of all was the Premier, R. J. Seddon: 'The men must remember', he said, 'that they were civilising agents, and he was confident that the only way to beat the Boers was to put the New Zealanders in the front.' He believed that the New Zealanders 'would strike terror into the hearts of the Boers'.[47]

Besides forming or confirming a self-image, the New Zealanders also developed or validated attitudes towards other national groups, notably the British and Australians. The British were believed to be lacking in some of the supposedly colonial qualities such as initiative and adaptability. A report from London said that Canadians, Australians and Boers 'had the capacity of acting for themselves'. The British troops, who were 'bred in or near towns mostly and accustomed to act by order and routine, arrived on the field absolutely ignorant and dependent on their officers at every step'.[48] The *New Zealand Herald* quoted a British correspondent saying that 'Brave and well disciplined as the regular troops are, they lack the knowledge of bush or veldt craft, and the resourceful habit of acting when necessary on their own initiative, possessed by the colonials. They are also far less mobile.'[49]

There was, however, little criticism of the fighting qualities of British troops (as there was later to be at Gallipoli), but there was frequent criticism of British generals, elderly men who failed to adapt to new conditions. This comment was sometimes repeated from British newspapers, but New Zealand troopers agreed. One of them said that British officers were 'brave enough, but treat their subordinates like dogs'.[50]

This was the general opinion among the NZMR. One trooper wrote in his diary, at Mafeking in 1900, that the sanitary arrangements were shocking: 'now we are among the Imperial authorities, the comfort of the men is quite unconsidered.' He wrote that the British officers ate in town and did not camp with the men.[51] Some of the New Zealanders regarded the British officers, with their upper-class accents, with loathing. Twistleton spoke of the absurdity of putting 'boys over seasoned men'. He regarded the officers as so many 'nincompoops'. He hated to hear 'the sharp, insulting tone of some prig who has never seen anything, suffered anything, or done anything, except make an ass of himself.' The people of Great Britain, he thought, would be astonished 'at some of the things they send out as officers'. It should be added that he did not think much of some of the British troops either. He was scornful of the Imperial Rough Riders 'or the London Bushmen, as they have been called', who were on one occasion on guard and firing away at nothing all night.[52]

The British officers treated their men with a cold aloofness, the New Zealanders felt. By contrast, the New Zealanders generally prided themselves on the good relations between officers and men. One trooper said that the regular army officers were often astonished at the 'freedom of their intercourse'. For instance, when one major was in hospital his men used to visit him. The 'regulars' said that the only class in their service like the New Zealanders were 'gentlemen rankers'. The major told them that that was just what all his men were.[53] (This difference between New Zealanders and British was to persist at least until the Second World War, when it was a subject of frequent comment among the former.)

The popular civilian image of the troops in South Africa was nicely illustrated by a *tableau vivant* put on in a Christchurch theatre. It showed a beleaguered Tommy Atkins being rescued by men of the Third Contingent.[54]

It need scarcely be said that some of the British became aware of colonial attitudes which often were mere conceit. A man in the Colonial Office wrote in 1904 that the colonials regarded themselves as 'independent nations quite as capable of defending themselves as the mother country is of defending them . . . . I have talked to Australians and New Zealanders & they all consider that they saved the Empire in the S. African war, that they will *if they consider any future war a just war*, say it again, that no real training or preparation for war is necessary for such admirable Crichtons as they are . . . .'[55]

Towards the Australians, the New Zealanders were ambivalent. They felt a noticeable rivalry towards the Australians, and sometimes asserted a superiority. A trooper wrote that the New South Wales fellows were not well liked. Another was surprised when he lost his belt and money and it was returned by a New South Wales Bushman: 'Supposed to be a rough crowd!'[56] Another thought the New South Wales Lancers were 'a standing disgrace'. 'They answer their officers back, and the noise they make at night when men on either side of them are trying to go to sleep is awful.'[57] Sergeant Trumpeter Fox and other troopers reported that on one occasion an operation had to be abandoned because the Lancers arrived late. 'They said they never signed articles and no one could force them to get up at such an ungodly hour. The general said he had a good mind to send them back disgraced.'[58]

Occasionally troopers' letters give the impression that they preferred the British to the Australians. Trooper Dickenson wrote that General French said that the New Zealanders were 'the best volunteers in the world, which was rather a slap for the New South Wales Lancers, who consider themselves little kings. The regulars do not like them at all, but come to our tents every evening.'[59] But such remarks were rare. Generally, the troopers praised all the colonial troops, including the Canadians. On one occasion Joseph Linklater wrote:

March 10th.—Standerton. Still halted. Victorians move out of camp to entrain. The greatest good feeling has always existed between the two regiments – indeed the same remark can well apply, to all the Australians we met. We were truly 'brothers in arms.' 'We are all one,' they said, when they found we were New Zealanders, and to that we readily agreed.[60]

The troopers' letters often make flattering comparisons between themselves and other allegedly inferior mortals. Very occasionally they refer to Great Britain or the Empire; after all, it was an imperial war. But 'the Empire' belonged, rather, to the rhetoric of politicians and editors. To take an extreme example the Auckland newspaper, the *New Zealand Herald*, was super-imperialist. It celebrated 'our racial cradle that lies . . . rocked by the Atlantic surges' and proclaimed, 'We do not want to found a new nation nor to fill the world with New Zealand's glory. We want, if it may be, to be chief among the children.'[61]

Obviously this sort of sentiment was remote from the opinions of the troopers, nor was it typical of newspaper comment. This editorial was almost certainly written by the journalist, William Lane, who had just arrived to become a leader writer for the *Herald*. No one could have been a less reliable guide to New Zealand opinion.

The soldiers' letters were very repetitive: the soldiers had developed a strong consensus on many issues. This is typical of units in the armed forces, where the same experiences are constantly discussed. The widespread publication of their letters meant that their views came to be widely known and, indeed, adopted in the community. The letters gave the public a sense of intimacy with the soldiers probably not exceeded before the days of television.

Major Jowsey had written home from the war that the contingents had been kept in the most advanced positions 'and the men felt proud to be called New Zealanders.'[62] There can be little doubt that their good reputation made other New Zealanders proud too.

It is difficult to exaggerate the importance of newspapers in stimulating national sentiment. They create a sense of community. They enable us to sense – to feel that we *know* – what the other members of our community, quite unknown to us as individuals, are doing. We share our roles in an 'imagined community' with them. We feel a fellowship.[63] Perhaps this is most easily explained by reference to television. In each news programme we see and hear what our fellow nationals are doing all over the country. In the days before television and radio, newspapers performed the same role. Even in the 1850s and 1860s the newspapers not only reported news (often weeks old) from other settlements; they also reprinted news reports, just as in 1899–1902 they reprinted soldiers' letters printed in other towns.

Perhaps more important, nationalism is a way of coping with death in war-time. This is one reason why nationalism has been called a 'secular religion'. The *Lyttelton Times* said that, despite all the carnage and misery, war had always been 'one of the chief foundations of national inspiration': 'For us colonials this war has been like the awakening of youth when we first "put away childish things." We too now play a part in the pageant of history ....'[64]

A Christchurch professor and a minor poet, Arnold Wall, wrote:

This country passed beyond the infant stage
And did deliver her first act and deed,
Then – when the harassed mother seemed in need,
She joined the quarrel without heat or rage,
And wrote her first firm lines on History's page ....[65]

Floral fete, Dunedin, 1900. *Turnbull*

Waimataitai School Patriotic Band, parading in honour of the relief of Ladysmith, 1900. *Turnbull*

Participation in the South African war encouraged national unity in other ways. Huge crowds, the biggest in the country's history up to that time, turned out to farewell the contingents. The crowd in Wellington when the first contingent sailed was estimated at 40 000. These crowds must in themselves have helped to strengthen a sense of community. Patriotic fervour was also aroused on such occasions as the relief of Ladysmith, the relief of Mafeking and the occupation of Pretoria. These days were declared public holidays. There was much hoisting of bunting, bands, singing and processions.[66]

The war had a powerful effect in establishing and strengthening social cohesion in many other ways. The third contingent and the fourth were equipped and transported at the expense, not of the government and taxpayers, but of the public. About £113 000 was raised by public subscription. Large numbers of people were kept busy fund-raising. The contingents took their own horses – over 8000 of them – and these had to be donated or purchased too.

Children assisted with the fund-raising. Little girls paraded in daisy bedecked dresses, at floral fetes. The money was raised so quickly that one magazine glowed at the 'dash and decisiveness of New Zealanders'.

Many Maoris were eager to volunteer and at one stage it was announced that they would do so. An 'ex-trooper' wrote to a newspaper saying that the 'coloured element' should be kept out, as this was recognised as 'a white man's war'.[67] This was far from true. By the end of the war the British had armed nearly 10 000 Africans to kill Boers.[68]

Nevertheless, the British authorities declined to accept Maori troops. It was felt, in the Colonial Office, that they were 'merely children & though they might fight as well as any coloured troops officered by Englishmen they would soon become a great trouble in a garrison.'[69] The *Lyttelton Times* regretted the decision, praising the Maoris' valour and suggesting that a war might 'infuse new vigour into a decaying race'. The Maoris did, however, raise large sums of money for the War Fund.[70]

As each contingent sailed, souvenir programmes or albums were printed, with photographs of all the men. Some of them became household names. Photographs of New Zealand casualties and war graves also featured in the newspapers and in albums.[71] Thus the war became a personal event for a large part of the population. When the first troops were killed the *Evening Star*[72], in Auckland, said that everyone wished 'to claim brotherhood with these gallant boys'.

To some extent a conscious effort was made to strengthen national feeling. By mid-1900 newspapers were discussing the 'cultivation of New Zealand patriotism' by the erection of monuments to the fallen and honours boards in the schools so that 'this epoch-making war' should cultivate the right spirit in the next generation.[73]

The flag, with its four stars, which was to become the New Zealand flag had, since 1869, been used by vessels as the New Zealand ensign. Sometimes it was flown ashore and called 'the New Zealand flag'. For instance, when the first contingent marched to the wharf in 1899, it was flown alongside the Union Jack and – interestingly enough – the Stars and Stripes.[74]

During the Anglo-Boer war the custom of raising and saluting the flag was often performed in the schools. Generally, but not invariably, the flag used was the Union Jack. In Canterbury, when the New Zealand flag was hoisted, the children sang 'Boys of the Southern Cross'.[75] In 1900 the blue ensign was adopted by Parliament as the New Zealand flag, with specific advice that it should be used in the schools.[76] Because of some legal problems, it was not formally introduced until 1902. The *New Zealand Journal of Education* in 1903 gave some rules for primary school children to do 'flag drill', marching in formation and waving flags.[77] In 1905 the Government provided New Zealand flags for the schools.[78]

One further influence exerted by the war needs to be mentioned. The veterans began publishing their own journals, such as the New Zealand Mounted Rifles' Association's *Bulletin*, which lasted from 1901 to 1954. *The Veteran* continued from 1925 until 1978. At their reunions, and in their journals, the veterans ensured that the Boer war was remembered, even after the horrors of 1914–18.

It is not and could not be asserted that, by this time, New Zealand had achieved nationhood. Certainly New Zealanders were not, outside the colony, thought of as a separate people. All that may be stated is that clear steps had been taken towards a national sentiment. The Anglo-Boer war built up feelings of solidarity, of unity, which contributed to national sentiment. It also fostered a sense of establishing a New Zealand tradition, which included the idea that New Zealanders were as good as their ancestors. Working towards a common goal involved New Zealanders in acting collectively. They began to assert that they were a distinct group.

Nineteen hundred was the fiftieth anniversary of the foundation of

Canterbury. When some troops were returning in that year, landing in Dunedin, the *Press* regretted that they were not arriving in Christchurch:

What could have been more touching and significant than the spectacle – the aged pioneers who had fought the battles of life so strenuously in this province, and the stalwart young New Zealanders fresh from the war, where they have been acquitting themselves so well on behalf of the Empire and their Queen, marching together in a joint act of hearty thanksgiving?[79]

The New Zealand Natives Association in Christchurch marked the jubilee by publishing a history, *Canterbury Old and New*, about the deeds of the pioneers. In linking the pioneers with the troopers the press was making a first step towards what was to become New Zealand's 'secular religion'.[80]

Chapter Ten

'PEACE HATH ITS VICTORIES': SPORT

In analyses of the rise of nationalisms in Europe a century or two ago, sport is rarely mentioned. In more modern national histories, especially in studies of Australia or New Zealand, it can scarcely be ignored. Its importance in an Australian sense of identity was recognised long ago. When the Commonwealth government opened its first office in London in 1906, Miss C. de Thierry wrote an article on 'The Hellenism of the Australian', asserting that the Greek love of sport had been inherited by the Anglo-Saxons and now by the Australians.[1] The Australian national spirit, she supposed, arose from success at cricket, in the absence of a war on Australian soil. The Canadians, South Africans and New Zealanders had gained their self-respect in their internal wars.

In the press there was much speculation about whether New Zealanders would prove to have inherited the British love of 'manly sport'. The *Southern Monthly Magazine* lamented, in 1864, that so far the bar and the billiard room were the 'chief resorts of our youths'. 'The nobbler reigns supreme', whereas vigorous sport should constitute their principal amusement.[2]

By the end of the century rugby football had clearly become the chief sporting love of New Zealand males, a fact greeted with widespread approval. There was, *Zealandia* declared, no danger of New Zealand 'rearing a nation of milksops, effeminate fops, luxurious dandies . . . .'[3] Some, however, criticised the craze for rugby. The *New Zealand Graphic* complained about 'The Tyranny of Football', which dominated local conversation. It wondered whether 'three months of football hardens all the finer feelings in a youth's nature and develops the tigerish animal side of him' and encourages 'larrikin instincts'.[4] The connection between sport and war was widely appreciated. Rugby could be seen either as a preparation for war or as a substitute. Tom Ellison, a Maori lawyer who was captain of the first official team to tour overseas, wrote in a book on the art of rugby in 1902 that it was 'a soldier-making game'.[5] Soldiers were to make the same connection. Captain J. A. Cross, a former Wellington College boy, was fighting at Gallipoli in 1915 when the men on each side of him were killed within seconds. Fortunately, he wrote, the excitement of battle clouded a man's reason and his duties as an officer kept him from thinking of his own danger:

The New Zealand Natives Team, 1888–89. *Turnbull*

My own sensations just before we get the word Go! are just the same as you all know on the football field on the day of an important match. Once the whistle has blown, and you are off, the worst is over.[6]

A 'prominent member of the Canterbury Battalion' wrote from Gallipoli to ask why all the athletes competing at home did not join up, as so many had done:

Yes, it thrilled us when practically the whole of the Christchurch Football Club and the Old Boys' Football Club offered their services. And I thought of that thrill when I saw the remnant afterwards here and at Cape Helles. And when we talked of the race across the red poppy patches near Sedd-ul-Bahr, I pictured the passing rush across 'The Park' in Christchurch, and I thought of the many playing there who might be playing the game of life here with the seashores for trench lines, rifles and bayonets for weapons, and freedom for the goal.[7]

Rugby did not begin to grip the New Zealand imagination until the 1890s. The first overseas tour, to Australia in 1884, resulted in eight victories in eight games, three of them against New South Wales. This tour was arranged by the several Rugby Unions. The next, in 1888–89 a private speculation which lost money, brought little credit to the game. The New Zealand Natives team was a Maori one, but it included four Pakeha. They played an extraordinary number of games both in Great Britain and Australia, a hundred altogether, of which they won seventy-two, lost twenty-two and drew six. Then they played further games in New Zealand. They lost to England and Wales but beat Ireland. They were criticised for rough play. During the game against England an English try was disputed by the Natives, several of whom angrily left the ground. They later returned and their captain apologised. It was feared in New Zealand that the British were getting 'an altogether wrong impression about our colonial style'.[8] On the way back to New Zealand four players, who were named in the press, were suspended for 'shady practice' in Brisbane. It was alleged that they took a bribe to lose a game, though this was denied by the team's secretary. The Otago Rugby Union looked into the allegations and was satisfied that they were untrue. However, the rumours had originated in the team and were widely reported.[9]

One member of this team, Tom Ellison, is said to have invented the 2–3–2 scrum and the use of a wing forward, which became features of the New Zealand game.[10] The team he captained in 1893 won a game against New South Wales but was well beaten in a second because, the New Zealanders claimed, so many of their players had been injured. Reinforcements were sent and they won the third game as well as several in Queensland. In Wellington a special reception committee was set up. The team was met at the wharf by thousands of people. After much cheering and the singing of 'See the Conquering Hero . . .' the team responded in Maori, 'Ake! Ake! Kia kaha, e'.

At the official reception which followed the Prime Minister, R. J. Seddon, and the Leader of the Opposition, William Rolleston spoke to them. It was, the latter said, 'a great national congratulation'.[11] The press wrote about the tour in terms worthy of a war: there had been 'gallant deeds', the team had 'covered themselves with glory'.[12]

In the next tour, in 1897, the New Zealanders again lost only one game, one out of three, against New South Wales. In 1903 they won all their games in Australia, including the first test match against Australia. A crowd of several thousand greeted the returning team at the Auckland wharf.[13] By now they were confident that they could beat Australians, but could they beat the British? There was much discussion in the newspapers about whether they had retained the traditional British vigour in sport.

In 1888 a British team made up of Englishmen and Scots played nineteen games in New Zealand including two against the South Island, which the British won, but did not play against a New Zealand team. The 1888 Natives team was not fully representative of colonial

The famous full-back George Nepia. *S. P. Andrew Collection, Turnbull*

talent. The first time when a New Zealand team played a British team was in Wellington in 1904. This game aroused extraordinary excitement, according to press reports. It was the one topic of conversation, the sole subject of thought, in the colony. An enormous crowd estimated variously at 15 000 to 40 000 turned out. The Governor-General, the Prime Minister and other ministers were in the grand-

The All Blacks who played Wales in 1905. *Turnbull*

stand. The 'black jerseys' won nine to three. It showed, said the *New Zealand Times*, 'that in this distant land the vigorous and manly pastime of the parent stock has worthy exponents; that in the migration of the race the vigour of its children has not diminished.' The *Press* said that the standard of local rugby was clearly much higher than most people could have hoped – how much better would not be known until a New Zealand team had been Home.[14] It was said that this game was the most important sporting event in the history of the colony so far.

The Gallipoli of New Zealand sport was the famous game against Wales in 1905 – a defeat to be forever celebrated as, if not a kind of victory, at least a draw. It was a major episode in the mythology of New Zealandism.

When the first All Blacks went to the United Kingdom in 1905, they soon conceived the ambition of not losing a game. In their early games against English clubs they amassed enormous scores. Within three months they had scored 802 points against 22. They beat Scotland, Ireland and England with only the Scots scoring any points. Indeed, only five out of twenty-seven opposing teams had scored. The New Zealanders were ecstatic, celebrating in verse as well as beer:

The Moa and the Lion: the 1905 All Black tour of Great Britain. *Turnbull*

Our 'two–three–two' formation strong
Broke up their feeble packs;
They couldn't stand our style ding-dong –
They couldn't stop our backs.
Our five-eighth cut their tacklers down
Like woodman with an axe!

And when 'no-side' was blown, you know,
After a struggle hot
The Britishers would puff, and blow,
And pant, and wheeze, I wot.
You see OUR boys were fully trained,
The beefy ones were not![15]

But then they went to Wales, where rugby was worshipped with a New Zealand or South African devotion. The Welsh games were the hardest. The All Blacks were said to be tired and stale. On 16 December Wales won three–nil, in the most famous game in New Zealand's rugby history.

So great was the public interest in the tour that post offices were opened on Sunday morning so that the cabled results of the Saturday games could be posted up. On this occasion, in Christchurch, 'a steady stream of enthusiasts' turned up to await the result. Then little groups stood about, talking in subdued tones, as if about some dire tragedy. The news 'spoiled the flavour of many a Sunday dinner'. In Wellington passengers arriving on a ship, 'saw dejection writ large' on the 'usually radiant countenance' of the Prime Minister, who was meeting some of his ministers. Dozens of passengers yelled out, 'Who won?' When told, they cried, 'Go on, you're "having us".'[16]

The first Press Association report of the game, received by 'electric telegraph', did not suggest that anything controversial had happened, although it mentioned that at the end of the game Deans had missed a chance to score by passing forwards. A month later, however, copies of the British papers arrived by sea. Several of these asserted that Robbie Deans of Canterbury had scored an equalising try. The 'special correspondents' of New Zealand newspapers agreed. Nevertheless, it was generally said that the Welsh had played better. Further accounts described the unnerving effect on the All Blacks of hearing the entire Welsh crowd singing 'Land of our fathers' before the game: it sounded like the Scottish army praying for victory before Bannockburn. It was alleged that the All Blacks 'listened spellbound' and never recovered from the hypnotic effects of 'the weirdly beautiful incantation'.[17]

What had occurred is famous in the New Zealand secular religion of nationalism. Robbie Deans of Canterbury had grounded the ball, according to him, six inches over the line. According to the Welsh captain, who was near-by, he was a foot short of the line, and 'rabbited' over. Both sides agreed that he was pulled back by the Welsh forwards, and that the referee could not see.[18] The episode was interminably discussed in the newspapers then and since as well as in numerous books. In the absence of film, it is a problem that can never be solved.

In Great Britain the All Blacks were gaining an enormous amount of publicity for the colony. The *New Zealand Herald* said that they 'were fighting our national battle for recognition in the Old Country' and providing 'the most remarkable advertisement ever secured among athletic nations'.[19] The Prime Minister, Seddon, certainly shared this view. He had been an athlete himself and revelled in the All Blacks' successes. At New Year, 1906 (just as New Zealand beat France in that country's first rugby international), the Government offered to pay for the team to return via North America.[20] The offer was accepted and New Zealand beat British Columbia as well.

When they arrived back in Auckland, and when the southern players reached Wellington two days later, they were met by great crowds, the like of which had not been seen since the South African war. Seddon greeted them in Auckland where he declared, about the All Blacks in Wales, that 'in their hearts, and in the opinion of most people, it was recognised that this was not a defeat, but a try to try.'[21] In Wellington the *New Zealand Times* proclaimed that 'Peace hath its victories .... There is no need to apologise for the predominance that sport has achieved in our national life.'[22] Two thousand turned up at a reception at the town hall. The mayor said that 'they were met there to mark a great national occasion, for to welcome a team of men, most of whom were native-born, who had made their mark at Home under difficult circumstances was a national occasion ... the work done by the team was of national importance.'[23] The High Commissioner in London, W. P. Reeves, said that they were all native-born.[24]

The tour was a considerable achievement for a team from a colony of less than a million people. It led to endless discussion about 'the New Zealand type'. Before the team had returned a book was published in London on *Why the 'All Blacks' Triumphed*.[25] Reeves, who had played both cricket and rugby for Canterbury, attributed the success to the fact that in New Zealand the young men all played the game instead of watching it. He thought good combination a factor, 'but we are never machine-like for the sake of machinery. We leave a great deal to individual initiative ....'[26] He thought physique was important – certainly the strength of the All Blacks made a considerable impression. One English paper reported that the 'real, typical New Zealander in height hovers somewhere in the neighbourhood of 6 ft., is broad in shoulder and clean in limb.' They were not lanky like the 'Cornstalks'![27]

In a sermon in London on 'The New Zealanders', the Revd W. Carlisle of the Church Army attributed the success of the New Zealanders to the fact that they were 'as hard as nails. They avoided over-feeding and over-drinking and other kinds of indulgences. England must wake up and do the same', he said.[28] The idea that the British were degenerating was popular.

Mr P. A. Vaile, from Auckland, wrote an article in the *Daily Mail* expressing a version of this theory, giving as reasons for New Zealand victories that

the New Zealander lives a more natural life than the Englishman, that he takes more exercise, that he has plenty of originality and resource, and that he is full of an 'overflowing vitality and virility.' The New Zealander plays football as the Japanese played the game of war – 'for all they were worth.' He beats the Englishman because he lives nearer to nature, and England will be beaten more and more by colonials as time goes on, 'unless she wakes up to the fact that men, and women, and children are of more importance than partridges, and pheasants, and grouse, and gives them the chance, that every Maorilander has, of getting their fair share of fresh air, and 'the smell of earth.'[29]

The notion had a wider currency. The French weekly, *La Vie au Grand Air*, asked whether European civilisation itself was decadent.[30]

There was a good deal of criticism of the All Blacks in the popular British press. There was controversy over the use of the wing forward, who was accused of 'wilful obstruction'. The All Black captain, Dave Gallagher, said that English teams played wing forwards but called them 'halves'. He was accused of putting 'bias' on the ball when putting it into the scrum. He replied that this was an impossibility. The All Blacks were often suspected of 'trickery'. His reply was that their scrum was so quick that sometimes even the referee could not follow the play. Gallagher was jeered at and hooted by the crowds and an ex-president of the Welsh Union said that he had played an 'absolutely dirty and unfair game'.[31]

But mainly the All Blacks were praised, especially for their modesty and gentlemanly behaviour. They were 'good sports'. The *New Zealand Times* celebrated 'a victory of character':

It may be an easy thing, in a nation that plays its games with the same strenuousness as it fells its forests and builds its cities, to produce a type of men physically more capable and mentally more alert than the natives of an older and less enthusiastic community. But it is a more difficult thing to produce a type of manhood that can bear itself in the difficult and often fatal hour of victory with the dignity and restraint that have long been thought to be the peculiar trait of the modern Englishman. Success, overwhelming success, is the hardest thing a young man, or a young nation, can be called upon to bear; and we may justly be proud that in our hour of triumph equally as on the football field, our representatives have quitted themselves like men.[32]

One other aspect of the All Blacks' success widely praised in New Zealand was that they were amateurs. The *New Zealand Times* hailed their return in this way:

The men whom we are welcoming today are no hired gladiators, but amateurs playing the game for the game's sake. It is professionalism in sport that is the bane of modern civilisation; and the wonderful record of our team in the Old Country points the moral. Without detracting in any way from our representatives' success, it must be apparent that had the professional element not crept into English football, we would have had a larger and more difficult field to beat. Our team's tour is a triumph for the purity of our football.[33]

If there was any doubt before, there was none after 1905 that rugby football had become the national game. It was praised as teaching 'self-control and unselfishness'. 'The striving in a manly game to win the honour of an All Black jersey is no small influence in the building of virile manhood.'[34]

War and sport are about the only international contests in which people from one nation can measure themselves physically and directly against others. The New Zealanders felt that they had been tested and not found wanting. Rugby stimulated national pride and national feeling. It brought the nation together, providing a focus for a feeling of unity. It brought Maori and Pakeha together. The views of women are unknown, but certainly many women were keen spectators; many must have shared the feelings of national pride. Mothers and sisters were also involved in the game in numerous ways as helpers.

The ex-servicemen's journal, *Quick March*, said in 1923 that, just as a man is known by the company he keeps, 'so is a country by the standard of good pure sport there'. So many of New Zealand's 'best sports' had been killed in the First World War that there followed a period of 'lean years' as new sportsmen grew up.[35] Dave Gallagher, for instance, was killed, and another of the 1905 All Blacks, E. T. Harper. The visit of a South African team in 1921 provided fresh stimulus. The two national teams won a game each and then drew one. The apotheosis of New Zealand rugby came in 1924 when the All Blacks went 'Home' again. This time they had a stuffed and mounted kiwi for a mascot. A special haka was composed during the voyage by Wiremu Rangi of Gisborne and Judge Acheson of the Native Land Court. One line announced that 'the New Zealand storm is about to break' – 'Ko Niu Tireni e haruru nei.'

This team won every game. Wales was beaten nineteen–nil. The newspapers ran large headlines. The *Daily Mail* proclaimed the team 'the greatest rugby side on earth'. They were the 'champions of the world'.[36] This time they were welcomed by crowds at the Wellington wharves, where a Harbour Board speaker declared that the All Blacks were 'the greatest asset New Zealand has had, excepting the Expeditionary Forces'.[37] There were processions, a jazz ball and a parliamentary banquet. Then, as the team broke up, its members received fresh welcomes in their home towns. For instance, when the West Coast All Black, Jack ('Frosty') Steel, arrived at the Greymouth railway station,

Top sportsmen: tennis player Anthony Wilding and runner Arthur Porritt. *Turnbull*

he was met by a crowd and taken to a mayoral reception in the Opera House. The names of the official guests at this and other receptions were published in the newspapers.

The point need not be elaborated that the role of sport in the community was not only a stimulus to competitiveness and a source of national pride in international success. Rugby provided the biggest public rituals and celebrations. Played at its best it aspired to art, if not religion.

Other sports as well as rugby provided the success that fuelled the national fires. In the 1890s several hurdlers and sprinters did well at the British and Australian athletic tournaments. In 1924 A. E. Porritt won New Zealand's first Olympic medal, finishing third in the hundred metres. We have, said the *Evening Post*, 'a place in the light of other suns than Rugby'.[38]

At the same time an outstanding middle-distance runner, Randolph Rose, was making a name for himself. In 1926 the American, Lloyd Hahn, one of the best milers in the world, competed in New Zealand.

From the *Chronicles of the N.Z.E.F.*, 27 March 1918. *Auckland Public Library*

Rose beat him four times out of five, setting a New Zealand record of 4 min. 13.6 sec., which broke the Australasian record by 4.8 seconds. At that time the world record was held by Paavo Nurmi at 4 min. 10.4 sec. Rose's record stood until 1950. A fund was raised to send Rose to Europe, where, it was hoped, that he would run against Nurmi. He failed to reproduce his best form, and the race against Nurmi did not eventuate. Rose's races against Hahn were the most memorable athletic contests in New Zealand up to that time.

A few other once-famous athletes inspired New Zealand enthusiasm. A champion cyclist, marksman and sculler, J. D. Arnst, won the world single sculls championship several times, most notably in 1910 in a race on the Zambesi river. The *New Zealand Herald* was moved to say:

before Home-bred writers bewail the physical degeneration of the colonial-born they might explain why it is that so many of the athletic championships have passed to New Zealanders, Australians, or Canadians, or to New Zealand, Australian, or Canadian teams.[39]

In 1890 an Aucklander, 'Torpedo Billy' Murphy won the world featherweight boxing championship in San Francisco. In 1928 Tom Heeney lost in eleven rounds against Gene Tunney in a bout in New York for the world heavyweight title.

Perhaps the most acclaimed success was that of a tennis player, Anthony Wilding. Like Porritt, who was at Oxford, Wilding, a student at Cambridge, had the advantage of adequate international competition, the lack of which was the great handicap of most New Zealand athletes. Wilding won the Wimbledon men's singles title each year 1910–13. He and his partners won the 1907–8 and 1910 men's doubles and the mixed doubles once. He and Norman Brookes of Australia won the Davis Cup as an Australasian team in 1907–8 and 1914. He won numerous other tournaments. He trained very hard and was supremely fit; he preached moderation in all things.[40] He was very good-looking and had many fans. He has been called 'the forerunner of the Bjorn Borg era'. He was killed at Ypres in 1915.

Chapter Eleven

CAIRO TO LE QUENOY, 1914–18

New Zealand was fairly well prepared to take part in the First World War. The 1909 Defence Act had introduced compulsory military service for all males from the age of fourteen to thirty. They served first in the Cadets and then in the Territorials. Both cadets and 'Terries' were part-time soldiers; they had periodic parades, training and camps. Colonel (later General) Alexander Godley was brought out from England to take charge of the system. He brought with him some staff officers and created the New Zealand Staff Corps and the Permanent Staff. The army was well equipped and well armed. Of the Main Body which sailed for Egypt in 1914, 82 per cent had had previous military training. Seventy-four per cent were New Zealand born.[1] The expeditionary force included a Maori contingent (a fact to be referred to in a later chapter) and men from Niue and Rarotonga.

Once again, as in South Africa, the New Zealanders had an opportunity to compare themselves with other men and rarely found themselves wanting. They stopped at Colombo, where they found the Cingalese men 'remarkable for their diminutive size'.[2] In Egypt national prejudices had a field day.

From the first there was 'bad blood' between New Zealanders and Australians. There was frequent trouble: 'If we meet or see them in a restaurant or anywhere in town there is generally a row of some kind.'[3] (It should be added that it is extremely common for trouble to arise between troops from allied countries running into one another on leave.)

Lieutenant H. H. S. Westmacott wrote that they had seen little of the Australians at work and 'had formed a very poor opinion of them when we met them on leave, when they thronged the streets of Cairo and seemed to us very boastful and noisy.' While they were on a route march in close formation, a 'disreputable Australian' in the Light Horse tried to pass through the ranks. He was brushed aside and his comment, '"F..k this I am out for fun" only gave us a sense of superior contempt.'[4]

When an Australian soldier was reprimanded by an Australian officer for molesting an Egyptian the other Australians 'counted him out'. Several New Zealanders recorded such incidents. Lieutenant C. S. Algie, who saw one episode, wrote, 'These fellows seem to have a tremendous hooligan element among them.'[5] This clearly was the case. There were endless complaints from generals and numerous arrests. Several hundred Australian drunkards, shirkers and VD cases were sent home.[6] (Twenty-four members of the Wellington regiment were repatriated for refusing to be vaccinated!)[7]

It was often said by New Zealand and British observers that the New Zealanders were, on the whole, more disciplined. Even the Australian newspaper correspondent, C. E. W. Bean, thought the New Zealander 'more urbane, less of a child of nature than the Australian'.[8] Nevertheless, he recorded various examples of New Zealand drunkenness and riot in his war diaries.[9] Probably the behaviour of Australians attracted more attention simply because they made up the great majority of the Australasian troops. Soldiers from both countries were noted for not saluting officers.[10] Obviously the New Zealanders had their share of ruffians. One member of the Auckland Mounted Rifles described how New Zealanders stole beer. They would enter a bar, and one of them would jump on a table and shout 'Rough house!' The others would start smashing chairs, shouting and fighting. The Egyptians would run away with the money; the New Zealanders would roll out the forty gallon kegs.[11]

New Zealanders caught VD in startling numbers.[12] In April 1915 the New Zealanders and Australians rioted in the brothel district, wrecking and burning furniture and other property, apparently in retribution for VD contracted by their friends. Bean believed that it was started by some New Zealanders. Numerous soldiers recorded this episode in their diaries.[13]

There were, of course, New Zealanders who had a favourable opinion of the Australians. Captain H. K. Hatrick, for instance, wrote that there was an Australian brigade on the ship, sailing to Gallipoli, and 'I never saw a finer class of soldier.'[14] Nevertheless, the fact that there was trouble between the two armies has been recorded in books in both countries and well documented in soldiers' letters and diaries.[15]

Equally well attested is the fact that feelings of rivalry or hostility evaporated after the landing on what came to be called Anzac cove. There 'an alliance of brotherhood was forged . . . .'[16]

It is clear from soldiers' papers – and from press comment – that, despite the appalling casualties in France in the actions of 1914, New Zealanders had not the slightest idea of what modern war was like. They did, however, strongly believe that honour was to be sought in the cannon's mouth.

Mateship at the front. *The Kia-Ora Cooee*, March 1918.

In January 1915 the Turks advanced towards the Suez canal: 'Of course it was good news for us . . . everyone was in a great state of excitement and joy . . . .' The 12th Nelson Company was 'honoured' to be selected as first reserves and was in action, suffering a few casualties.[17] The men were 'not taking their war against the Turks very seriously': they referred to the night raiders as 'a harmless lot of orange sellers'.[18]

On 25 April, as the convoy steamed towards Gallipoli, Sergeant Richard Ward wrote in his diary, 'This I have no doubt will be the greatest day in our lives.'[19]

The first Australian division landed before dawn, but the Royal Navy had taken them to the wrong beach, facing cliffs and steep hills, a tangle of ravines and slopes covered with scrub. They took the beach by assault and drove inland, suffering severe casualties. By mid-day the New Zealand division followed. They lost 600 casualties on the first day – more than during the three years of the Anglo-Boer war.[20]

An engineer, E. C. Clifton, wrote in his diary that the Australians had 'covered themselves with glory' – 'one would hardly know the Australians, officers & men, as the same who were in Egypt haggling at one another.'[21] After this day, criticism of the Australians is rarely found in New Zealand war diaries. The change of attitude may be illustrated by one example. Back in Egypt, in 1916, Fred Voitre Kofsky wrote to his girl-friend, Florrie, in Hawera, that he and two friends had tried to rescue a drunken Australian sergeant who was being beaten up by a crowd of 'natives' near the 'Nigger quarters'. They were having a rough time themselves when 'about a dozen good old Australians came up with a rush .... I can tell you the Australian chaps are good fellows, & always go to anyone's assistance no matter how many are against them.'[22] Men of the two new nations had come to trust each other, which they continued to do throughout the war.

Whether Australian conduct in Cairo or at Gallipoli was in fact worse or better than New Zealand is irrelevant in a nationalist scrutiny. That the island troops did indeed feel themselves superior, or at least equal, to those from the Trans-Tasman continent was part of a nation-building exercise and a later mystique.

The other side of New Zealand's question of identity, as we have seen, was the British connection. Again, jealousy, suspicion and prejudice were to be favourably modified by successive experiences. The New Zealanders' first sight of British soldiers was in Egypt when some of Kitchener's New Army began to arrive. The most common comment by New Zealanders was that they seemed astonishingly young, 'mere boys'. Most of the New Zealanders were over twenty-one.[23] The New Zealanders saw few of the professional British soldiers, for instance, the Guards. These were the 'terriers', the territorial army. One soldier wrote that they were 'not in the same class as the Australasians, the average height being about 5 ft. 4 ins. and 17 years old ....'[24] Colonel W. G. Malone of the Wellington regiment wrote, 'Our men seem like Giants alongside them.'[25] The British soldiers were, indeed, generally smaller, but few of the New Zealanders could have known that, because of the appalling casualties suffered in France in 1914, the British had reduced the minimum height for a soldier from five feet eight to five feet three.[26]

At Gallipoli the New Zealanders were profoundly unimpressed with the fighting qualities of the British troops there. They criticised the British for retreating from positions that the New Zealanders had won. This was a constant Australian complaint about the British too.[27]

The main thrust of Australasian criticism of the British, however, was directed against their officers and, eventually, the whole command. Basically the Australians and New Zealanders resented the intrusion of the class system of Great Britain into its army, where the officers were almost a caste. The Australians and New Zealanders prided themselves upon having citizen's armies, where social equality ruled as far as possible. As in South Africa, the New Zealand troops were said to be the social equals of the officers, which was far from being the case in the British services.

Major F. M. Twistleton wrote, in 1917, 'The weak place in the British army is the officer, he seems to think he is of different clay to his men. I would sooner trust my Lance Corporals with a crowd of men where things have to be done than any officer of theirs I have seen.'[28]

There can be little doubt that the New Zealanders had been taught by their parents, or had otherwise acquired, a strong dislike of the speech, manners and attitudes of the higher British classes. Thus there was a lower, or non-upper, class element in New Zealand perceptions of the British. To give one example, a New Zealand soldier, Cecil Malthus, was on leave from a hospital in Cairo:

> *My first outing was marred by a clash with a little bounder of a British officer of the futile but self-important type, complete with monocle, which placed him on a higher plane in the animal kingdom. He was deep in a doorway as I passed, but came bounding out after me and accused me of* lèse-majesté*: '. . . You stroll past one . . . You don't salute one, etc., etc., etc. Do you call yourself a British soldier?' To that I am afraid I answered, 'No, thank God', upon which he muttered, 'Oh, you are one of these colonials', and modified his attitude a bit. But I turned away and left him still gobbling like a mongoose. This incident put me in a very bad humour.*[29]

What finally ruined the reputation of the British in New Zealand opinion was their behaviour during the actions at Chunuk Bair and Suvla Bay in early August 1915, battles described at length in various books.[30] A new offensive was planned to seize the heights which commanded both sides of the peninsula, with several coordinated assaults. The British were to land an army at Suvla Bay, to drive across the plains and link up with the Anzacs on the heights. The Australians were to attack opposite Lone Pine. The New Zealanders were to take the outposts in the foothills and then take the commanding height of Chunuk Bair.

The New Zealand Mounted Rifles, with attached platoons of

Maoris, were brilliantly successful. Despite heavy losses, they went in with the bayonet and took several key hills. The Turkish hills rang with the Maori cry, 'Ka Mate! Ka mate! Ka ora! Ka ora!' (The Pakeha usually fought silently, but they too, on occasions, shouted a haka. When the Turks attacked, shouting 'Allah! Allah!', Major P. J. Overton wrote, 'We responded with a good old 'Ake Ake Kia Kaha').[31] Private Kohi Hemana wrote from a Cairo hospital. 'It is just like football. We had colours on too [for identification].' 'You can never imagine the fun we had that first night .... Every trench we took you'd hear the cheer before charging and the Maori war-cry .... Our Maori officers did some good work with our white New Zealand brothers and Australians by us. Nothing would stop us.'[32]

In one of the most famous actions in New Zealand military history, the Wellington infantry, led by Colonel Malone, took Chunuk Bair and looked down upon the Narrows of the Dardanelles, leading to Constantinople and the Black Sea. The allies seemed on the brink of victory: the Turks were almost encircled. Tragedy followed. The Wellingtonians could not be reinforced in time. They were shelled by a British destroyer, which, it was believed, caused the death of the colonel. Some of the New Army battalions, coming up to reinforce the New Zealanders, broke and fled the action. On one occasion several hundred Englishmen ran towards the Turks with their hands up. The New Zealand machine guns opened fire on them 'to prevent the whole front collapsing', a major wrote. They returned 'at some cost in life'.[33] Eventually New Zealanders, British and Gurkha reinforcements, were all driven off in disarray by a massive Turkish counter-attack. This time New Zealanders ran too.[34]

The British New Army Corps landed at Suvla Bay where it was pinned down by light Turkish forces and did not succeed in driving inland to draw in Turkish reinforcements. The failure of the new British units to fight effectively was the subject of bitter comment in the diaries of many New Zealand soldiers. One wrote to his mother, 'Would God we had 100 000 Australasians led by own officers and long ere this we would have been back in Egypt ....'[35] Some of the soldiers' letters were hysterical in their denunciation of English cowardice: 'A large number of the poor mothers in N.Z. can thank Kitchener's Army for the death of a number of their sons': 'They are damn curs and cowards ....'[36]

The New Zealanders' criticism of the British now extended to the High Command – even more than to the 'Tommies'. Major A. E. Alexander wrote of Suvla Bay, 'it was quite obvious that the troops in the landing were badly led, their officers were weak & they funked it . . . .' He blamed the Higher Command.[37]

Colonel Malone realised that in modern war at that time the advantage had swung to those on the defensive.

We and the other troops have suffered tremendous losses because our directors failed to quickly appreciate that this is the day of digging and machine guns and that prepared positions cannot be rushed . . . . now it is going to be sap sap dig dig. The war of Flanders again. I expect every day to be told to, in our Brigadiers words 'Fix Bayonets and go right through no shilly shallying about everybody going on'. If I do there is a 500 yd slope in front of me over which my men must pass and it is absolutely commanded and enfiladed by a number of Machine Guns across a big gully.[38]

The British High Command continued to believe in massed infantry assaults until the end of the war.

Denunciation of British leadership was to continue throughout the war, but there is little criticism of British troops after Gallipoli. This was partly because the New Zealanders saw some of the crack British regiments in action, partly because there were so few New Zealand survivors of Gallipoli, who had seen sections of the New Army crumble. Not many Main Body soldiers survived to fight in France.

In these actions both sides suffered fearful casualties. A few days before the Chunuk Bair action Lieutenant H. H. S. Westmacott was badly wounded. He told his sergeant to leave him: 'I'm finished' – 'You must take command of the platoon now.' Sergeant Ward replied, 'I beg your pardon Sir. It is no use talking like that . . . there is no platoon left.'[39] On Chunuk Bair the Wellington battalion was virtually wiped out. There were only ninety out of 750 to answer the roll-call the next day. By the end of the month there were only fifteen. In the end, at Gallipoli there were 7400 casualties out of 8500 who had fought.[40]

The battle at Gallipoli had profound effects on the 'home front'. At first the landing by the troops was hailed with naive 'joy and pride', much the same emotions as were expressed by some soldiers. At last 'our young New Zers' were being given the chance to prove themselves as good as the Canadians had been at Ypres.[41] Within two months soldiers' letters from the war began to be published in the newspapers, describing their 'feelings and actions' during 'The Baptism of Fire'.[42] But news of what had occurred came through only very slowly and partially. Ominously, the first casualty lists, in mid-May, contained only the names of officers. A month later the *New Zealand Herald* was

Anti-German feeling at home. *Turnbull*

still complaining that the names of officer casualties were cabled through at once while the names of other ranks arrived five or six weeks later.[43] These delays caused great public anxiety. What the public could not know was the difficulty, in the gullies and scrub of Gallipoli, where thousands of bodies lay for weeks, months – even years – of determining who was dead. Very few New Zealand dead were buried in individual graves.[44] But by mid-July the first wounded were returning and the people began to learn about the realities of war.

Knowledge, far from depressing, stimulated a widespread passion for victory. There was virulent talk of the 'satanic preconceptions' of the Germans and of their propensity to rapine and to bayoneting babies.[45] Citizens of German extraction, like Professor von Zedlitz at the Victoria University College, were persecuted. Even New Zealand-born men of German parentage were badly treated: one man, Frank Ackerman, who fought with the New Zealand Division, said that 'his life with the Forces was rendered most irksome by the continual taunts levelled at him . . . .' His brother was imprisoned in New Zealand for refusing to obey orders.[46]

When the level of the casualties became clear, a first concern of the Government was recruiting. By November the Prime Minister, William Massey, was promising to send about 2500 men per month to front up to the guns. An undignified dispute broke out in the press as to whether New Zealand was sending, proportionately, as many of its men as Australia. By late 1915 it was estimated that New Zealand might need to 'supply' 100 000 men – which was not far out – and newspapers were asking whether we should rashly promise more.[47]

A powerful campaign was launched for recruits.

URGENT APPEAL

1000 MEN WANTED

FOR THE FIRING LINE

So a newspaper headlined a Defence appeal for more infantry for the 11th Reinforcements.[48]

As in other countries, women played a major role in recruiting. And they were caught up in the national – and imperial – war in innumerable other ways, some as simple as knitting socks and wrapping food parcels. Lady Annette Liverpool, the wife of the Governor, published *Her Excellency's Knitting Book*, which proclaimed:

For Empire and for Freedom
We all must do our bit;
The men go forth to battle,
The women wait and knit.

A Volunteer Sisterhood was established to encourage women to work as clerks, shop assistants, waiters and so on to release men for the front.[49] The National Efficiency Board urged women to join the work-force. And women did increase their share of the employment field at the expense of men, a change which continued up to 1921. However, by 1926 there was a decline in the number and the percentage of women working.[50] All over the country different districts elected 'Queens' and then embarked on fund-raising for the Patriotic Fund, holding Queen Carnivals, auctions and the like. For instance, in a ten weeks' carnival period, the Auckland Queens raised £269 000.[51]

In New Zealand, which had as recently as 1912–13 been socially divided by strikes and violent anti-strike action, the war was cohesive. The Prime Minister, W. F. Massey, said that there was scarcely a family not represented at the front.[52] In country districts and in suburbs each party of soldiers was farewelled at gatherings in the local halls.

Support from the women: *Her Excellency's Knitting Book*; 'She Helps Her Boy to Victory'. *Turnbull*

Returning men were often driven in motor processions through streets lined with cheering crowds.

Not all males were eager to die, as had been shown by the replies to an official questionnaire in 1916. Only 58.4 per cent of the eligible males who replied (187 682 men) were willing to serve overseas in the armed forces; 77 999, or 41.5 per cent were unwilling to serve in the armed forces, or willing to serve only in a civil capacity. Over 18 per cent were unwilling to undertake any war service.[53] However, in 1916 conscription was introduced.

Beneath all the militaristic fervour, there must have been many people with grave doubts as well as broken hearts. Even in 1915 there was much criticism in the newspapers about British staff blunders in Gallipoli, especially at the time of Chunuk Bair. Some of this originated from British reporters like Ashmead Bartlett, but New Zealanders had the same opinion.[54] New Zealand press comment became harsher when the Dardanelles Commission later made public the disastrous series of mistakes that had been made. New Zealanders became more conscious of 'the losses and sufferings needlessly inflicted upon our own heroic soldiery'.[55]

Early in 1916 the New Zealand division was reorganised, mainly from fresh troops, in Egypt. The Maoris, who had been divided up among four New Zealand regiments, were now turned into a Pioneer Battalion, that is, a non-combatant labour force. It was, the historian of the Division wrote, 'a happy solution' – presumably to the problem that the British did not approve of non-European troops fighting against Europeans. Maoris did, however, take part in patrols when the Division moved into the line near Armentières.[56] Others served in NZEF units other than the Pioneers.

In July the New Zealanders took part in the battle to capture Pozières. There was a terrifying artillery barrage, said to have been the worst in the war. It was 'the most horrible night the soldiers had ever experienced'. The Anzacs, Scots and London Territorials faced 'a wall of iron' and went through it. The New Zealanders helped to capture Flers and drove the Germans back several miles. The casualties were appalling. In the first battle of the Somme the New Zealanders suffered 7400 casualties, the Australians 23 000 and the Canadians 24 000.[57]

It is not possible here to chronicle the story of the New Zealanders' role in what were once famous battles, now remembered mainly by very elderly veterans. Few nations have ever been so reckless with their youths or their youths with their lives. They fought at Messines and

In action. *Australian War Memorial*

claimed to have stormed the ridge. This the Australians disputed. It was even brought up in Parliament in Wellington.[58] The *Press* had no doubts.

HAIG'S LATEST BLOW.

NEW ZEALANDERS' MAGNIFICENT PART.

"SLASHING DEFEAT INFLICTED ON THE ENEMY."

Most Important Victory of The War.

4th Year–69th Day.[59]

In the appalling battle of Passchendaele in October 1917 New Zealanders waded through waist-deep mud (in which the wounded drowned) and hurled themselves without avail against barbed wire. Many were shot by snipers from the élite riflemen, the green-clad Jaegers.[60] We lost 2500 men; some 640 lay forever in Flanders fields.

During the last great German offensive in March 1918 the Germans forced a passage between two retreating British armies and advanced towards Amiens. The New Zealanders were thrown in to close the gap. Bombadier B. D. Stokes wrote in his diary, 'We passed Australians,

Canadians and South Africans – all the Colonials seem to have been called to check the beastly Hun.' He wrote of the retreating British troops, that the Tommies 'seemed to have lost all confidence – they seemed to have let "Fritz" come all the way as he liked.'[61] Flushed with victory, some of the German troops encountered by the New Zealanders near the village of Mailly-Maillet scarcely bothered to take cover. 'The shooting for a couple of hours that morning was very good,' wrote a New Zealand war-hero, Second Lieutenant Ormond Burton, Military Medal, Medaille d'Honneur (who was to be a leading pacifist during the Second World War). Large numbers of Germans were killed. The New Zealanders established a new front line in some old trenches, and the gap was closed.[62]

The Germans were soon in retreat almost everywhere. At a place called Trescault Spur they made a stand, bringing in two crack divisions, one of them the Jaegers. They were attacked by the New Zealand Rifle Brigade, the 'Dinks', so-called, originally in derision, by the veterans of Gallipoli. The Governor-General had announced that the newly recruited brigade was the finest body of troops in the world. In other words, they were 'fair dinkum soldiers'. After the Somme they bore the label like a medal.[63]

There was bitter fighting, of which Burton wrote:

the Jaegers made a grand attack and poured down every sap in a desperate attempt to win back the lost ground, but the riflemen held on grimly and at last, as darkness fell, the enemy sullenly gave up and the fight rested. Three days later the Rifle Brigade attacked again, and despite desperate resistance, carried the greater part of the ridge. The Jaegers lost heavily and their dead lay thickly through all the trenches and in the cemeteries behind. All honour to these brave German men who fought a hopeless fight and stood like a strong wall when all about them their army was breaking and their cause lost. They were very valiant men.[64]

The New Zealanders advanced to the east, besieging the walled town of Le Quenoy. They took it 'in old-fashioned style', scaling the ramparts and capturing the German garrison.[65] Soon they marched and entrained into Germany.

The New Zealand Division had become highly professional soldiers, skilled at trench warfare. Pride in their skill shines out in their books such as Ormond Burton's *Silent Division*. The colonial divisions were frequently used as shock troops. During the war the Canadians lost 103 per cent of their original strength, the Australians 96 per cent, the New Zealanders 95 per cent, the British 81 per cent. New Zealand's war

Taking shelter. *Australian War Memorial*

effort was astonishing. 124 211 men, 11.4 per cent of the population, were mobilised for service overseas, over 100 000, some 10 per cent, actually served abroad.[66] By 1917 there were only 2400 out of the original 23 200 still on active service.[67] By the end of the war there had been 58 000 casualties. Of all New Zealand men aged twenty to forty, nearly one out of every three had been killed or wounded.[68]

The English journalist, Ashmead Bartlett, wrote in 1915, that the Australasians with their 'amazing physique', which Europeans could not match, were 'not so much an army as a community come together for a job'.[69] Certainly many New Zealanders felt something of the sort. Trooper Roderick McCandlish wrote, 'It seems great to be such a long way from home but we are all New Zealanders and now that we are away from our own country we all stick together like glue'.[70] That was strikingly true of New Zealanders during all their wars abroad and doubtless true of men from most other nations sent to foreign wars.

As a community they invented their own names or were given them by others. They were often called 'Pig Islanders' or 'Maorilanders', probably more often by the 'Aussies' than by themselves. Occasionally, for instance, in *Punch*, they were called 'Fernleaves'. A white fernleaf on a black circle was the tactical sign used, for instance, to identify the New Zealand Division's trucks. The soldiers' journal, *Chronicles of the*

NZEF, referred to 'Wiri Fernleaf' going to Paris and to 'the average Fernleaf'. On a couple of occasions that name was used in soldiers' letters,[71] but it is very unlikely that they used it as a form of address. It is difficult to imagine a New Zealand soldier calling his mate 'Fernleaf'.

In 1917 some of the New Zealand men in a working battalion which was burying cables began to address one another as 'digger'.[72] The name caught on among both the Australians and New Zealanders, perhaps because digging was such a constant occupation, and became the almost invariable form of address. The name survived into the Second World War as 'dig'. The 'digger' was called a 'kiwi', and represented as one in cartoons.[73] The army pierrot troupe, led by Corporal Tiri Katene, came to be called the Kiwi Concert Party. In the *Chronicles of the NZEF* the New Zealanders called themselves 'Kiwis', 'diggers', 'Pig Islanders' and 'Enzeds' interchangeably.

It is noticeable that there is much less vainglory in soldiers' letters and diaries from France than from Egypt or Gallipoli. They had now seen the Guards and Scots Highlanders and other famous units, as well as the Australians, in action and were now less likely to think themselves superior to other troops, but simply, as good as the best.

Like the South African war, but more so, the First World War was a powerful stimulus to national feeling. It encouraged nationalism in many ways, especially among the men in the army. They lived close together and shared danger – both experiences encouraging a sense of community. They formed numerous social bonds and personal ties. Above all regular drill helped to form them into a coherent community. Though most of the men detested it, close-order drill encouraged *esprit de corps*, a feeling of belonging to a unit, acting as a unit. 'There is something irresistible and confidence making in the company of marching men in close formation', Lieutenant Westmacott wrote.[74] The men identified with their unit, the NZEF, and they regarded it as a national unit, not, for example, as a mercenary might identify with the army in which he serves, as an end in itself.

On his first day at Gallipoli Frank Cooper wrote, 'Today Australia and New Zealand have earned their place amongst the nations that breed heroes.'[75] Captain H. K. Hatrick wrote, after the fighting on Chunuk Bair, 'You will hear NZ boys praised and after what I saw let me tell you that we *are* a race on our own, "New Zealanders".'[76] The soldiers' heroism, the Prime Minister, W. F. Massey said, 'had made New Zealand a respected country with all the nations of the earth . . . .'[77]

There is a negative nationalism – dislike of other peoples – but there is also a positive nationalism, love of country. 'I don't think I shall ever want to leave N.Z. again . . . .' wrote Lieutenant Chris. Carrington, who was never to return from the war.[78] And Corporal L. D. Fitzmaurice wrote, 'If I come out of this allright I am coming back to N.Z. again there is no place like it in all the world for me.'[79]

The high praise the troops received abroad boosted national pride: for instance, in *The Times History of The War* or in the poet-laureate, John Masefield's *Gallipoli*, which said that the Australians and New Zealanders and the Royal Naval Division were the 'finest body of young men ever brought together in modern times. For physical beauty and nobility of bearing they surpassed any men I have ever seen. They walked and looked like the kings in old poems . . . .' Others, like the General, Sir Ian Hamilton, found classical analogies hard to ignore, so close to Greece. He wrote that 'Antiquity has no more glorious story'; 'The plains of Troy never echoed to the feet of such heroes.' It became a standby of editorial writers and speakers at Anzac Day ceremonies to call the Gallipoli landing the Thermopylae of the New Zealand and Australian soldiers. Or Crecy, Agincourt and the Light Brigade could be alternatively invoked.[80]

The idea was widely believed, as Eileen Duggan wrote in her poem, 'Invasion', that 'War shows what each man's country means to him.' It became accepted wisdom to write that the nation was born, as O. E. Burton wrote, 'Somewhere between the Landing at Anzac and the end of the Battle of the Somme'. It was then that 'New Zealand very definitely became a nation.'[81] In *The Silent Division*, Burton made many comments on this theme. He believed that New Zealanders were unaware of national unity; that some catastrophe was needed, some great suffering, some great deed done in common, to make them conscious of their identity. They found it on Chunuk Bair. Among the troops, a sense of nationalism and identity deepened between the murderous battles. He wrote movingly of the 'quiet intense pride, a certain elation and exultation; but over it all, deep sorrow for all the dear friends who were gone.'[82] Historians took up the theme. The new nation, wrote W. P. Morrell in 1935, first 'wrote its name on the page of history' on Anzac day, 1915.[83]

Occasionally historians have discovered data from questionnaires or referenda collected long before they became popular, offering answers to questions about public opinion thought unanswerable, not decisive answers, but perhaps the only ones we will get. In 1916 the Minister of Defence, James Allen, circulated to army officers, chaplains, YMCA

Marching towards Germany. *Australian War Memorial*

secretaries, and some NCOs, a questionnaire about the moral, mental and social changes in the troops resulting from war service. Only twenty-two men replied so a revised questionnaire was recirculated in 1917, eliciting twenty further replies, two of them from men who had answered in 1916. The detailed replies of forty men enable us to give a tentative answer to a very difficult question – what did the troops believe that they were fighting for and dying for? In 1917 one question was about the patriotism and pride of country and race, both as New Zealanders and as citizens of the Empire, of the average man on arrival in camp.[84]

Of the replies, twelve stressed patriotism, four stressed both factors and four did not comment. Only one, as an afterthought, put the Empire first. Lieutenant Drew emphasised the 'intense patriotism and pride, first of race, then of country' of the soldier: 'He feels a superiority in the fact that he is a New Zealander' but 'above even this pride he places . . . a pride of citizenship of the British Empire.'

H. T. Peat, a Methodist chaplain, stressed patriotism, as inspired by the heroism at Gallipoli – 'the average man is not an Imperialist', he wrote, 'because New Zealand had been treated, not as a partner, but as a child.' Major Johnson thought the soldier had a 'keen sense of patriotism generally' but 'Vague and indifferent ideas as to what the Empire means'. This was the most common opinion. Captain W. P.

Johnston said that the men had 'a full sense' of being New Zealanders: 'As a citizen of the Empire – except a few, I do not think the average man thinks much about it . . . .' Several other replies said the same thing. Colonel H. R. Potter stressed 'pride of country' too, but thought that 'the Empire spirit' was slowly developing.

The replies to other questions, such as the one about the differences between New Zealand-born and British soldiers and about whether the former were morally superior, produced repetitive assertions of the New Zealanders' patriotism and superiority.

These replies reinforce a conclusion already suggested in this book, that most New Zealanders were indifferent to imperial federation, to imperialism. The Empire belonged to an official rhetoric, to newspaper editors, to school teachers, to politicians, to Governors and Governors-General. 'The Empire' was for most people no more than an abstraction. It has recently been argued that much the same was true in Great Britain. The mass of the people were unmoved by imperial questions, which failed to become electoral issues.[85]

V

Interlude: Dates and Emblems

An entry in the competition for a national coat-of-arms. *National Archives*

Chapter Twelve

HOLY DAYS

There has been a view, widely accepted in New Zealand, that the population was relatively inhibited and puritanical. Moreover, it has been thought that it is right to be so. As M. K. Joseph said in his clever, satirical poem, 'Secular Litany', which interprets New Zealand's 'civil religion':

From all foreigners, with their unintelligible cooking
From the vicious habit of public enjoyment
From kermesse and carnival, high day and festival
From pubs cafés bullfights and barbecues
From Virgil and vintages, fountains and fresco-painting
From afterthought and apperception
From tragedy, from comedy
And from the arrow of God
  Saint Anniversaryday
  Saint Arborday
  Saint Labourday
    Defend us.

In the public behaviour of individuals or crowds, joy rarely found expression, except under the influence of alcohol. How to express feelings in public was a problem. Consequently, the choice of a national day involved not merely the selection of a date, but of appropriate forms of behaviour on that occasion.

In the nineteenth century the settlers used to celebrate the Queen's birthday with a holiday. After the death of Queen Victoria, Lord Meath pushed the idea of continuing this celebration on 24 May, calling it Empire Day. That day was first celebrated in New Zealand in 1904, but it never aroused much enthusiasm. It was not a public holiday and, although some offices and warehouses closed, most of the shops stayed open. In 1907 the *Lyttelton Times* reported that the celebrations were 'rather half-hearted'.[1] The trouble was, the *New Zealand Herald* observed in 1905, that the day was not associated with any 'tangible personality or tangible event which can most readily be seized upon by the popular mind.' It went on, 'If our untrammelled liberties had been won by bloodshed and battle we should celebrate them.'[2] What was needed, in short, was a good war or revolution.

When Edward VII died in 1910, Empire Day was allowed to lapse. Thereafter it aroused little interest, perhaps because of its proximity to King George V's birthday, which was a public holiday, on 6 June. Empire Day was said to be much more popular in the United Kingdom and in Canada.[3]

The most popular holiday, apart from Christmas and New Year's Day, was Anniversary Day, which was different in each province. In Auckland, for instance, the establishment of the settlement in 1840 was celebrated annually by a regatta on 29 January. This marked, not the arrival of the 'First Ships' as in Canterbury, but of the first Governor, William Hobson, at the Bay of Islands in 1840. That date had been gazetted as a public holiday as long ago as 1842. In January 1890 it was gazetted as a public holiday throughout the colony to celebrate the jubilee of the establishment of the colony.

This decision met with a very mixed reaction. The Wellington *Evening Post* thought it absurd that 'the arrival of a half-pay naval captain at Kororareka as Consul-General accredited to the sovereign chiefs of New Zealand should be celebrated as marking the establishment of the colony of New Zealand.' The Wellingtonians claimed that the proper date was the anniversary of the arrival of the first New Zealand Company settlers, Wellington's anniversary day, 22 January. The Auckland *Star* denied that the Wellington settlers had been founding a colony – rather, they aimed at setting up a 'bastard republic'. In an interesting editorial, almost certainly written by its editor, the future historian, William Pember Reeves, the *Lyttelton Times* reviewed the events of 1840. It said that Hobson was not really a governor when he landed, for he had nothing to govern. The day on which sovereignty was transferred to the Queen was undoubtedly the day on which the Treaty of Waitangi was signed, 6 February 1840. This was later to become the national day of what the editorial called 'a nation well knit together'.

In the event the jubilee was largely ignored in the South Island – neither Otago nor Canterbury had been settled in 1840, and their people had no sentimental attachment to 29 January. In Auckland there were great crowds, haka, yacht races, Maori canoe races between Waikato and Ngatiwhatua Maoris (the Ngapuhi refused to come) and out-rigger canoe races between Rarotongans. Rewi Maniapoto was among the visitors.[4]

So far there was no truly national day to celebrate. In 1907 the Prime Minister, J. G. Ward, tried to invent one. At the Imperial Conference in London in that year Ward argued that New Zealand had 'well outgrown the "colonial" stage'. It was as much entitled as the Commonwealth of Australia or the Dominion of Canada to a separate designation. He suggested 'Dominion of New Zealand', and he wrote to the Secretary of State for the Colonies, to urge the colony's case. Speaking in favour of a supporting resolution in Parliament, he referred back to Julius Vogel's efforts to create a New Zealand Polynesian federation in 1874. Vogel had looked forward to New Zealand becoming 'the head of a new dominion'. (Canada had become a Dominion in 1867.) By becoming a Dominion, New Zealand's status would be raised to a 'higher plane' than that of a colony. Ward said that in Great Britain many people thought that New Zealand was part of Australia and were unaware of its 'independent destiny'. Some people, like C. E. Major, the MP for Hawera, thought the name 'colony' had always been 'offensive'. Ward argued that in 'the Old Country' the term 'meant a new unsettled country' – not one of the self-governing colonies.[5] Other people also admitted to hating the name 'colonial'. The name 'colony' had come to seem appropriate, not to self-governing colonies of settlement, but to Crown colonies mainly inhabited by 'people of alien speech, manners, and habits'.[6]

Political opponents of the change thought the term too grandiose – 'bombastic'. The Leader of the Opposition, William Massey, an ultra-imperialist Ulsterman, preferred the term 'colony'.[7] There was much discussion of other possible names. The *Lyttelton Times* thought that the title 'Dominion' was associated with Canada. It canvassed the names 'territory' or 'domain'. Others suggested 'state', 'realm' or 'united provinces'. Some New Zealand-born MPs wanted just the name 'New Zealand',[8] a view which was, shortly after the Second World War, to be accepted.

The change of title, for which there had been no public demand, produced little public interest. It was widely regarded as Ward's personal show. The lack of interest is easy to understand, for the change of name was not accompanied by any constitutional change, such as occurred when some of the British North American colonies joined together in the Dominion of Canada. It was merely cosmetic. Nor is it clear now, if it was then, that the word 'dominion' implied a lesser subordination than 'colony'.

The public reaction to the change was very mixed. The *Lyttelton Times* acknowledged that some people valued 'a touch of grandiloquence in politics'. A 'colony' was no longer to be envisaged as a convict settlement – the name rhymed with 'felony'.[9]

When the Government proposed that 26 September should become a public holiday, Dominion Day, to mark the change, there was widespread debate. The *Lyttelton Times* conceded that the country would now have 'a native holiday common to all the provinces'.[10] Other papers spoke of 'a great national festival'. The *Auckland Star* suggested that Auckland's Anniversary Day should become Dominion Day, as January was a good time for a holiday.[11] Few people publicly supported the idea of adding an additional statutory holiday to the existing six. In Wellington Mr Whitcombe of Whitcombe and Tombs thought there were too many holidays. Mr Kirkcaldie of Kirkcaldie and Stains suggested abolishing Labour Day. In Auckland Mr Choyce had interviewed sixty fellow drapers, mercers and furnishers who all agreed that the day was most inconvenient for a holiday. Moreover, his employees had voted 182 to 48 against closing.[12] Ward's view was that perhaps the new public holiday could be merged with another. The only holiday at about that time of the year was Labour Day, on the fourth Monday in October, so naturally the Trades and Labour Council objected.[13] Many local bodies favoured a special celebration as, no doubt, did public servants, since they were to be paid.[14]

Ward urged that citizens should make Dominion Day a grand celebration. Only Wellington really took up his challenge. The proclamation declaring New Zealand to be a Dominion was publicly read by Ward. A military review followed, consisting of 1600 men, the Permanent Force, a Naval Brigade, the Volunteers, including the Zealandia Rifles and the school Cadets. Maoris from all over New Zealand, performed the haka, 'Ka mate, ka mate!' Later there was a big meeting in the Town Hall at which Ward outlined the country's ideals, notably to preserve 'the purity of the race .... We should resist to the last man any intention of any Eastern horde, which, by mixing with our population, would produce in this beautiful British country of ours a race of half-breeds.'[15]

In Christchurch, too, there was a big military parade, followed by an evening concert provided by the Garrison Band. In Auckland there was another parade, but some of the Volunteer Companies did not turn out and only two or three thousand people went to watch. It seems that most of the stores remained open. An aluminium Dominion Day medal was struck for every school child and Ward pronounced the day a wonderful success.[16]

On the whole, in 1908 too, the population declined the government's invitation to be demonstrative. In Christchurch the celebration was left almost entirely to the Volunteers, most people contenting themselves with watching rather than participating. A

Military Revel, Bazaar and Art Union was opened for a fortnight in the Barracks.[17] Wellington again showed more enthusiasm. Some 20 000 people turned out at Newtown Park to watch the parade. Over 5000 children carrying coloured flags formed a living New Zealand ensign. At night Parliament and other buildings were brilliantly illuminated, symbolising the country's 'bright future'.[18] In Auckland there was a marked lack of interest. The *Herald* used the occasion to denounce the Liberal Government. However, a good crowd attended the Avondale races.[19]

Sometimes Dominion Day was an occasion for nationalistic self-assertion, as in the *New Zealand Times* in 1911 when 'Tiru' discussed what the day meant. It was 'not an occasion for Imperial thoughts. It is a celebration all our own. It is a day upon which we can recall and be thankful for, the many advantages that attend our youth.' However, he said its significance could really only be understood by one who had travelled. 'Tiru' went on to express horror at the servility of the British poor towards the rich, the poverty to be seen in Italy, and the sight of women labouring in the fields in Germany.[20] But on the whole the day failed to find acceptance in the feelings of the public. In 1909 the *Dunedin Star* expressed the hope that it would disappear from the proposed list of statutory holidays. By the Public Holidays Act in 1910 it was 'Mondayised' – that is, the celebration ceased to be linked to 26 September, but to the nearest Monday, thus creating a three day week-end. William Massey, who led the Reform Party to power in 1912, had disapproved of the change of the country's name to Dominion. The new government did not promote the holiday. By 1912 it was marked mainly by the closure of government departments, banks and legal offices. Saluting the flag became a regular custom in schools; indeed, the significance of Dominion Day was strongly emphasised in the schools, and may have made a lasting impression.

Why Dominion Day failed to catch on is a matter for speculation. It might be thought to indicate the weakness of nationalism, and certainly some people considered that Empire Day was more important.[21] Probably the major factor, however, was that a change of title, without any other significant change, failed to arouse any emotional reaction. Also the weather in September was not holiday weather, whereas Labour Day in late October was clearly the spring festival.[22] Becoming a Dominion did, however, have an eventual effect. Now there were two Dominions, Canada and New Zealand. After the First World War the term 'dominion status' was adopted as a label for the constitutional position of the former self-governing colonies and the Irish Free State.

On Empire Day, in May 1915, there was a large military parade in Wellington, as the Anzacs were fighting in Gallipoli. A genuine national day was in the process of being born.[23] A year later a half-holiday on Anzac Day was gazetted in New Zealand. Anzac Day was also celebrated in Cairo (in 1918 it was called 'Gallipoli Day').[24] On this day, the *Press* in Christchurch proclaimed in 1920, New Zealand 'achieved nationhood, in the eyes of the world,' an assertion made repetitively and annually from that day to this.[25] In 1985 at the Dawn Ceremony of Remembrance at the cenotaph in Auckland it was announced that 'the service proclaimed our belief that the landing at Anzac was the dawn of nationhood to New Zealand and Australia.' At dawn the Anzac dedication was then pronounced. In part it says 'At this hour upon this day Anzac received its baptism of fire and became one of the immortal names in history.'

At the end of the war the Returned Servicemen's Association pressed to have Anzac Day declared a 'close' holiday, with no business transacted, hotels closed and sports functions forbidden. It was suggested that perhaps Anzac Day should replace Dominion Day.[26] At first there was opposition from some businessmen to the declaration of another holiday so close to Easter.[27] The British were considering introducing one holiday for the whole Empire, but the RSA wanted Anzac Day, to express a separate nationalism.[28]

In 1920 Parliament passed the Anzac Day Bill which would, in its original form, have made the day in all respects like a Sunday. However, the Government feared that if restrictions were too severe there might be a reaction, and the Bill was modified so as to close only hotels and prevent race meetings. Anzac Day in 1921 caused much dissatisfaction, for some businesses did not shut, and hotels closed while picture theatres remained open.[29] In 1921 the Act was amended so as to make it a 'close' holiday, 'a sacred day'. It was to be, said the *Evening Post*, not a holiday but a holy day.[30] In 1916 the commercial use of the name Anzac had been forbidden.[31]

During the early 1920s a ceremony to be adopted on Anzac Day was evolved. In 1920 Dr Boxer, the President of the RSA, suggested a ritual that was widely though not universally adopted.[32] The fundamental feature was to be that the whole service was sacred. It was not a commemoration of Gallipoli only but a tribute to the memory of all those who fell. The ceremony was to be 'as fully military as possible'. There was to be a parade in which a firing party with reversed arms at the trail would lead a gun carriage with wreaths and bearers. The ex-servicemen wearing their medals and ribbons would follow. The firing party was to enter the hall, which would be draped with flags, to Chopin's Funeral March and stand with bowed heads round a table, a symbolic bier, with wreaths on which was laid a soldier's hat. After two hymns a padre was to read part of the burial service. Three volleys were to be fired and the Last Post played. The service was a symbolic reenactment of a burial at the front.

Once Anzac Day was made a close holiday the ceremonies became even more impressive than before. In 1922 in Auckland some 2000 bemedalled veterans marched up Queen Street from the wharves to the Town Hall, through a great crowd of citizens. Many of the veterans carried poppies – it was the RSA's first Poppy Day, to remind people of Flanders Fields as well as of Gallipoli. Large numbers of serving sailors, airmen and representatives of the Australian and British services also marched. Outside the Town Hall a replica of the cenotaph, the empty tomb in London, had been erected. Just as today, four servicemen guarded it. The Governor-General, the Prime Minister, two VC's, the RSA executive and Army nursing sisters occupied the platform. One of the hymns they sang, Kipling's 'Recessional', soon became a constant element in the Anzac rituals. The audience listened to two speakers, before the playing of the 'Dead March' from *Saul* and then the Last Post. Other ceremonies followed later in the day.[33]

In Wellington on 23 April there was a large church parade of veterans of the Anglo-Maori wars, the South African war and the Great War. Some of the older men also wore medals from imperial campaigns in Egypt and 'the East'. On Anzac Day there was no march. A crowd of 4000 attended a children's ceremony, at a cenotaph erected in front of Parliament Buildings. Numerous wreaths and poppies and other floral tributes were laid at its foot. Often, in years to come, Brownies and Boy Scouts took part in Anzac Day rituals. Later there was an Assembly in the Town Hall. There were services in all the state schools – generally a prayer, hymn and a short address by an ex-serviceman. At night there was a sacred concert in the Town Hall.[34]

In Christchurch the ceremonies at this time included a larger religious element than in most places. There were, in 1922, early morning memorial services and communion in the Cathedral. Later there was a large procession of about 4000 ex-servicemen to a combined service in the Barracks.[35] Dunedin followed much the same procedure as Auckland. A parade of ex-servicemen marched to a replica of the cenotaph. After the laying of the wreaths there was an address and the burial service was read. Numerous church services followed.[36] Similar ceremonies were held in most small towns and country districts as well as in many suburbs. For instance, at Petone, a monument of Coromandel granite was unveiled in memory of local boys who had died.[37]

On all these occasions and on the thousands that have been held since, ministers, ex-servicemen, governors-general, generals and politicians have pronounced upon the meaning of Anzac Day.

The symbolism of the Anzac Day ceremony was explained by Pastor W. F. Nichol at Waimate in 1937: 'The bugler sounds the "Last Post"; the good night signal, "Lights Out." Your comrade has fallen asleep. But is that all the bugler sounds? No sooner has the last note of the bugle sounded but you hear another note. Triumphant with a ring of joy and certainty about it. THE REVEILLE .... And in that simple ceremony you are witnessing ... the Resurrection.'[38]

Anzac Day was, of course, an expression of sorrow; the ceremony enabled people to express their grief. But it was also held to be a kind of celebration, of the glory and the great victory won at last by the servicemen.[39] It was affirmed annually that 'Their Name Liveth for Evermore.'[40] It was often said that the men had answered the call of freedom and, in dying, had ensured that the nation could continue its democratic life.[41]

Many people, especially ex-servicemen, saw a deep moral purpose in Anzac Day. The war had been fought for justice and righteousness, which must now be preserved in peace-time. The ex-servicemen were the custodians of the nation's memories and its ideals. The RSA was the keeper of the dreams. The dead had fallen in defence of an ideal of a better world. Pastor Nichol said to the veterans: 'But we have grown weary of dreaming that dream. In this post-war world it seems so impossible and we are settling down to the old condition of things again. It is your task to keep that dream before us and, however difficult the task is, to keep us to it.'[42] Anzac Day was the day of dreams. The living must keep faith with the dead. Their work was unfinished. 'We must strive to carry on the unfinished work for which they had given their all. The challenge of Anzac was for us to live the sacrificial life', said the President of the Christchurch RSA, the Revd W. Walker, on 25 April 1922.[43] Moreover, the message must be passed on to future generations.

It has often been remarked that nationalism is a 'secular religion'. A South African has written about the 'civil religion' of the Afrikaners, with its catalogue of heroism, victories and grievous wrongs.[44] The Irish have a similar historical chronicle. The New Zealanders, too, have a secular religion. It celebrates first of all the heroic work of the pioneers, in 'breaking in' the land. Their achievements are saluted by stone monuments erected in many parts of the country, for instance, at Waipu and Okarito. Victories in sport and victories and defeats in war, however, are the principal causes of celebration. Most of New Zealand's monuments are war memorials.

As has been remarked, New Zealanders were not notable church-goers. In 1891, for instance, only 28 per cent of the population attended church, a significantly smaller proportion than in Great Britain.[45] In response to Sir James Allen's questionnaires about the soldiers in 1916 and 1917, of whose few who commented on the influence of religion on the men, seven said it had none at all, six thought it strong, but they included two chaplains and a YMCA secretary.

In New Zealand nationalism fulfilled some of the roles of religion. It helped to make the death of so many men meaningful, while offering a kind of immortality to the dead. It was based upon suffering and heroism. More than on any other day of the year, on Anzac Day life took on a fuller dimension and purpose. In the light of the past, the present assumed a grandeur in the imaginations of many people surpassing anything to be seen in the light of day.

From the first the ex-servicemen had resisted the introduction of denominational services: they wanted a simple service like those at the front. By the 1930s the RSA had increasingly gained control of the Anzac Day ceremonies: the military aspect increased in importance and the religious element was reduced. It became more common to select a speaker from the armed forces. In 1939, following Australian precedent, the Dawn Service was introduced throughout the country (a few towns had adopted it earlier).[46] It reminded the veterans of the dawn stand-to in the trenches, but might, indeed, have been some pagan ceremony. The men march in procession towards the hushed crowds in the dark. The Last Post sounds and then, as dawn greys the horizon, the Reveille.

The notion of paganism is greatly strengthened if one looks at the monuments erected in memory of the dead in all parts of the country. They are neither churches nor chapels; the cross is rarely employed. Rather, they look back to the Greek cenotaph, the empty tomb, or to the column. The Auckland War Memorial, like the National Museum in Wellington, was inspired by Greek temples. Each is placed on a hill, like the Acropolis. The obelisk looks back to ancient Egypt. Some monuments are arches, like the triumphant arches often erected in nineteenth-century New Zealand to welcome distinguished guests.

War memorials: the Carillon, Wellington, *c.* 1932; 'The unveiling of soldiers' memorial 30.6.21 – Havelock-Marlborough.' *Turnbull*

These, too, derive from the pre-Christian world.[47] In many countries, these war memorials played a major role in strengthening nationalism. The nation was imagined as a community in which everyone shared, and to which everyone owed an equal duty. For men, that duty included, if necessary, the supreme self-sacrifice.

Chapter Thirteen

SIGNS AND SONGS

The new nations in the British dominions all sought for symbols of identification, like those in British armorial bearings. Generally they adopted British (and, in the case of Canada, traditional French) elements, as well as adding local emblems such as the maple leaves in the Canadian coat-of-arms.

In the late nineteenth and early twentieth centuries New Zealand was sometimes represented in cartoons as a small boy, or as a lion cub.[1] Frequently the country was represented as a moa, occasionally envisaged as an avian camel. In the *New Zealand Graphic and Ladies Journal* in the 1890s New Zealand was billed as 'The Land of the Moa'.[2]

By the late nineteenth century a fernleaf (from the 'silver fern') was widely adopted as the national emblem – the 1888 New Zealand Natives rugby team and the succeeding All Blacks wore a fernleaf on a black jersey. A fernleaf was a badge of the army volunteers and was worn by some troops both at the South African war and at the First World War. The 'green fern-leaf' was, a poet declared, 'Our National Flower'. Others argued for the pohutukawa, the kowhai and the rata.[3] The symbol that was eventually most widely used for New Zealand and its inhabitants, the kiwi, took some time to be accepted. The kiwi appeared on some regimental badges during the South African war.[4] It featured more commonly on First World War badges.

In 1905 the kiwi was used to represent its country in a cartoon in a London newspaper which was republished in the *New Zealand Herald*. It shows a kangaroo and a kiwi going to a Colonial Conference in London. A few days later the *Herald's* cartoonist, Trevor Lloyd, drew what is at present believed to be the first New Zealand cartoon portraying New Zealand as a kiwi, almost, but not quite, swallowing Wales in the famous test match.[5] It is not clear whether Lloyd derived the idea from the *Westminster Gazette*, but certainly he popularised the identification by using kiwis repeatedly in his cartoons. He liked the emblem so much that he also drew it inside his own books.

For some reason, at present mysterious, the kiwi was acquiring a new appeal to the New Zealand imagination, as a uniquely national emblem. In 1905 the Students' Association at the Auckland University College launched a new literary journal, *The Kiwi*, which was to last, with brief interruption, for sixty-one years. They took the name,

The moa and the kiwi featured early as national emblems. A painting by J. E. Ward, early this century, from the *Auckland Star. Turnbull*

perhaps, from the College Seal adopted in 1887, when three kiwis were substituted for the three stars suggested by the London designer.[6]

As we have seen, New Zealanders began to be called, and to call themselves, 'Kiwis' during the later stages of the First World War, at the same time that the term 'digger' came into use. In August 1917, for example, a New Zealand soldier in a convalescent depot in France wrote that the 'Ossies, Kiwis, Canadians, and South Africans' formed 'quite a happy family'.[7] At the same time the word 'kiwi' was receiving much publicity as the name of a shoe polish. 'Kiwi' polish was originally made in Melbourne, in 1906, by a man with a New Zealand wife. During the war millions of tins of the polish were sold to the army and it was widely advertised in London. The New Zealanders sometimes said that they 'kiwied' their boots.[8]

The New Zealanders continued to identify their country with other symbols, such as the fernleaf or the Southern Cross, which had been accepted as a national emblem in 1869, when it was adopted as the badge of the colony, for instance, on the Blue Ensign. But certainly by the Second World War, they generally identified themselves as Kiwis, and were so-called by other English-speaking peoples. Their self-identification with a flightless, nocturnal bird was not totemic. There was no mystic association; no identification of the New Zealand man

The Kiwi and the Cage, a Prohibition poster from 1928. *N.Z.*: 'How many times must I tell you I *won't* be caged? Take the darn thing away.' *Turnbull*

with nature. The device was not totemic but heraldic. It was obviously chosen because the bird was unique to New Zealand and – unlike some other local species, the weta or the tuatara, for instance – was thought to have a certain charm. It was also easily recognisable.

Two competitions for a design for a New Zealand coat-of-arms, held in 1906 and again in 1908, provide a guide to the symbolic state of the New Zealand psyche at that time. Why the competition was repeated is not known. It was reported that the 1906 entries had been destroyed when the old Parliament buildings burned down in 1907, but that was incorrect.[9] Both lots of entries are in the National Archives.

In 1906 there were twenty-eight entries and seventy-five in 1908. Some contestants put in multiple entries which were given a single number. Some of the contestants explained the choices they had made.

Winning entry by 'Whakairo' in the coat-of-arms competition. *National Archives*

In 1908 entrant no. 43 explained that 'the Kiwi is shown as the emblem of the oldest New Zealanders extant (that is to say representative of these Islands).' Entry 44 said that 'The Kiwi on the escutcheon is typical only of N.Z. and is already used as a mark of the Dominion.' Entry 14 in 1906 explained that the design symbolised 'the operations hopes and aspirations of New Zealand as a nation, an idea quite compatible with that of Imperial Unity.' Some of the entries used an artistic shot-gun, hoping to hit the national target somehow. Entry no. 42 in 1908 was a shield with the New Zealand flag in the centre and squares depicting a cabbage tree, the tui, fantail, tree fern, raupo, flax and nikau, plus a kiwi, a volcano and lake with a canoe and a pastoral scene with sheep. There was Mitre Peak, a steamer and mining gear. The shield was surmounted by a crown and two huia and flanked by kauri trees. There was a taiaha and a toki. Below was botanical decoration, manuka and toe toe. In addition the Aurora Australis may be seen, as well as a moa, pukeko, tuatara, cows, wheat, huntsmen and kidney fern. In addition, gun carriages, kauri gum and a pohutukawa were pictured.

The entries include 75 to 100 recognisable symbols – and, because of poor draughtsmanship, not all are readily identifiable. The most popular, in the two competitions, were:

Southern Cross (three, four or five stars)	57
fernleaf or fern	49
kiwi	45
crown	39
sheep	32
moa	28
sheaf of wheat	26
Maori chief (usually tattooed)	25[10]

There were numerous representations of Maori women and canoes; some of taiaha, tiki, Maori carvings and patterns. There were lots of landscapes, lions, ships, flax bushes, cows, fleeces, pioneers and flags. The numbers are only approximate – for instance, it is not clear that all groups of stars represented the Southern Cross. But they give a general idea of what New Zealanders thought of as suitable symbols of their nationhood.

The winning entry was less imaginative than many – no. 75 of 1908. Perhaps it was selected because it fitted easily into heraldic conventions. It was a shield surmounted by a lion. In the centre were (and are) three lymphads (sailing ships). The quarters showed the Southern Cross, a sheep, a sheaf of wheat and mining tools. It is flanked by Zealandia, a young lady in white, and a Maori chief with a taiaha. Below were some 'curlicues', later replaced with fernleaves. There is no kiwi, though the bird features in the coats-of-arms of some of the cities. The coat-of-arms was adopted in 1911.

The search for a national symbol was paralleled by the quest for a suitable song. Few New Zealanders have felt able to write of either result with enthusiasm, not that that is unusual. Few national anthems are inspiring if considered in a calm and literary frame of mind, as opposed to at emotional moments.

What was, in 1940, to be adopted as the national song, was written by Thomas Bracken and published in 1878. For more than a generation his best-known verses were the maudlin 'Not Understood', a compulsory recitation for high school children. Before Bracken's anthem

Ferns were also seen as symbols of New Zealand, as on this photograph of New Zealand rower William Webb.

was accepted, numerous other versifiers and musicians tried their colonial hands at the task.

William Pember Reeves published his 'New Zealand' in 1898. The sentiment expressed by the author of the Industrial Conciliation and Arbitration Act failed to find national favour:

Though young they are heirs of the ages
Though few they are freemen and peers,
Plain workers – yet sure of the wages
Slow Destiny pays with the years.
Though least they and latest their nation,
Yet this they have won without sword,
That Woman with Man shall have station,
And Labour be lord.

Nevertheless, it was more vigorous than contemporary rivals. Francis H. Valpy's 'All Hail Zealandia' (music by Frederick Leech) asserted that an 'empire shall arise' in Zealandia. Charles S. Thomas's 'New Zealand National Hymn', first performed at the New Zealand Industrial Arts Exhibition in 1885, alleged that New Zealand's sons were 'resolved to emulate England's glorious enterprise'. Herbert B. Bridge's 'Jubilee Hymn' (composed for the 1890 jubilee), asked God to 'Raise up a Nation, here'. R. Thompson's 'Zealandia. Recitative and Aria' (music by Harry Rossiter) proclaimed, 'New Zealand for New Zealanders from sea to sea'. W. R. Lawson and F. D. Fenton's 'Maoriland' praises the 'Britain of the Southern Sea'.[11]

Most New Zealanders know only the first verse of Bracken's 'National Hymn' (1875), which calls on the 'God of nations' to defend them, but it does express other thoughts:

Men of every creed and race
Gather here before Thy face,
Asking Thee to bless this place,
God defend our Free Land . . . .

Peace, not war, shall be our boast,
But, should foes assail our coast,
Make us then a mighty host,
God defend our Free Land . . . .

Guide her in the nation's van,
Preaching love and truth to man,
Working out Thy glorious plan
God defend New Zealand.

VI

The Peripheral Majority

A reminder from St Patrick's School, Hastings: '"Peace on Earth to Men of Good Will"' Don't Forget! We Helped to Win the War.' *Turnbull*

Chapter Fourteen

MAORIS

That Maoris were 'native-born' was indisputable. They were the tangata whenua, the people of the land, whose ancestors had lived in the country for about 1000 years. How were Maoris accommodated in Pakeha ideas about the nation? Did they belong in the same nation as the Pakeha? Was the nation bi-racial? And what did the Maoris think about these questions?

European attitudes towards the Maoris had throughout the nineteenth century always been ambivalent, mixing fear, admiration and contempt. Most commonly they had been regarded as a superior kind of savage. The novelist, Anthony Trollope, thought that in 'their savage condition' they were of all savages 'the most civilised'.[1] They were, said a correspondent in *Zealandia* in 1889, 'naturally a more intelligent race of people than those of any other uncivilised country in the world'.[2]

In an age when theories of racial superiority and inferiority, of racial classification of civilisation, were widely accepted, the Maoris were frequently placed high in the scale and not far below the supposedly superior Europeans; always well above the Australian Aborigines or the peoples of southern Africa. (This attitude has not everywhere changed. The author has often been told by South Africans that they have to deal with 'Kaffirs', not Maoris.)

That the Maoris were superior fitted in perfectly with the evolving New Zealand national sentiment: it had often been claimed that the settlers were 'selected stock', having survived the voyage on the longest migration route on earth. Similarly, the heroic Maoris had sailed across the great Pacific Ocean, 'Vikings of the Sunrise'.

How to explain the superiority of the Maoris exercised the minds of many European New Zealanders. The first missionary in New Zealand, Samuel Marsden, had concluded that the Maoris were of Semitic descent.[3] Soon it was held that they were one of the lost tribes of Israel. This opinion was to be shared by several Maori prophetic movements, whose study of the Old Testament had revealed analogies between their plight and the persecutions of the ancient Jews. Some of them called themselves Teu or Hurai (Jews). Some early amateur ethnologists and historians concluded that the Maoris were of Indian extraction, because of supposed resemblances between Indian and

Rewi Maniapoto, June, 1879. *Turnbull*

Maori languages. The most spectacular of such theories, however, was that of Edward Tregear, an amateur ethnologist and linguist who was later an important public servant. In 1885 he published *The Aryan Maori*, which called upon Comparative Philology and Comparative Mythology to decipher the mystery of the origins of the Maoris.

Tregear believed that he had discovered Sanscrit, Greek or Latin origins for numerous Maori words. Thus he claimed that *taurus* (bull) was ancestral to the Maori word tara (courage). The Sanscrit word for cow was *gau*. Tregear believed that it survived in the Maori kahui (a flock). Tregear claimed that the Maoris had embalmed memories of cattle and other Euro-Asian animals. He also claimed that some English and Maori words had a common origin, for instance, 'kete' and 'kit' or 'ngau' (to bite) and 'gnaw', or 'kuri' (dog) and 'cur'. Tregear claimed that the ancestors of the Polynesians were Aryans, nomads of central Asia who had passed through India on their way to the Pacific. According to Tregear the Maoris had preserved 'in an almost inconceivable purity' the speech of their Aryan ancestors. In New Zealand 'the Aryan of the West [the Briton] greets the Aryan of the Eastern Seas.'[4]

Perhaps not many people swallowed all of this. However, it was widely believed that the Maoris were 'a branch of the Caucasian race'. The historian, M. P. K. Sorrenson, has speculated that this belief may help explain why the Maoris were not a target for the vicious anti-Chinese and anti-Asian propaganda of the late nineteenth century.[5]

The conception of Maoris as heroes persisted into later historical elements in the New Zealand tradition. The wars against the Maoris in the mid-1840s and the 1860s did not stimulate Pakeha nationalism. For one thing, the Maoris too often won battles. The war did not arouse pride so much as guilt or shame.

As early as 1865 Mrs Ponsonby, the Principal of the Scotch College for Young Ladies, in Dunedin, wrote in an article on Female Education:

> *With regard to the disastrous war in New Zealand, the only proper and consolatory light in which so dark a page in the history of the colony can be regarded, is to view it as connected with the adorable sovereignty of God, and as a means in His hand for the spread of knowledge and religion amongst the native tribes, and throughout the colony generally.*[6]

It is very striking that the only hero to arise from the war was Rewi Maniapoto, whose courage at the battle of Orakau is one of the most famous New Zealand national stories. Another story very well-known in the nineteenth century was that of the Maori heroine, Huria Matenga (Julia Martin) who in 1861, swam out in a terrible storm at Nelson 'to take ashore a rope from a sinking ship, the smart brig Delaware'. Almost all of the crew were saved by her daring. She was called 'the New Zealand Grace Darling'.[7] By the late nineteenth century the Maoris were not always or even generally regarded, in Pakeha minds, as the 'baddies'. New Zealand white children rarely, if ever, played Settlers and Maoris. Strangely, perhaps, they did play Cowboys and Indians, once they fell under the influence of Hollywood in the 1920s and 1930s.

In New Zealand literature the Maori is often portrayed as the noble savage, or at least idealised. As early as 1832 the artist, Augustus Earle, had written that the Maoris reminded him 'of the fine models of antiquity' immortalised by the Greek and Roman sculptors.[8]

In magazine short stories, in the *New Zealand Graphic* during the 1890s, there are to be found fine young, pre-European chiefs; also tall, muscular, mission-educated heroes, and some brave half-caste beauties.[9] But there are also some terrifying savages, especially in stories about Te Kooti's attack on the settlers (and 'friendly' Maoris) outside Gisborne.[10] This was a theme providing powerful images of Maori barbarism.

Other Pakeha stereotypes of Maoris influenced how they were thought to contribute to the nation. It was frequently asserted that the Maoris had been well treated by the white man – unlike the Bantu or Aborigines. In this respect, the *New Zealand Herald* claimed in 1906, New Zealand was 'the experimental colony'. 'Here, for the first time, the savage man was treated as one who had some of the natural rights of property, which our race has always claimed for its own people. And here, therefore, a colony was begun which was founded on a great and novel experiment.' But alas, the editorial continued, the Maoris had only been partially civilised; at best their civilisation was only skin-deep. 'It is by no means evident that . . . humanity gains anything by the perpetuation of a race of lazy, half-civilised people, who do little for themselves, and nothing at all for anybody else.'[11]

The aspect of Maori life which received the worst publicity was the dangerously low level of hygiene in Maori kainga. Maori health was much worse than that of Europeans; outbreaks of typhoid were frequent; the rate of infant mortality was bad. Maori leaders were as well aware of this as Europeans. Maori medical practitioners, like Dr Peter Buck, devoted much time preaching the need for higher standards of hygiene. By 1909 there were also two Maori nurses,

Huria Matenga. *Turnbull*

A district nurse checks a baby's progress at Waihara. *Northwood Collection, Turnbull*

qualified in mid-wifery, working in the villages. One of them, Akanei Hei, wrote two articles about her work and the problems of superstition she encountered. The Maoris believed that death, other than by war or accident or 'natural death', was caused by witchcraft. Unfortunately she contracted typhoid while nursing near Gisborne and died.[12]

Pakehas generally believed that Maoris, especially women, at least before marriage, were sexually promiscuous, a characteristic widely condemned in a society less male-dominated than in colonial times and increasingly 'respectable', at least in profession and intent. The *New Zealand Illustrated Magazine* reported in 1901 that 'the surroundings of a Maori village are demoralizing in the extreme, and it is the aim of the Young Maori Party to remove as many girls as possible from such immoral influences, and place them in a school where they may receive teaching.' The need for education for Maori girls was often stressed. The same journal said, 'With education that will teach them morality, with a household régime to impart ideas of health, sanitation and cleanliness, there is great hope for the preservation of Maori womanhood. And if its women are pure, the race will be saved morally, and mentally, as well as physically.'[13]

Most commonly, it was assumed that the Maoris were dying out, and they would survive only as people of mixed European and Maori descent. Innumerable newspaper and other references to this expectation can be cited – even years after their population was observed to be rising, as Maoris acquired resistance to introduced diseases, in the census of 1901. In 1905 the poet, Dora Wilcox, proclaimed that they were doomed, their passing marked by 'a greenstone arrow'![14] As late as 1919 the Minister of Health published a book saying that, because of bad hygiene, the Maoris were dying out or 'being absorbed into the white population'.[15] So decided was the Government that the Maoris were dying out that it commissioned a sculptor, Nelson Illingworth, to make bronze busts of 'prominent Maori types' to serve as a 'national memorial'. When they were placed in the National Museum the Director, Augustus Hamilton, had them painted, so that they looked like 'defective figures in some night-mare waxworks show'.[16] In the museum in Cape Town are numerous statues of 'bushmen' and 'hottentot', the Khoi-san, representing the same belief.

There were other attitudes towards the Maoris which reflected and influenced Pakeha perceptions. For instance, there was the lovable Maori of the 'py korry, I te plurry fine fella eh!' school of humour. This was not usually ill-intended. For instance the *Chronicles of the NZEF*, which praised Maori troops, also published stories about 'Private Puripeef' (Bully beef) of the Pioneer Battalion and about the 'Henares' (that is, Henrys) in what was supposed to be Maori-English. 'Puripeef' concludes his account of a two-hour army course on cooking and its tasteless consequences:

It all t'e same Sunday-school picnic in New Zealan', only I'm wery sorry I never take t'e bottle of beer wit' me. W'en you eat t'at kai, you t'ink he t'e real kai. You never t'ink he t'e bully beef an' t'e biscuit. T'e only trouble for me is t'at I'm behin' w'en t'e plate come to me, all I can taste is t'e finger of t'e front row. But he wery good. Yes, I get t'e good education t'at time all right.[17]

It would be wrong to imply that there was only one Pakeha attitude towards Maoris, but it is safe to assert that there was a general recognition that they had not yet been integrated fully into the European community. The 'amalgamation' of the races, the aim of the early nineteenth-century humanitarians, had not been achieved.

By 'amalgamation' the missionaries had, in substance, assumed that the destiny of the Maoris was to be absorbed into the European culture, converted to European ways as well as to the worship of the European god. It was assumed that the Maoris would benefit from European civilisation: in other words, the coming of Europe would be a blessing, freeing the Maoris from savagery and idolatry. The Maoris would survive as a people, as brown Europeans, but the destruction of their culture was to be almost total.

A good example of this destruction was the assault on the Maori language. The early mission schools had used Maori as the language of instruction: the Maoris became literate in their own language. But the government saw this as a barrier to the official policy of Europeanisation. In 1871 an Act prohibited the use of Maori in schools. Generations of Maori children were punished for speaking te reo Maori.[18]

Sometimes it was hoped that events were bringing the two races closer together. For instance, when New Zealand became a Dominion in 1907 the *New Zealand Times* observed that the Maoris had never been 'colonists' and that the word 'colony' must have seemed alien to them, but that now they could lay equal claim with the Pakeha to the word 'Dominion'.[19] Occasionally Europeans asserted that Maoris and Pakehas were one people, as Hobson had said at Waitangi in 1840. For instance Kate Sheppard, one of the most distinguished women in the country, said, as President of the National Council of Women in 1901, that the bitter feuds of the past had died out. 'Maori and pakeha have become one people, under one Sovereign and one Parliament, glorying alike in the one title of "New Zealander".'[20]

Certainly the settlers wanted the Maoris to feel part of the nation. For themselves, they adopted some elements in Maori culture as national symbols. The haka, for instance, was a major New Zealand ritual. But the Maoris were peripheral to Pakeha society. They lived apart, mostly in rural districts where there were few Europeans. They were not central to Pakeha thinking about their own national identity.

It is more difficult to discuss Maori views about whether they belonged to the New Zealand nation. Certainly the Maoris shared many things with the Europeans, as well as a country. They shared sport and war and Anzac day. The Maoris, who exalted rugby and war, and were big men, could easily be fitted into the Pakeha idea of the nation. There was a considerable degree of intermarriage, so that there were thousands of people of mixed descent who could, and did, identify with Maori or European society, or both.

When 'the Great War for Civilisation' began it was assumed that

Maoris would not enlist because of the reluctance of the British to use 'native' troops. However, the British accepted a New Zealand offer to send a Maori unit. Originally it was believed that it would be non-combatant and the first contingent was for a time sent to Malta on guard duty. The enlistment of Maori volunteers and their despatch to the war received much publicity in the newspapers. At the farewell in Wellington of the second Maori contingent Sir James Carroll, a part-Maori, exhorted the men in the name of the mana of Tu, the war god, to 'Go forth with your pakeha brothers. Our blood has been spilt on the Peninsula of Gallipoli.' He called upon them to 'find satisfaction' that is, utu.[21] The arrival of the first Maoris at Anzac created a stir among the other New Zealanders. Here they were, the Official War Correspondent wrote, among the ghosts of Xerxes and Alexander, Hector, Achilles .... General Godley exhorted the Maoris to prove as valiant as their forefathers. Another journalist recalled the heroism of the great Maori leaders of the past: perhaps the Maori soldiers were 'much closer to their real ancient home than the ethnological world once believed'![22]

And Te Hokowhitu a Tu, the warrior band of the war god Tu, did prove as valiant as their ancestors. While it is difficult to prove, there is evidence that the Maori and Pakeha soldiers felt united in pride in their heroism and achievement. Dr Peter Buck, whose Maori name was Te Rangi Hiroa, said, when addressing the Maoris at Gallipoli, 'Though we are only a handful, the remnant of the remnant of a people, yet we consider that we are the old New Zealanders. No division can be truly called a New Zealand Division, unless it numbers Maoris among its ranks.' (Loud applause from the members of the New Zealand battalions who were looking on.) 'We, therefore, ask you, as the old chiefs of our people would ask you, to give us a chance for active service with our white kinsmen from New Zealand. Give us a chance!'[23]

References to the Maoris by the other troops were, to the writer's knowledge, uniformly complimentary. Alexander Aitken, for instance, wrote a moving account of the second Maori contingent being welcomed by the first.[24] When the first Maori contingent joined the New Zealanders at the Zeitoun camp near Cairo they felt strongly that they were part of a larger whole. Te Rangi Hiroa wrote, 'One of our full-blooded Maoris shook his head sadly and said: "Yet some of the Maoris ask for mana motuhake, the right to govern themselves. Let them travel with the Expeditionary Force, and they will never open their mouths again!"'[25] In a ship-board journal, *The Waitemata*

The Maori Pioneer Battalion greets Prime Minister Bill Massey and Sir Joseph Ward in France, June 1918. *RSA Collection, Turnbull*

Wobbler, was published he whakahau – an invocation or order – to the thirteenth Maori reinforcement:

1. *Hapainga te patu a o koutou – tupuna*
2. *Kia kotahi te haere me to whakaaro*
3. *Kia tutuki ai ia koutou – te tonoa to tatou Kingitanga.*

1. *Take up the weapon of your ancestors.*
2. *Be united in thought and deed*
3. *So that you may fulfil the command of our Kingitanga.*

In the late twentieth century the term 'Kingitanga', kingship, would be thought a reference to the Maori King movement, but at that time the Maori King was opposed to sending Maoris to the war. The translation published in the same journal was 'Empire'. The King referred to was the King of England.[26]

The Maoris had leaders, of great mana, about whom the Europeans knew little. On the other hand there was a new Maori élite, sometimes of part-European descent, like Peter Buck and James Carroll, who moved at ease and effectively in both cultures. Most of them were politicians, as well as being professional doctors or lawyers or ministers of religion. The latter group frequently commented in public on the relations between the races, and especially so during the First World War.

Early in the war two Members of Parliament, Apirana Ngata

(Eastern Maori) and Taare Parata (Southern Maori) said that many Maoris wished to volunteer.[27] Indeed, some had already done so, and served. After the Gallipoli landing Parata said that the 'misunderstandings' between Pakeha and Maori had been swept away forever. Dr Maui Pomare (Western Maori and a Member of the Executive Council) said in 1916 that he had helped to send over 1000 Maoris to the front: they were coming to help Great Britain so that the Treaty of Waitangi could be kept inviolate.[28] Parata could be heard referring to Britain as 'the Mother-country'.[29] Maori politicians quite frequently expressed a strong loyalty to the Crown. They seem to have stopped short, however, of saying that Maori and Pakeha were one people. They often described the two races as standing 'side by side' or 'back to back' in the war.[30]

Ngata could say in the House that there was 'some competition amongst the tribes' as to which could raise the most volunteers.[31] While true, as everyone knew, this was far from being the whole truth. Whereas Ngapuhi, Arawa and other tribes volunteered in considerable numbers, a few tribes resisted strenuously, especially those who had had their lands confiscated during the Anglo-Maori wars, notably the Taranaki tribes, the Tuhoe and the Waikato. Rua Kenana, the Tuhoe Maori prophet, for instance, discouraged his people from enlisting. In 1916, at least partly because of this, the Government sent in an armed force of police to arrest him. He was prosecuted and imprisoned.[32]

The Maori people recognised two kings. Parata, a South Island Ngaitahu, said that his people acknowledged only the King of England, not the Maori King.[33] Most Maoris agreed with that. But in the Waikato, in the central North Island, the Maoris followed their own King, Rata, who was opposed to sending his men to fight in an imperial war. Some Maoris from the 'King Country' did volunteer. In 1917 the Government introduced the conscription of Maoris as well as Pakeha, who had been conscripted since 1916. In the end some Waikato Maoris were imprisoned as military defaulters for refusing to serve.[34]

The Maoris responded tribally to the call to arms, but it must not be supposed that those who went to war were necessarily always pro-Pakeha. One of the roles of the Maori Members of Parliament was to articulate Maori grievances to a European audience. In this respect the Ngapuhi and the Ngaitahu were as resentful as the Waikato, whose land had been confiscated. In 1915 Parata was complaining that his people had not been fairly paid for their land.[35] Nor did the aureretanga, the groans of the Maori, cease. In 1939 Paikea was saying that his people, the Ngatiwhatua, could not sing 'God Defend

New Zealand' with enjoyment because of the way their Orakei lands in Auckland had been acquired by the Crown. And Ngata said that in 1840 a chief had said that, under Waitangi, the shadow of the land went to the Queen, but the substance remained with Maoris. Now they had only the shadow.[36]

In discussing the attitude of Maoris towards belonging to the New Zealand nation it is impossible to ignore Maori separatism. In the 1850s there had been a Maori nationalist movement, an attempt to rise above tribalism which did not succeed, although it led to the election of a Maori King and to a powerful inter-tribal Maori resistance movement in the central North Island. Maori nationalism was not, at first, anti-European, but even then it envisaged a separate role for Maoris. One of its founders, Matene Te Whiwhi, travelled about the North Island in 1853 bearing the message, 'the Lord is the ridgepole, New Zealand is the rafters of one side, England is the rafters of one side, thus resembling a house.' By 'Niu Tireni' (New Zealand), Te Whiwhi meant the Maoris, and by 'Ingarangi' (England) the Pakehas. They were seen as separate, joined in Christ.[37]

Similarly, the most notable other Maori religious and political movements of the later nineteenth century envisaged some kind of separate organisation for the Maoris: a Maori King motto was 'te mana motuhake' – a separate destiny or mana. This was, in different ways, the aim of the Great Council or Kauhanganui set up by the Maori King and of the Kotahitanga or Unity Movement which set up a Maori Parliament in the years 1892–1902. Many – probably most – Maoris did not want to be culturally absorbed by the Europeans. They wanted some measure of political independence too. Those aims were incompatible with New Zealand nationalism as envisaged by the Pakehas. They were not, of course, incompatible with the idea of a bi-cultural or multi-cultural nation, but that idea seems not to have occurred to Pakehas in the early twentieth century.

Chapter Fifteen

WOMEN

Not only was New Zealand society in the nineteenth century, like many others, male-dominated, but this characteristic was greatly reinforced because of the shortage of European women. Consequently society was male-oriented; the central nationalist ideals were male. Moreover, the events which first inspired strong national feeling, imperial war and international sport, concerned men more immediately than women.

One major role of women was more subtle. As painters, and above all as writers, they played a leading role in defining the New Zealand identity, in a national myth-making. They taught their people how to see their lives. The role of writers is discussed in other chapters. But how did women fit into the general perception of the national destiny? And was there a distinct feminine view of the subject?

As we have seen, some women, like Edith Searle Grossmann, clearly articulated the ideals of the native-born, and could be as nationalistic as the men. In 1896 'Wahine' wrote a long letter to the *Evening Post* about the formation of the New Zealand Natives Association, which pleased her very much. The Americans, she said, had appreciated the need to form a national spirit and in their state schools children began the day by saluting the flag. She doubted whether New Zealand children knew that their country had a flag. Yet their destiny was to 'found a nationality'.

Let our young New Zealanders learn more about their country, and take a pride in its development and advancement, and we shall soon have mastered the problems of poverty and injustice, and stand out as the most advanced and the most enlightened country in the world, and one in which the people are most happy and contented.[1]

Some women accepted or fitted easily into a masculine perception of the nation. For instance, women could be as militaristic as the men. The *Citizen* reported, in a woman's column – 'A WOMAN'S CAUSERIE' – in 1909,

It was with very great surprise that one read in the papers the report of a meeting of women held in Mrs David Nathan's house last week to consider ways and means of helping on the movement of compulsory training. Possibly

it is proof that one belongs to prehistoric days by right, but somehow one has always regarded war and all that appertains to it as a field belonging solely and exclusively to men, save in the most exceptional and compelling circumstances. The more one examines the idea of women working up their enthusiasm in the cause of the compulsion of military training for men, the more distasteful it becomes. Have they any right to do so? It is the men who fight, not the women. Aren't these ladies stepping into one of the things that completely and totally separate men from women? That women should think it necessary to bestir themselves and agitate in order to rouse men's fighting spirit so that they, their children and their homes may be defended, strikes one as being curious.

These 'Militant Matrons' (as the journalist called them) were not alone. The same journal had a fortnight earlier reported that

A strong plea for military training was made by a woman the other day in an Auckland paper. She says: 'Women are not bothering their heads to see that their sons and husbands possess or can even hold a gun. The sooner women spend less time in the trivialities of modern easy life and devote a few more hours to the inculcation among boys of the spirit of fighting for their country and the encouragement amongst their menfolk of an organised system of training, the sooner we shall be prepared to resist an enemy and the more secure our homes will be.[2]

During the First World War many women entered into the martial atmosphere with a powerful intensity. Mary Boyle Barclay wrote in to the *Evening Post* describing the call of the men overseas for '"Men, more men! Hurry up mates; we know you'll come. The colonial tradition is, We'll stand by our mates!"'[3] 'A Mother' wrote that she had heard men say that they would go when 'all the mugs have gone'; and, 'Let Mr Fat fight his own battles.' Her exhortation was, not to think of 'mugs' or 'Mr Fat' 'but go and fight for the women of this country and nation; it is we who need protection.'[4]

Following an English precedent, women formed White Feather Leagues in a number of towns to shame men into volunteering. Many people, however, deplored such tactics, especially when feathers were posted to men who happened to be returned soldiers. The women should use tact: 'The methods have to be those by which our women hold their high place of honour in the esteem of men. Therefore, the "white feather" and similar offensiveness, unworthy of women or men, have to be avoided.'[5]

A further manifestation of a war-like spirit was an Anti-German League founded by women in Wellington in 1916. It expressed extreme views about the need to punish Germans, even when they were naturalised British subjects. The leader in this activity was an overseas visitor, but Lady Stout, formerly a member of the Natives Association, was active too.[6] It should be added that not all women were chauvinistic. For instance, at the National Council of Women's conference in 1901 Kate Sheppard urged that they should 'discourage this rampant war spirit' and urge 'the principles of Peace and Arbitration'.[7]

For many women the war presented opportunities to work in wider spheres than previously. A young woman doctor, Doris Gordon, wrote later, that

The men wanted to get into khaki and the women realized that a unique chance of community service was opening for them. Prejudice against petticoats and preference for pants died a sudden death when the Kaiser tore up his historic scrap of paper. Hospital Boards, hitherto loath to employ women doctors, would be scrambling to engage us.[8]

The women's group that fitted best into the men's world were nurses; they, too, shared in the hardships and dangers of war. In New Zealand the nurses organised and received legal recognition very early. A remarkable woman, Grace Neill, was appointed Assistant Inspector of hospitals in 1895. She was impressed by the need for a register of trained nurses and convinced the Government of this. In 1901 the Nurses Registration Act was passed. It provided for a three-year course of training, a state examination and a register of qualified nurses. Three years later a Midwives Registration Act was passed. Both Acts provided protection against untrained nursing. It was believed that the 1901 Act was the first in the world. Nurses were also proud of the fact that the Australians had copied the New Zealand system of organising visiting nurses.[9] A national Trained Nurses' Association was formed in 1909; some provincial organisations had been established a few years earlier.[10]

When the 'main body' sailed for Egypt there were, it seems, no army nurses, though six were with the expeditionary force that seized German Samoa. A deputation from the Association waited upon the Minister of Defence to ask that some nurses should be sent to the war: 'When New Zealand's sons were serving the Empire in the field it was only right that her daughters, who were able and willing, should be allowed to do so too.' Altogether some five hundred nurses served overseas.[11]

The nurses provided their own national heroes. One was awarded

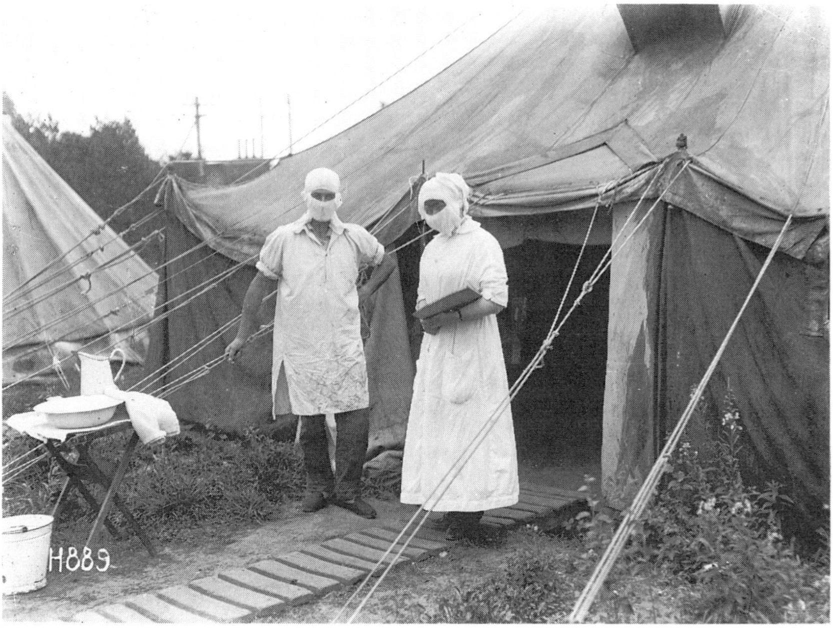

New Zealand nurse and orderly outside a diphtheria ward during the First World War. *RSA Collection, Turnbull*

the Croix de Guerre, another the Military Medal. In October 1916 a troopship, the 'Marquette', transporting the 1st New Zealand Stationary Hospital to Salonika, was torpedoed and sank. Ten New Zealand nurses were drowned.[12] Some of the nurses made the 'Tommies' get into the life-boats first. The *Evening Post* urged the New Zealand male to follow their example of 'supreme self-sacrifice', or else 'blush for his weakness every time he sees a woman ....'[13]

Like the men, often for the first time the women were able to compare New Zealanders with a wide variety of people from other English-speaking countries. Like the men, they did not always admire what they saw. A New Zealand nurse, Elsie Grey, was caring for British officers in a hospital in France. She had Lord Bury and Lord Dalkeith in the ward, and 'the Hon this that or the other':

... 'awfully jolly don't cher know' sort of style, but really in my heart of hearts I wish they were the New Zealand boys.

The latter, she wrote, were dying one a day at a New Zealand hospital in Gosford:

The British people are driving us [some New Zealand nurses] mad. Oh they are the limit. The orderlies are all idiots. Have absolutely no idea how to do anything and as for getting a move on. Well I think they all ought to go out and meet Fritz. Perhaps he would make them smart. The medical officers are as bad . . . won't do anything on their own – refer to somebody a little higher up. Oh if our own people would only send for us!![14]

Like the men, the women prided themselves upon their adaptability. Shortly before the war the nurses' journal, *Kai Tiaki*, had remarked that 'some English nurses working in the colonies appear to expect a great deal of waiting upon.' By contrast, in the Home papers, colonial nurses were 'commended for their readiness to put their hands to anything'.[15]

When the nurses returned from the war there were the same 'grouses' about the promised 'rehabilitation' not being carried out. Ex-servicewomen as well as men could not always get their jobs back. The most notable example was that of the Matron-in-Chief of the New Zealand military hospitals in England, Miss Thurston. She had previously been the Matron of the Christchurch Hospital, which had appointed a replacement during her long absence. There was a public protest meeting about her treatment. Over a year later the North Canterbury Hospital Board explained that it had been impossible to appoint a temporary replacement to such an important position.[16]

There was another type of woman who fitted readily into the masculine idea: the sports woman. An article in the *Otago Witness*, subtitled 'In the Land of Fine Sport and Good Women', said,

The Outdoor Woman promises to become a rapidly increasing expression of her sex in New Zealand. Climate, surroundings, the influence of modern education, opportunity, and, most of all the subtle penetration of an exhilarating freedom, which is an integral part of the air of our islands all combine to this end. The present generation of young matrons in New Zealand is of more imposing height as a rule than their mothers have been; the young girls, and their still younger sisters, many of them, promise to be in very truth 'daughters of the gods, divinely tall, and most divinely fair.'[17]

In the *New Zealand Graphic* in 1890 the question of 'Girls' Rights' was debated, with journalists and correspondents writing for and against women's cricket and tennis. Some people thought cricket unladylike. There had, however, already been a team of women cricketers in the Waikato.[18] And there were some excellent women athletes. Kathleen Nunneley, for instance, won the women's tennis singles championship thirteen consecutive times, 1895–1908. Anthony Wilding thought her outstanding.[19] In 1909 a New Zealand women's team beat New South Wales at tennis, but international competition for women was rare before the First World War.

Apart from fitting or being shoved into a masculine vision, women had a separate history and role as the mothers of the nation. This role could be viewed in several different ways. One common opinion, often expressed by women, was that, in New Zealand, the women were regarded by the men as equals. A columnist, 'Olivine', wrote in the *Ladies' Mirror* that in New Zealand men and women were 'upon much better terms with each other than are those of other allegedly civilised countries. Here the politeness of the members of both sexes to each other is the rule rather than the exception; a spirit of *camaraderie* exists between the sexes that is frequently a matter of surprise to new-comers.'[20] A much more formidable woman had explained why this was the case. Lady Stout had written in 1910: 'The pioneer settlers recognized that their wives were noble types of womanhood, who had unselfishly left home and civilisation to help their husbands to reclaim the wilderness; that but for the help of the women their task would have been well-nigh impossible. That is one reason, I believe, why the men of New Zealand have always treated women as equals.'[21]

That women shared equally in the hard work of pioneering was a frequent theme in New Zealand fiction. In *Miranda Stanhope*, Mrs Mactier stressed the 'terribly isolated life' of pioneering women.[22] In *Ponga Bay* Sophie Osmond wrote that 'They had to do men's work, and they did it with the souls of men to the glory of womanhood, without thought of self-sacrifice or weariness or unending work, but only regardful of their mates and the marriage tie.'[23] Moreover, the lives of settlers were just as harsh in some districts in the twentieth century. In discussing the hard life of Taranaki 'cow cockies' and their wives in about 1918, Dr Doris Gordon wrote, 'The lying-in period [in childbirth] was the only holiday that Taranaki farming women expected.'[24]

Hard though the work was, it has been argued that colonial women derived a high degree of satisfaction from their lives. The colonial 'help-meet' had to accept many unaccustomed tasks. She contributed substantially to the family income – for instance by selling eggs or butter – and standard of living. Women felt a greater sense of personal worth and independence than in Great Britain. One woman wrote that she felt 'in her element' in the colony.

Just Out of Reach. *The Prohibitionist*, 1892. *Turnbull*

I consider myself a much more respectable character than I was when I was a fine lady, did nothing for anyone but made a gt. many people do things for me . . . . I am so proud at finding how easy it is to be independent . . . . I really feel myself less a slave now that I see I can do everything for myself, than I ever did before.

And not all of the women were wives: in 1874, 245 women were running their own farms or sheep stations.

New Zealand was the first country to give women the vote. It has been argued that this was, in part, because the feminists accepted that the role of women was in the home and did not threaten the family or other institutions; that men agreed to the female suffrage. The men freely acknowledged that the women deserved the vote because they were, indeed, equal.[25]

There was nothing new about the idea that the duty of women was to preserve the moral fibre of the nation within the walls of two sanctified institutions: home and family.[26] But, two historians have claimed that, in the late nineteenth century, 'Mother became a cult figure, her temple the home.'[27] Attempts were made to establish a scientific basis for this 'cult of domesticity and true womanhood', not only, of course, in New Zealand. Domestic 'science' was one aspect of this effort; so, too, were the teachings of some medical men and women.

'What We Aim At': 'Woman's supreme and unchallenged domain is the home – feminine art and grace have their abiding place here, and within its walls are mirrored the very soul of its chatelaine. We will have much to say concerning the Home Beautiful . . . .'[28] The authors of such assertions were usually women, as were the readers.

Such attitudes were not always sentimental pap. It was constantly asserted that women were morally superior to men. The *Graphic* said, 'Most women demand a higher standard of morals than men, and rightly directed, this little idiosyncracy of theirs ought to be of immense service to the country.'[29] Women were the bulwarks of civilisation in a world threatened by male violence and vice. A principal female mission was to protect society from the use of alcohol by supporting the prohibition movement. It was widely held that the female franchise would help to purify politics: corruption would be punished.[30] A cabinet minister, G. W. Russell, wrote in 1919 that 'the personal character of members has been raised' by the women's vote. 'It is of little use for the dissolute man, the drunkard, the man who is a notorious free-liver, to appeal for the votes of the women. Sooner or later they find him out, and his political end comes.'[31] Just as the moral tone of pioneering societies had been raised by the infiltration of women's influence, so politics would now be civilised.[32]

In a remarkable passage in her autobiography, Dr Doris Gordon explained that women were spiritually superior because of their role as mothers. Referring to the pangs of birth, Dr Doris Gordon wrote that in her creed she placed 'all mothers closer to the Godhead than the males of this world, for mothers have all had their Calvaries.' Childbirth was the moment of facing death, a moment of sacrifice like war. And – as one of the leading professional women – she went on: 'Chase all the careers you like, tell yourself you are best serving God by remaining single, but you'll die a disappointed woman unless you marry and go down this awful, painful, glorious road of suffering that new life may come from you.'[33]

A reading of newspapers and periodicals in the period from about 1890 into the 1920s shows an extraordinary level of discussion of the role of women, unprecedented in New Zealand and not repeated until the 1960s or later. There were several issues, at first the franchise, but then other concerns. One was the falling birth-rate, which aroused fears of a national decline. The *New Zealand Illustrated Magazine* regarded it as 'an ugly thing', a reproach to New Zealand women:

'The Summit At Last'. *NZ Graphic*, 21 July 1894. *Turnbull*

One would have thought, that in a land like ours, where the slaves of convention might shake off their fetters, that our women would have grown morally clean. But no sooner is our growth established than this canker of an effete nation appears and threatens the British race . . . . Women brought up in New Zealand's pioneer days, who knew the plainest of living and who were never accustomed to servants, who had a simple faith, who knew how to work with their hands, and who said very little about their affections, but who, nevertheless, took pride in having clean homes and clean, healthy children – these are the women who establish a race. And it is cruel to think that after their endurance, which they knew as not endurance, but only ordinary life, their daughters should make the chief desires of their hearts, social position, luxury, laziness, absence of responsibilities, white hands, and no children . . . .

I know the burden to many, of an abnormally large family, but the woman who cannot rear four or five children is a poor specimen of a woman, and perhaps it would be to the benefit of the race that she should be out of the struggle.

The article went on to say that any intelligent woman who shirked the family responsibilities, ignored 'the nobility of motherhood', was 'morally deteriorating'. This is from a regular feature, 'My Lady's Bower', by 'Alma'.[34]

Men could be equally worried. In 1919 G. W. Russell, in a book on *New Zealand Today*, wrote a chapter on the declining birthrate. He made some striking observations:

That much of the decrease is deliberate on the part of the population is certain. In the early days large families were common. Now they are rare indeed. Allowing for the lessened fecundity of women which invariably accompanies the higher development of the intellect, and making further allowance for the open-air life which women in New Zealand are able to enjoy, and which undoubtedly disinclines them to motherhood, it would appear that this problem of the deliberate limitation of families is one that must be dealt with from an economic as well as from a moral and religious standpoint.[35]

The anxiety about the possibility of a static or declining population placed an additional emphasis on the importance of motherhood. It returned in the 1930s when Dr Doris Gordon was co-author of a book on the danger of septic abortion. She also wrote two articles in the nurses' journal, *Kai Tiaki*, about 'Modern Problems of Maternal Welfare in N.Z.' and 'The Abortion Evil'. She preached the need for more babies to combat the falling birth-rate. It was estimated that there were at least 6000 illegal abortions annually: about a quarter of the babies were being destroyed before birth. The nation needed four children per healthy family. 'The remedy [more babies] involves sacrifice . . . women's true destiny is sacrifice and from such service alone comes personal happiness, civic usefulness and Empire stability.' She advocated salary, tax and rent benefits for families with four or six children.[36] Nearly thirty years earlier a trade union group had similarly suggested a state bonus for large families.[37]

Related to the fear of national suicide, was a separate anxiety about the possibility of 'national deterioration', to which the nurses' journal referred in 1915.[38] This fear was not confined to New Zealand. There is a considerable literature on this topic with regard to the USA and Great Britain, and two New Zealand scholars have recently referred to it.[39] Possibly it derived from Darwinian ideas about the survival of the fittest; certainly being fit was a New Zealand masculine obsession. Soft

Conference of the Women's Christian Temperance Union, 1916. *F. J. Denton Collection, Turnbull*

urban living as well as contraception or (male) masturbation might weaken the race. Increasing civilisation could weaken women's natural instinct for maternity.

Apart from the falling birth-rate there was also concern about the high infant mortality rate: in 1903, for instance, eighty-one infants died for every 1000 births. In 1904 Seddon produced a 'Memorandum on Child-Life Preservation', recommending various reforms such as the provision of day homes for children. This memorandum was probably inspired by Grace Neill.[40] Undoubtedly, all of these fears about children's health and the birth-rate were heightened by the casualties during the First World War. There was a new anxiety about children.

In New Zealand society the medical doctors were the High Priests. Above all others, they felt it their right to teach women their duties. The women doctors tended to agree with the men on the central importance of the home and on the 'proper spheres' of the sexes.

One topic upon which they pronounced had, from early colonial days, been an obsession of journalists and middle-class women, 'the servant difficulty'. Domestic servants were prone to marry young. Later in the century the colonial-born girls would not work as 'slaveys' (pronounced in New Zealand as in 'Slav'). In shops or factories girls worked shorter hours, for slightly higher pay, and had more independence.[41] An article on 'Labour in New Zealand' in the *New Zealand Official Handbook* observed, in 1892, that this was a preference which did not 'tend to fit them for the care of a home when they marry and have to provide for the comfort of husband and children.'[42]

Some of the doctors – doubtless short of servants themselves – linked domestic service with marriage in the same way. In making submissions to a Sweating Commission in 1890, three doctors stressed that factory work was unhealthy for women. Working sewing machines was particularly injurious to the uterine organs. Service 'in respectable families' was far more healthy than factory work. One doctor thought female commercial labour in any shape or form was a misfortune. A girl in domestic service was much more likely to prove 'a suitable helpmate to a working-man'.[43]

In 1909 Dr F. C. Batchelor, a leading specialist in women's diseases, asserted flatly that serving girls made better mothers. Dr Emily Siedeberg, the first woman graduate of the Otago Medical School held that work as a domestic servant, or as a house-wife, were vocations requiring proper training. It was 'impossible to teach house-keeping in a school'.

The State will require to make compulsory training essential, with a certificate of efficiency, given after practical examination, before a woman can claim wages as a domestic, or before she is entitled to a house of her own by marriage. The care of the baby could easily be taught in the course of elementary physiology ....

Women would not work as domestic servants because of its 'want of status'. This must be improved.

On the influence of Dr Truby King in New Zealand Erik Olssen has written:

The Society for Promoting the Health of Women and Children, better known as the Plunket Society, played a decisive role in defining the new duties and obligations of motherhood. Founded in 1907 by Truby King and his wife, the Society insisted that women ought to be trained for motherhood and that every mother 'should, if possible, fulfil her maternal duties'. The home and the mother existed for the sake of the child. In several widely-read pamphlets and books, and in their regular newspaper column, the Kings spelt out in detail the responsibilities of the mother from conception until adulthood. In particular, however, King stressed the importance of the first five years and the enormous significance of the mother's role.[44]

Dr King and the Plunket Society preached a very conservative view of scientific domesticity. They stressed the dangers of young women working outside the home:

As the Central Council reported in 1930, where women attending ante-natal classes 'have been office, shop, or factory girls before marriage . . . [they] are utterly unlearned in the "profession of motherhood"'. King had stressed this message since the 1890s. 'Home-making and motherhood is the finest and most important calling for girls,' he wrote on one occasion, and both roles required 'adequate preparation'.[45]

Sometimes the male doctors went too far for their female allies. On one occasion Truby King, and the Minister of Health, Sir Maui Pomare, toured the Dominion advising women how to have babies without sepsis. The Minister advised women, 'Go back to nature's ways; no doctor, no anaesthetic. Even if stitches have to be inserted these do not hurt much!' And Sir Truby King proclaimed, 'Wear low-heeled shoes, avoid corsets, take a swim daily, never have any drug or anaesthetic in labour.' Dr Doris Gordon later wrote:

> *These curious dicta were challenged by the New Zealand branch of the British Medical Association; and it is safe to say that many women wondered, in a tolerant irony, just how the honourable Minister, a* man, *knew how much or how little the insertion of stitches might hurt at the end of a strenuous twenty-four-hour labour.*[46]

The Plunket Society achieved an extraordinary dominance over child-care in New Zealand which will be the subject of further comment. As far as the role of women was concerned it powerfully reinforced the emphasis on motherhood. That maternity was women's destiny was scarcely questioned, even within the contemporary feminist movement. This is not to suggest, however, that women were always content with their lot. On the contrary, their leaders had catalogues of women's disabilities. In 1893 they had no seat on Boards of Education, School Committees, Hospital Boards or Juries, as Kate Sheppard said in an interview.[47] There were numerous other grievances. They were excluded from the Anglican synod; they could not stand for Parliament. The laws, made by men, favoured men in numerous ways. Moreover, as the years went by, women became acutely aware that not much had been achieved since the gains in their legal status in the late nineteenth and early twentieth centuries.[48] So some women had a nagging feeling that motherhood was not enough; that in other aspects of life they were achieving little.

There was a more radical cutting edge to the feminist movement. In 1897 the National Council of Women resolved that married women should share their husbands' incomes – which men saw as a threat to the institution of marriage.[49] A short-lived radical women's journal, *Daybreak*, cited the Dunedin Women's Franchise League, in 1895, advocating the use of the 'lash' to punish 'certain offences against women or young girls'.[50] This demand sounded like something in the 1980s in the sense that women's radicalism, by calling for a single standard of sexual morality – namely that men should adopt women's standards – could support repressive and puritanical mores rather than a more expansive and perhaps more permissive role for women.

Such issues were much debated at meetings, in newspapers and journals. It does not seem that there was much support for any women's views suggesting a radical change in their role. 'Olivine' praised the educated Bachelor Woman, well-informed upon the affairs of the day,[51] but much more frequently 'blue stockings' were denounced as over-educated.

In 1908 there was an interesting comment in a journal, *The Triad*. A male journalist wrote that there was 'not a solitary capable women journalist in New Zealand', and went on, 'for all our talk of advanced women and all the rest of it, we still have a sort of idea that a woman who does anything well cannot be quite respectable.'[52] There is a sense in which this goes near the heart of the matter: women's creativity was supposed to be expressed in parturition.

Chapter Sixteen

CHILDREN

To an extent which may be unique in a modern society, in the early to mid-twentieth century New Zealand came close to having a national system of child-rearing. This was the Plunket system invented by Dr Truby King and his wife. He was arguably the most influential man in Pakeha society.

The Plunket system stressed the importance of fresh air, good food and long walks for the expectant mother. If possible the birth should be without instrumental assistance. The baby was to be breast-fed, every four hours by day and ignored at night. It should not be fed merely because it cried. Toilet training must commence within the first six weeks. Babies should not be rocked, tickled or otherwise 'spoiled'. Everything was supposed to be organised by the clock. The emphasis was upon health, self-control, discipline. Great stress was laid upon cleanliness and hygiene. An army of Plunket nurses called at the parents' homes, measuring and weighing the babies and recording their progress.

The Government backed the Society for Promoting the Health of Women and Children. It commissioned King to write *Baby's First Month* and issued copies to all mothers soon after child-birth. Another of his books was given to every applicant for a marriage licence. King was appointed Director of Child Welfare. By 1930 about 65 per cent of all non-Maori children were cared for by the Society; 85 per cent by 1947.

The result – no one doubted that it was a result – was a spectacular decline in European infant mortality to one of the lowest in the world. The Maori rate was much worse, though Dr Maui Pomare, who was several times a cabinet minister, was urging King's ideas upon the Maoris too.[1]

A major aim of the Plunket system was to 'build character' in the babies. This aim was to be pursued in their later upbringing too. From the age of two all children were to have a daily cold water bath followed by twenty minutes' exercise.[2] King strongly recommended cold baths for everyone – they were character-forming.

King had firm views on education: most of his opinions were definite. For one thing he stressed physical rather than mental training, arguing that the 'hideous' evil of 'over-pressure' or 'cram' in the

Karitane nurse visiting a family, Dunedin, 1949. *Turnbull*

education system was responsible for 'terrible evils' in the form of mental collapse. The 'craze for examination' led to pressures which had 'a most pernicious effect upon the growing brain': 'in hundreds of cases it causes lifelong injury of the most serious character.'[3] Intellectual work should be indulged in only moderately.

There was nothing new about this opinion. A book on *The Science of Life*, first published in 1883, had stressed the danger of nervous collapse faced by imaginative and intellectual boys. They must be obliged to exercise. Moreover, physical activity would repress any inclination to masturbation, which itself was believed to lead to physical decline.[4]

King's view that the education system was detrimental to the children's health was welcomed by the *New Zealand Herald*, which remarked upon 'the notorious fact .... that prize-winners as a body do not make the leaders of men, that the scholarship boys are generally outstripped in after life by the lads who reflected no examination credit upon their school.'[5]

Much more influential however, and widely accepted, was King's opinion that it was a 'preposterous farce' to give boys and girls the same education. Their roles in life were different and so were their intellectual capacities. King believed that too much intellectual effort impaired 'the potentialities of reproduction and healthy maternity'. Keen female scholars would grow up flat-chested and unfitted for maternity. They should not receive an academic education after puberty. Dr Batchelor seconded these views. Excessive study, he held, resulted in an inadequate development of the reproductive organs.[6]

These opinions, too, were readily acceptable to the philistines. The *Observer* was shocked to discover, from a survey in 1905 of twenty-two schools, that girls were top in nineteen. It observed, 'The amazing facility with which many New Zealand girls learn by rote without exercise of any faculty but that of memory is no cause for congratulation.' The 'motherhood of the girls' was being 'sapped by school competition with the boys'. It concluded that the education system was defeminising women, which would prevent the country from being 'strong nationally'.[7] The *New Zealand Graphic* complained that the education system prepared girls for every occupation except housework and cooking. They should have less head and more hand work at school. Wife desertion was becoming quite common because girls learned arithmetic and could buy cheaper meat but could not cook it.[8]

Similar opinions were advanced by more serious commentators. It was argued that the education of girls should be different from that of boys because the 'female mind' had different characteristics. In 1917 a sub-committee of the national Council of Education brought out a report on 'Differentiation in the Education of Girls'. This war-time report, perhaps a product of a new emphasis on the importance of children, occasioned much debate. It claimed of the sexes that 'Their mental capacity and physical strength are unlike. The boy is more original, the girl is more imitative, and there is more danger of the girl suffering from overwork.'[9]

There is no doubt that girls generally received less education than boys. They were likely to be sent to school later and allowed to leave earlier than their brothers.[10] In the event of family illness they were likely to be kept home as nurses. Emily Chaplin, BA, a member of the Council, explained to the Otago Educational Institute in 1917 that it was impossible to know what occupation, out of thousands, a boy might adopt, but that, 'We know as an absolute fact that the girls in our schools today will be the mothers and the home-makers a few years hence. They may be side-tracked for a few years into some occupation where they become independent wage-earners, and rightly so, but there is no manner of doubt as to their future destiny.'

She went on to urge, as the report had done, that there should be

Left Mrs F. E. Baume, first woman member of the Auckland Education Board. *N.Z. Capital and Labour Review*, 1 Oct. 1917. *Auckland Public Library*

Right A domestic science class, St Margaret's College, Christchurch, 1914. *Steffano Webb Collection, Turnbull*

more differentiation in the education of the sexes. She said that 'If we do not bend all our energies towards the highest development of the girl nature, the race cannot progress in the best way.' She supported the view of the Council of Education that girls should be taught, as far as possible, by women teachers, especially in the higher classes, then generally taught by men.[11]

The views of the Council were criticised on various grounds, for instance that because a lower level of attainment would be required of the girl, she would be handicapped as a wage-earner. A man attacked the report because it implied a segregation of the sexes rather than co-education,[12] but there is little doubt that he was one of a minority. Another critic pointed out that a narrowing of the education of girls was implied.

Phoebe Myers wrote in reply to the critics, strongly supporting Emily Chaplin. It was established by leading biologists, she claimed, that the fundamental difference between the sexes was 'that the male is disruptive and the female is constructive.' Consequently their needs

were different. The boy must be the 'home-builder' and 'home-protector', the girl the 'home-maker'. The girl must be educated so as to be 'physically, mentally, and morally efficient for motherhood'.[13]

Rosetta Lulah Baume, PhB, a graduate of the University of California and widow of F. E. Baume, the former NZNA president, wrote an article in 1917 arguing the case for 'differentiation'. She denied, as a critic had alleged, that it meant rivetting 'the shackles of household drudgery and slavery' on women. Their life's work was 'home-making'. What was needed was further education beyond primary school. Of the 8000 or so girls leaving primary school at the age of thirteen or fourteen only 800 went on to secondary school. Mrs Baume suggested that all the others should have compulsory domestic science classes for three hours, once a week, between the ages of fourteen and seventeen. This would teach them their duty to society which the boys learned at their military training.[14]

The idea that girls were intellectually or physically weaker fitted perfectly into the opinion that since their destiny was different, so should be their education. It is noticeable that these attitudes were expressed particularly vigorously towards the end of the First World War, when there was a great concern not only about the future of the nation and of the children, but about the need for 'national efficiency' if the nation were to survive and strengthen in the post-war world. However, such views continued to be expressed into the 1920s.

Boys were thought of much as high-spirited animals needing taming. A newspaper in 1872 published some verses, 'Our Boys':

Who ape with pride the airs of men;
Who smoke and sometimes drink at ten;
Who spoken to, retort again?
Our Boys . . .

Who band together after dark;
Nor fear the honest watch dog's bark;
But play the devil for a lark?
Our Boys.[15]

From time to time, throughout the nineteenth century, there was concern about larrikinism. *The New Zealand Schoolmaster* in 1884 defined '*mischief* (the delight of the larrikin) as *superfluous energy misdirected*' and argued that cure of larrikinism was more education – presumably to keep wild boys busy.[16]

There was a very strong emphasis in the schools on physical education for boys and girls. In 1901 by Act of Parliament physical drill was made compulsory for children over eight in all schools. In 1913 a Physical Education section of the Education Department was set up. It provided courses of instruction for teachers, who would return to their schools fired with physical enthusiasm.[17]

A president of the Institute of Education asserted in 1909 that every boy in the Dominion ought to be able to harness and ride a horse, to shoot a rifle and to milk a cow.[18] That was no longer possible for every boy in the towns. However, in the previous year the Boy Scouts Association had been established to inculcate loyalty and obedience, observation and self-reliance. In 1909 the Girl Peace Scouts, later the Girl Guides, were also inaugurated. Many thousands of children learned out-door skills through these associations.

The connection between scouting and warfare, like that between sport and war, was obvious. The 'Song of the Scouts' referred to marching, drilling, learning signals, building a fort and rescuing the wounded.

Some day the scout will be a man!
Some day a war dog is let loose!

And well he knows the bugle call,
A gallant man to face the foe,
Once he was a happy scout.

Chorus:- For Zealandia's glory lads we sing,
We carry the flag of the free ....[19]

In 1900 a school cadet scheme was introduced by legislation. Military drill became compulsory for all boys aged twelve or more. Those under twelve could drill if they were four feet seven inches in their socks. They drilled with dummy rifles, but small bore rifles and live ammunition were issued for practice at the firing range. By 1916 there were over 14 000 cadets. In 1909 a Defence Act created Junior Cadets in the primary schools, aged twelve to fourteen, and Senior Cadets, aged fourteen to seventeen, whether at school or not. Service was compulsory for all British subjects.[20] The Junior Cadets lapsed in about 1919, but the secondary school cadet system continued until the 1960s, and in a few schools even into the 1980s.

The education of boys was extremely militaristic, but it was more than that. Colonel Sleeman explained in 1919 that 'Citizenship, not militarism ... is the real aim of the new Cadet Force.' The cadets were to do twenty-three hours of physical training, fifteen hours of musketry instruction a year, while infantry drill was reduced from thirty-eight hours to less than nineteen. During every parade there was to be a 'lecturette'. Among the topics laid down were: Citizenship, Advantage of Physical Fitness, Personal Hygiene, Folly of Swearing and Smoking, Sanitation, Playing the Game, Patriotism, Self-discipline, Evils of Selfishness, Debt Owing to One's Country, Physical Fitness and Individual Efficiency, Value of Punctuality and Smartness, Power of Concentration and Observation, Requirements for Health, Discipline as a Civil Asset, Healthy Minds and Bodies.[21]

The cadets' marching song was ambivalent. It proclaimed that their aim was 'Defence and self-reliance'; praising New Zealand's scenery, it asserted a determination to 'shield her and defend her'. However, it admitted to a still 'nobler ardour', vowing to love and serve 'An empire great in peaceful arts', but returned, at the end, to the affirmation that 'first of all, and best of all, We hail our loved New Zealand.'[22] A rivalry between and inter-twining of national and imperial loyalties was characteristic of opinion among English-speakers in all four 'white' dominions.

The emphasis in the education system – as in the Plunket system – was upon discipline, self-control and physical vigour. In 1916 the

Cadets at Richmond junior school *c.* 1905. *Jones Collection, Turnbull*

Council of Education produced a report on 'mentality tests', medical inspection and physical education. The aim said Phoebe Myers, President of the Women Teachers' Association, was 'a systematic building up of the physique of the nation'.[23] It was, said the *New Zealand Herald*, essential if civilisation were not to lead to 'national decay'.[24] It was, then, with great pleasure that the Director of School Hygiene, Dr Ada Paterson, announced at an Australasian Medical Conference in 1927 the discovery that New Zealand children were bigger than other children. *National Education* headed its report: 'A SUPERIOR RACE'. A survey of about a fifth of the primary schools had revealed that New Zealand children aged ten to fourteen were taller and heavier than children in Australia, Great Britain or the USA. According to 'available statistics' the only children as big were those in Toronto.[25]

The war-time and post-war years were a time of many parental and educational anxieties. For instance, the 'moving pictures' aroused new fears. Would the 'very objectionable' pictures being shown 'weaken the moral fibre of our young people'? The influence of the movies on morals was fiercely debated. Many people believed that 'unsuitable themes' shown in a 'vitiated atmosphere' until late at night must be demoralising.[26]

There was much concern about the sexual morals of children. A senior teacher urged in 1917 that 'Patriotism, Temperance and Sexual Hygiene' should be recognised as compulsory and not optional subjects in the school syllabus.[27] The teachers who made such remarks were almost always vague as to what sexual instruction should be given. When a doctor wrote a pamphlet on sex hygiene, and the Minister of Education, C. J. Parr, raised the subject, a teacher objected: 'Such teaching destroyed the innocence of children. Good parentage, refined teachers, and decent environment would go far to remove the necessity for sex teaching.'[28] A teacher said that 'The superstructure of a righteous nation' must be erected on teaching children how to behave, 'training them into the perfect exercise and kingly continence of their bodies and souls.'[29]

In 1924 the President of the New Zealand Educational Institute said that many people had 'a pathetic belief in the redeeming power of mere knowledge of facts of sex'. He thought that a sublimation of the sex impulse might more probably result from a vitalisation of the study of literature, music and art as well as biology. What concerned him most was the danger to society of feeble-minded adolescent girls, 'with no intellectual interests to sublimate the over-developed sex impulse'. Like many people he was impressed by the (spurious) evidence of the Juke family in the USA, breeding thousands of mental defectives, criminals and prostitutes. His solution was draconian – 'a census of those of feeble mind and lower, and the segregation of the girls especially into farm colonies.'[30] Mr Aschman's remedy did not become law, but a Mental Defectives Amendment Bill was before the House in 1928 setting up a Board to compile and keep a register of mentally defective persons. Those in the register might not marry and there were offences concerning having sexual intercourse with or supplying alcohol to these persons.[31]

The speaker was expressing the views of the eugenics movement, which enjoyed a vogue in New Zealand in the early twentieth century. It preached the doctrine of scientific breeding. Science was to be called upon, as the *New Zealand Herald* put it, to 'assist the blind efforts of nature'. It was logical to apply to humans the same care as was used in 'the breeding of valuable racehorses or cattle'. In order to 'stem the tide of national degeneracy' it was necessary, not merely to provide mental hospitals, reformatories and schools, but 'to begin with the child yet unborn'.[32] It was not merely important to ensure a good physique for the babies, but to ensure that the right ones were being born.

In 1903 Dr W. A. Chapple, the leader of the New Zealand Natives Association in Wellington, published a book, *The Fertility of the Unfit*, in which he advocated the sterilisation by tubo-ligature, not only of all 'defective women' but of the wives of 'defective men'. He did not recommend vasectomy for the males because it was 'a violent outrage upon the man's nature and sentiment'. He further suggested that couples proposing to marry must have certificates of health issued by a Central Board.[33]

Branches of the Eugenics Education Society were established in Dunedin in 1910 and soon in other towns.[34] However, although the movement attracted many professional and well-educated people, it did not enjoy a popular following.

The motto of the Educational Institute was, 'As in the school, so in the nation'. It was constantly said in the *New Zealand Journal of Education* and at Educational Institute meetings that the aim of education was to inculcate national ideals. Children were the nation's greatest asset. The public schools were the great unifying force in the state: 'For forty years [they had] . . . been welding our people into a united nation, in intellect, character, and public spirit at least the equal of any nation in the world.' The object was 'national self-realisation'. To achieve that a 'truly national system of education' must be evolved, reflecting 'the national character, temperament and aims'.[35] Yet not much was done in the schools to inculcate a sense of national identity.

Certainly the children heard about sporting victories, and the importance of sport was rarely under-estimated. The Prime Minister, George Forbes, said in 1931 – and was supported by a head-master – 'that a boy learned more in the sports ground than in the class-room.'[36] They were also taught about the significance of Anzac day. There were, for instance, essay competitions on that subject, and innumerable addresses at school assemblies.[37] There were also school flag-raising ceremonies, intended to impress the children with the importance, even sanctity, of the flag. Saluting the flag had been common in schools since the South African war. In 1921 it was made compulsory, once a week, in all public schools.[38] However, the flag which was honoured was often the Union Jack; the song that was sung was usually the national anthem, that is, 'God save the King'.[39]

From time to time teachers or journalists advocated that more New

Raising the flag, Kaukapakapa, *NZ Graphic*, 7 Aug. 1897. *Auckland Public Library*

Zealand history should be taught in the schools. The trouble was that the text-books used were British, so that the students had a heavy diet of Hengist and Horsa, but very little about Maui and Marsden.[40] While he was Minister of Education William Pember Reeves produced *The New Zealand School Reader* (Wellington, 1895). This was an anthology of New Zealand prose and verse, more suitable for secondary than primary schools. The early histories of the colony written for children, such as E. M. Bourke's *A Little History of New Zealand* (Auckland, 1881), were tedious to read, emphasising constitutional history and electoral dates, for instance.

When *Our Nation's Story* was written (anonymously) for Standard 6 (that is, the top primary school class) children, in the mid-1920s the 'nation' was the British. The book contained sixty-five pages about 'The Romance of New Zealand', but another 200 about the Portuguese, Spanish, French, Dutch and British Empires, and several chapters about British history. It concluded with a 'Table of English Sovereigns Since 1066'. A civics text-book, *The New Zealand Citizen* by E. K. and Alan Mulgan (Auckland, 1914) similarly contained a substantial section about the Empire. Nellie E. Coad's *The Dominion Civics* (Auckland, 1924) had a section on the League of Nations as well as the British Empire.

The children were given a massive and deliberate indoctrination in British imperialism. This may best be illustrated from the *School Journal*, which began publication in 1907. It was published in three parts for different age groups, monthly from February to November. In 1914 its use was made compulsory. Two surveys of the journal up into the 1930s reveal that the imperial and militaristic content was phenomenal – 55 per cent in 1911, over 70 per cent in 1916, and at least 26.6 per cent over a period of thirty years.[41]

A scrutiny of the *Journal* published for the older primary school children in 1920 reveals that there were a few articles on Maori legends, New Zealand birds, Anzac Day and sport, but the main emphasis was on the history of Great Britain and the Empire, the Celts, the battle of Jutland, the monarchy, the forthcoming visit by the Prince of Wales, and the like.

The imperial mission of the Education Department was ably assisted by various propaganda societies. The most influential was the Navy League. Its committee in 1936 consisted of top bankers, ex-prime ministers (Forbes and Coates) and former high commissioners. The League enrolled thousands of school children as honorary members, giving them badges. It published its notes and news in each issue of *National Education* and had an almost automatic right to instruct children during school hours. Its spokesmen would enter the schools on Empire Day, Trafalgar Day, and Nelson Day and preach the messages of imperial defence. When an Auckland School Committee refused the League permission to enter in 1921 because it was fostering a military spirit there was an outcry. The Prime Minister, the Ulster-born super-imperialist, William Massey, intervened personally.[42]

Another imperialist body was the League of Empire, which was established in 1901. It arranged for children to contact pen friends throughout the empire. By 1911 20 000 children were members of the Comrades' Correspondence section. It also ran a system of 'school-linking'.[43]

Children were also the target of an imperialist and royal bombardment spontaneously and often commercially inspired. Children's literature, like G. A. Henty's stories, and the children's papers, like the *Boys' Own Paper* were strongly empire-oriented. So were numerous films.[44] Imperialist pictures were constantly used in advertisements, on biscuit tins, tea and cigarette packets and on postcards.

What is not known is how much 'penetration' this publicity had; how far it produced imperialists. These questions are difficult to answer in any quantitative way. As we have seen, the Empire was so rarely referred to in soldiers' letters or diaries that the propaganda seems to have had little effect. It has been suggested in this study that imperialism was an official ideology rather than a popular enthusiasm.

Other aspects of the issue have also been touched upon. One is that, while to a modern student the imperialist propaganda might seem counter-nationalist, it did not seem so to most New Zealanders. As the

'British Commonwealth of Nations' evolved from, say, 1919 to 1939, it was official dogma that membership of the Commonwealth was not at all incompatible with dominion status, as defined by the Balfour Report of 1926, and complete sovereignty. It was by now widely recognised that distinct nations had evolved in the Dominions.

The two surveys of the *School Journal* referred to earlier noted that the imperial content dwindled to nothing by the end of the 1930s. That was symptomatic of deep-seated changes in New Zealand opinion during that decade. The *Journal* became anti-war, even pacifist, and internationalist, supporting the League of Nations.[45]

Similar changes may be observed elsewhere. The post-war young historians – the authors of school text-books and histories of New Zealand – J. B. Condliffe, J. C. Beaglehole, W. T. G. Airey – were liberal, internationalist, if not left-wing.

There was now widespread criticism of the education system, and frequent assertions in *National Education* that New Zealand had fallen behind other countries.[46] A new leader, C. E. Beeby, who was to become Assistant-Director of Education in 1940, was already foreshadowing extensive educational reform. The Minister of Education in the Labour Government, H. G. R. Mason, was now reported in *National Education* questioning the effects of saluting the flag.[47]

Almost wherever one looks at New Zealand society in the mid to late 1930s there is evidence of a rapidly changing climate of opinion. This is especially noticeable if we consider the political and literary activities of university students.[48] But, once again, a war intervened – not to stop, but to hold up change.

VII

Centenary

'Man Alone': the cover of the *Weekly News*. Christmas, 1920. *Turnbull*

Chapter Seventeen

THE SINGERS OF LONELINESS

On 6 February 1940 most New Zealanders celebrated the hundredth anniversary of the signing of the Treaty of Waitangi and the annexation of the country by the British Crown. The Taranaki and Waikato Maoris declined to attend the reenactment of the signing of the Treaty at Waitangi because the Treaty had not been kept.[1] There were protests about the loss of their land. Sir Apirana Ngata, an MP and a former cabinet minister, said that he doubted whether any 'native race' had been as well-treated by Europeans as the Maoris: that was why they had 'offered up the flower of the race for the Maori Battalion'. 'However, the Maori race wanted to retain its individuality.'[2] Thus, the demand for a separate identity, 'he mana motuhake', was again asserted. Nevertheless, the Ngapuhi (who had stayed away from the Jubilee ceremony in 1890), celebrated in grand style. There was a race between two war canoes, one was 120 feet long, with eighty paddlers, the other 50 feet, with twenty-five paddlers.[3]

Some of the celebrations were muted, or even cancelled, because the Second World War had begun. The First Echelon had been publicly farewelled in Wellington on 4 January. In Auckland a centennial procession, 'The March to Nationhood', was cancelled. Nevertheless there were pageants in most towns and cities, as well as in numerous rural districts. Often these centred on a procession of floats representing historical scenes – Kupe, Tasman, Cook, the pioneers and so on. In many places centennial parks were dedicated or halls erected. There were also some public thanksgiving services.

Needless to say, the centenary provided an excellent opportunity for the Government to seek a national consensus, 'above politics', after a decade of embittered political division. The Prime Minister, M. J. Savage, proclaimed on New Year's day, 'This young nation has come of age.' The Hon. W. E. Parry announced that all New Zealanders 'can be one big family'.[4] There was endless editorialising and speechifying about the meaning of Waitangi or of life in New Zealand. The Christchurch *Press* thought, 'It is pertinent now for New Zealanders to ask themselves if they can yet be called a nation.'[5]

The principal national celebration was a Centennial Exhibition in Wellington. This was no 'mere fair', but 'the measure of our worth, the evidence of national manhood that we present to the world.' Martyn

'Waitangi', cartoon by Minhinnick. *NZ Herald*, 7 Feb. 1940.

Finlay reviewed the Exhibition in an article, 'Nation or Colony?' in the journal *Tomorrow*.[6] He thought the Hall of Progress, recording a century of growth, very impressive. The Dominion Court, with its 'cool gloom', he felt was 'a nightmarish geography lesson'. The 'towering peaks of papier-mache mountainry' he felt were oppressive. All in all he thought the Exhibition 'very encouraging . . . to all New Zealand Nationalists'. He regretted, however, that in this exhibition of New Zealand's 'claim to nationhood', there was scarcely a reference to music, literature or art.

What he might have added was that, in arranging for the centennial celebrations, the Government had given a surprising emphasis to art and letters. A Centennial Exhibition of New Zealand art, beginning with the work of artists who came out with the first explorers, but not including Maori art, toured the country. Its organiser, A. H. McLintock, said that it was 'quite apparent that at the present time New Zealand is far from possessing an art truly national.'[7] There seems little reason to dispute this conclusion: there was no national 'school' of artists. The painter, W. M. Hodgkins, thought that local painters were handicapped by the absence of great collections of art in the colony, to provide examples and models.[8] Of some 220 artists whose work was represented in the Exhibition, less than one hundred were New Zealand-born.[9]

The literary celebrations were extensive. E. H. McCormick edited a series of books, the Centennial Surveys, the largest enterprise of the kind in the country so far. It summarised the results of ethnographical, historical and other scholarship in the Dominion in the past fifty or so years. Largely, but not solely, because of the appointment of historians in all four University Colleges, historical research was in the 1920s and 1930s at least beginning. In 1930 an ex-serviceman, J. B. Condliffe, had published *New Zealand in the Making*, an economic history. W. P. Morrell and J. C. Beaglehole began publishing history in the 1920s. In 1940 Beaglehole published *The Discovery of New Zealand*, F. L. W. Wood wrote the first survey of New Zealand in international affairs, *New Zealand in the World*. Even more notable was McCormick's own *Letters and Art in New Zealand*. Sir Apirana Ngata wrote *The Maori People*. Such works were at the intellectual cutting edge of the process of self-definition.

To mark the centenary the Government also sponsored several literary competitions. The short story contest was won by Frank Sargeson's story, 'The Making of a New Zealander', in which Nick, a young 'Dally' (Dalmatian immigrant), 'was saying he was a New Zealander, but he knew he wasn't a New Zealander. And he knew he wasn't a Dalmatian any more.' Third prize went to Roderick Finlayson's not quite convincing story, 'The Totara Tree', about an elderly Maori woman sitting and dying in her 'birth tree'. The essay competition was won by M. H. Holcroft's *The Deepening Stream. Cultural Influences in New Zealand*, which will be referred to later. What was surprising, and marked a considerable advance, was that it was in 1940 possible to hold a literary competition and to receive such interesting entries.

An Australian scholar has said that the heady nationalism of the 1880s and 1890s proved a false start and that after 1900 there was a revival of colonial dependence and a hiatus in the growth of nationalism.[10] Certainly a case could be made out that nationalism declined in New Zealand too, especially in the 1920s. Some writers have suggested that the severe casualties of the war caused a missing generation – in medicine and other aspects of social life, as though too many potential leaders were dead or badly hurt, so that creativity failed.[11] The evidence is inconclusive. But it is noticeable that few writers, for instance, were ex-servicemen, while some of those who were, like John

A. Lee and Frank S. Anthony had been severely wounded. Most of the well-known writers were older men, like W. P. Reeves and Alan Mulgan, or young men like R. A. K. Mason, or women. With few exceptions, the verse, in particular, of the writers of the 1920s was lamentable, what came to be known, after the title of an anthology, as *Kowhai Gold* poetry, sentimental, faded Georgian work, away in fairyland, full of archaisms. At least, in the 1890s, some of the writers, like Reeves, had tried to confront real life. It is at a few younger people, beginning to write in the 1920s, more of them in the 1930s, that we must look to find the origins of modern New Zealand literature.

In 1926 Count Geoffrey Wladislas Vaile Potocki de Montalk, poseur and claimant to the crown of Poland, was living in London and Paris. His grandfather, who was of aristocratic Polish extraction, had taught French and German at the Auckland University College. In that year another young Aucklander, A. R. D. Fairburn, who had been to primary school with de Montalk, began corresponding with him. They were young poets who took themselves very seriously. In his first book, *Wild Oats* (Christchurch, 1927), 'Prince' Potocki, as he then styled himself, affirmed that his work might be compared with that of the young Coleridge. He wrote to Rex Fairburn that he was 'the Byron of today'. The evidence for this assertion was presumably that he wrote verse and was to a high degree sexually obsessed. In Paris he wrote a poem 'just after naughtying Marcelle'.[12] He denied a cabled news item published in New Zealand that he claimed to be as great as Shakespeare, but wrote to Fairburn that he did think that New Zealand had 'the greatest living group of poets', and that his own was 'the best poetry on the world's market today'. Alas, the editors all turned him down and he was 'too much of an aristocrat to kow-tow' to them.[13]

De Montalk proposed that Fairburn come over and share Marcelle. In 1930 Fairburn came to stay with him in London. Two years later 'Monty' was sentenced to six months in prison for publishing an obscene libel. The case received wide publicity in literary circles as an example of puritanical censorship, but sympathy was restrained by the thought that, as a poet, he had no discernible talent. His waist-long hair, his cloak and his broad-sword, however, attracted much attention.[14] Charles Lahr, a bookseller and publisher in London, wrote to Fairburn that it was 'a pity it wasn't a real poet who came up against the authorities.' The 'publication' was merely a technical offence, of arranging for poems to be printed.[15]

Before Fairburn went to England, de Montalk and he constantly exchanged poems and views on poetry. At that time Fairburn, in his early twenties, greatly admired Rupert Brooke.[16] Later he was to repudiate that 'pale lily-white lad' in himself, who wrote 'Drinkwater-ish' verse, and he was to turn to stronger stuff.[17]

De Montalk had turned his back on his country of birth, but thought 'it would be all very well being back in New Zealand if one could do what one was presumably born there for, to make a New Zealand civilisation.' He thought that the New Zealand poets formed 'a grand and unique group .... All so young, so fair to look at, and gifted with so great a strain of song ....'[18] Rex Fairburn, too, all his life was concerned to build up a national literature.[19]

When he returned home he promised 'to preach economic nationalism as hard as my jaws will work.' After flirting with Marx he had become a follower of Douglas Social Credit. If the Labour Party refused to adopt that platform he would start a 'Nationalist, anti-Communist movement ... anti-big-business: with the ultimate object of cutting New Zealand away from the Empire and making her self-supporting .... Objects ... to get out of the clutches of the League of Nations; assert New Zealand's *nationalism*, and make her as far as possible a conscious and self-contained nation on her own account. I should try, for the time being to give the thing a strong military flavour. *No* pacifism, "idealism", passive resistance, or other such useless sentimentalities. Then, when the time came, a Fascist coup might be possible.'[20] He regarded democracy as a failure which should be knocked on the head, as was happening in Germany. This letter was written from England in 1932 to the Auckland poet, Ron Mason, who was a Marxist. It might be thought that Rex was baiting his friend, but it sounds perfectly serious. Certainly de Montalk had encouraged Fairburn in elitist attitudes. Of course poets much better known than Fairburn had similar political views.

One of New Zealand's best-known authors, Frank Sargeson, referring to travels in the 1920s, wrote, 'Like so many of my fellow-countrymen I had had to visit Europe to discover that I was truly a New Zealander ....' He felt himself 'only very indirectly a part of it all' – of 'so much civilisation'. He found that he preferred, to the old, the landscape of his own new world, where wandering on his uncle's farm he could wonder 'whether any human foot had trod there previously ....' This feeling of being first could be as romantic as the dream of the European past. In his uncle he perceived 'the seeds of a new kind of society, one in which I might eventually find myself at home ....'[21]

Charles Brasch, the poet, who went to Oxford University in 1927,

A new generation of writers. *From left to right:* Robin Hyde, J. C. Beaglehole, Frank Sargeson, John Mulgan, Jane Mander, R.A.K. Mason

wrote, 'It was New Zealand I discovered, not England, because New Zealand lived in me as no other country could live, part of myself as I was part of it, the world I breathed and wore from birth, my seeing and my language.'[22] One New Zealand writer after another has testified, not usually so eloquently, to the fact that you could not lose your country by leaving it. In 1932 Rex Fairburn wrote to Ron Mason, from Wiltshire to Auckland:

You know 'how nice it is to be near the centre of things'? Yes, damn fine. And NZ is a crude little hole, without doubt. But, in spite of the fact that I am tolerably happy in England, I'll tell you what I'd like to do now. I'd like to go back to NZ and be a New Zealander. Not a wistful student of French Impressionism and Post-Impressionism, as some of our young artists would apparently wish to be. Not a follower of the Bolshevik Revolution – which is about as irrelevant to NZ as ham to a Synagogue feast. Not a student of Anglo-Irish decadence – of Virginia Woolf, James Joyce etc. But just a New Zealander. I would like to live in the backblocks of NZ, and try to realise in my mind the real culture of that country. Somewhere where I might escape the vast halitosis of the Press, and the whole dreadful weight of modern art and literature. Because we really are people of a different race, and have no right to be monkeying about with European culture.[23]

Fairburn thought that New Zealanders should cease to live vicariously on 'culture memory'; that the painters, for instance, should come to terms with New Zealand's 'hard, clear light'.[24]

Like the New Zealand troops at war, the New Zealand writers, meeting people from other nations, became more aware of being New

Zealanders. Lady Ottoline Morrell wrote of Katherine Mansfield, 'When in England I think she was conscious of being a New Zealander, secretly proud of it and cherishing it as a lovely harbour of refuge for her thoughts and imagination to play in, but at the same time it perhaps prevented her from mixing with ease and friendliness amongst us here . . . .'[25]

A minor poet, Isabel Maud Peacocke, found that in England, she felt an 'alien'. Ian Milner felt it to be 'a foreign land'.[26] Most of the New Zealand writers developed independent attitudes towards the British. Alan Mulgan's sentimental book, *Home, A New Zealander's Adventure*, (London, 1927) was anathema to them. Fairburn said it marked the end of an era. The young poet and historian J. C. Beaglehole wrote about a post-graduate seminar in London: 'most of us are colonials or yanks too; the English highbrow girls I have met give me the pip, & the men on the whole aren't much of an improvement; give me a Boer or an Aussie any day.' This view of the English went beyond the seminar:

The more I see of the place the more I despise the English & the more I like England. The paradox I leave you to unravel. Stupidity everywhere, & the people intensely, passionately proud of it – about the only thing they are passionate about. They are the same in NZ of course, but there is a different shade of emphasis there.[27]

New Zealand during the depression did not loudly call its children home. Beaglehole wrote that it was 'not exactly encouraging for the free human spirit'. Moreover, 'once in N.Z. you're dead as far as history is concerned.'[28] He thought that returning home was 'the death of the mind'.[29] Nevertheless, like Fairburn, he did come home, both of them to periods of unemployment.

Verses by Mason, Beaglehole and Fairburn had appeared in Quentin Pope's cloying anthology *Kowhai Gold*. But Fairburn now became a spear-head of a new poetic advance. Beaglehole lived to become New Zealand's most notable scholar.

Although there had been numerous, generally short-lived literary journals in the past, in 1931 it seems that there were none. In that year an Auckland University student, Jim Bertram, suggested that the Literary Club should launch a new journal. Bob Lowry, a very talented young printer, who produced the new literary journal, *Phoenix*, wrote about Bertram to the young Christchurch poet and printer Denis Glover: 'He's a most refined young fellow, of the very perfectest thing in taste – in every dashed subject under the sun . . . .'[30] The aesthetes, led by Bertram, edited the journal in 1932. In 1933 a Marxist, if not already a Communist, R. A. K. Mason, became editor. Lowry wrote to Denis Glover, that Mason was 'a crack-brained socialist, with some literary ability'. He thought he was 'certain sure to land Phoenix into a rough-house with the College authorities . . . .' His prophecy was correct. The journal caused a stir, but failed financially and ceased publication after two years.[31]

Phoenix was important because, for the first time, it became possible to speak of a 'school' of New Zealand writing. R. A. K. Mason, Fairburn, Allen Curnow, Charles Brasch, D'Arcy Cresswell and J. C. Beaglehole all published in its pages. Charles Brasch wrote that, in effect, *Phoenix* said: 'Here we are: New Zealand literature begins here.' He went on to say that 'a group of able young people from all over the country were aware, for the first time since William Pember Reeves left Wellington for London in 1896, of the place of literature and the arts in the life of a civilized land . . . .'[32]

The writers of the 1930s were strangely unaware that they had any precursors. They often ridiculed those they knew of but, more than that, they seemed to suppose that they had invented New Zealand nationalism. Some older men perhaps resented that. Ormond Burton, a First World War veteran, having written that that was when New Zealand 'very definitely became a nation', continued: 'Twenty years later when our poets caught up with the feeling it was interesting to note that apparently none of them had been at all sensitive to the deep surge of feeling that had swept through the men who were their fathers or elder brothers. Too much in revolt perhaps.'[33] Another possible explanation is that the more literary and educated New Zealanders had been intellectually tied to British culture for longer than their people in general.

Phoenix was followed by *Tomorrow*, 1930–40, a left-wing journal of opinion edited in Christchurch. It published poetry and fiction, including Frank Sargeson's early sketches. The *New Triad, New Zealand New Writing* and other ephemeral journals followed, until Brasch established *Landfall*, in 1947, a journal still surviving nearly forty years later.

Why there was this new and unprecedented vigour in New Zealand literature is a question debatable rather than definitely answerable. One answer must be the birth of a new, post-war generation. Robin Hyde was convinced that the explanation lay in the depression. In an article published in Shanghai in 1938, from which the title of this chapter is taken, she wrote that the depression had a 'stimulating effect on the thought and culture of rebellious young minds, in a silent country which at least learned to be articulate.' She thought that this was 'probably worth all the hardship involved'.[34]

The depression was a blow to the pride of 'a people of plenty'. It led many people to ask radical questions about the nature of their society: why had it failed? It also could lead to criticism of Great Britain, overwhelmingly the country's chief market and the source of most of its overseas loans. It could be blamed for the plight of the Dominion. In Fairburn's long poem, 'Dominion', which promotes Douglas Social Credit ideas, he wrote,

We are the Empire's Junior Partner
and we have no gold:
what shall we do in the day when we shall be asked for?
Nothing. We shall not be asked. We shall be told.

It should be added that some of these writers, like Fairburn and D'Arcy Cresswell (although a consummate bludger), were often desperately poor, which did not encourage them to admire the social or political system.

These writers, and others, often wrote to one another, endlessly discussing literature. Moreover, some of them lived on Auckland's North Shore. Frank Sargeson lived in Takapuna. In 1934 Robin Hyde and another poet, D'Arcy Cresswell, lived at Castor Bay. At about that time Rex Fairburn and his family stayed in a local motor camp. The blind German poet, Karl Wolfskehl also lived on 'the Shore'. They constantly met and talked about their writings. This North Shore group was New Zealand's first regional 'school' of writers.

Not all of this discussion was high-brow. Fairburn and Glover, in particular, greatly enjoyed verbal and other clowning and – while very serious in their aims – were anxious not to sound pompous. Fairburn always hoped, as he wrote later, 'to relieve the dreadful solemnity of the New Zealand muse . . . .' He was also perfectly clear that his aim was to 'épater les bourgeois'. Hence his letters are full of references to 'literachoor' and the like.[35]

Glover and Fairburn strongly resented the influence of C. A. Marris, Alan Mulgan and J. H. E. Schroder, three editors who controlled literary pages and also (in Marris's case) selected annual volumes of verse. Glover wrote in *Short Reflection on the Present State of Literature in this Country* (Christchurch, 1935):

Three Men who hold within their hand
the Literary of the Land
and lead this little pilgrim Band,
Mulgan, Marris, Schroder.

Alas, these words will never bust
into the Literary Column:
Mulgan, Marris, Schroder must
keep it Solemn, Solemn, Solemn.

To break out from this supposed dictatorship was one motive encouraging Glover in Christchurch and Bob Lowry in Auckland to print and publish the new writers themselves. In 1934, for instance, Glover published *New Poems* by Curnow, Fairburn, Mason and himself. Fairburn hoped this new volume would establish 'a kind of *Criterion* . . . . A measuring rod . . . a sinister spectre at the junketings of the Menstrual School of Poets' (one of his pet hates).[36] When he wrote his long poem, 'Dominion', Fairburn thought of offering it to Glover: 'we ought if possible to keep this local publishing racket going. It's nicely under weigh now, and represents our *only* chance of Building Up a National Literature . . . .' In fact he first – unsuccessfully – sought a London publisher. In the long run the publication of poetry locally enabled the poets to abandon the practice of seeking London publishers, which meant a subjection to English taste.

Fairburn was a very large, genial man, with strong prejudices. One of them was a hostility to 'nancy boys', the 'Green International', who, he believed, boosted one another's writing and careers. He claimed, however, to have 'no objection to pansies as persons'. Since some of the writers, like Sargeson and Cresswell, were homosexual, he must have given great offence. His views certainly led to a rift with the former.

Cresswell was a very odd person, the son of a well-to-do Christchurch family, who had served in France. He was – with Katherine Mansfield – one of the first New Zealanders to devote himself entirely to the life of a writer. He wrote two interesting prose works, but his poetry, which he highly esteemed, was not notable. The archaisms of his prosody were as odd as his opinions. In 1936 he wrote to Glover that he was broadcasting on poetry, 'scarifying modern conditions – particularly machinery and the pursuit of wealth, and the ludicrous pre-eminence of women . . . .'[37] He held that everything had gone wrong since Copernicus, and preferred an ancient and pagan world. When Cresswell cadged some money off a friend and then denounced him anonymously in *Tomorrow*, Fairburn wrote to Glover that Cresswell's 'Nature is apparently only ill-nature, & his Pantheism merely Pansy-ism. And his satanic anger and aloofness only the bitter spite of a schoolgirl.'[38] In his youth Cresswell, like the others, had aimed at 'a national poetry', but now (like de Montalk) he professed a larger goal, which he was never to achieve.[39]

Cresswell and de Montalk left the country. Other writers returned. One was Jane Mander who, having lived for twenty years in the USA and Great Britain, came back in 1932. She was not well thought of in respectable circles – a reviewer had accused her of portraying 'morbid egoists' who lacked 'ordinary morality'; of writing 'the "sex" novel' portraying 'free love' which might mislead people unacquainted with 'the normal healthiness of the country'.[40] Nevertheless, she was probably the best novelist New Zealand had produced.

Jane Mander read an article by Fairburn in which he urged New Zealand writers to look to American writers for models, because they had a common colonial experience. It seemed that Sherwood Anderson, for instance, had influenced the stories that Frank Sargeson was publishing in *Tomorrow*.[41] Jane Mander replied in some articles in the Christchurch *Press*.[42] She wrote that every small town had its Authors' Club. There was a large number of writers, mainly women, but their writing was mostly amateurish and slip-shod. In her view, the New Zealand language was English, not American. However, a week later she was urging her readers to read Hemingway. It is clear that she was scarcely aware that the next generation of writers was as dedicated and professional as she had herself been, in perfect isolation.

Some of the new writers, notably Glover and Allen Curnow, had been influenced by modern English writers, especially W. H. Auden and Stephen Spender.[43] Curnow wrote, 'Whatever may be said or written about a national literature for New Zealand, England remains at the very least the "technical research laboratory" where the finest and most advanced work is done with that subtle material, the English language.'[44]

The leading Australian poets seemed to the New Zealanders to be untouched by post-'Wasteland' modernism. Consequently trans-Tasman literary relations were as marginal as the economic or political. The USA and the UK were enormously more powerful cultural influences upon the country than Australia.

One of Fairburn's prejudices was, as he wrote to de Montalk, that the Australians 'have no literature, & never will have. The national temperament . . . is quite incapable of grasping or absorbing the Hellenic tradition, which has built most English poetry. We in N.Z. can do this.' In short, 'The Orstrylians are a nation of larrikins.'[45] He also wrote in *Tomorrow* an ignorant article based on perusing the journal, *Art in Australia*, saying that Australian painting was mediocre. The young poet had perhaps not heard of the Heidelberg School.[46]

Perhaps the most striking characteristic of the new writing was that its authors dealt with real life. Gone – almost – were 'the Fairy Horse', tuis, gypsy girls and other romantic props. The writers had come out of fairyland. Fairburn, for instance, could write about New Zealand's economic problems in 'Dominion', its politics, its history, its land. In the 1890s Reeves had occasionally touched upon politics, but most New Zealand poets chose 'poetic' subjects. A number of the new poets sometimes wrote satirical verse: the ability to laugh at themselves or their country had rarely been evident, at least since the 1890s. In his persona, 'Whim-Wham', Allen Curnow made an industry of satire. Denis Glover and Fairburn also wrote some very amusing, satirical verse and, in Fairburn's case, prose.

Another important advance was that the new poets had, in general, abandoned the use of 'poetic' language. Their English was not only idiomatic, but often distinctively New Zealand. Especially in Sargeson's stories, but also in some of Curnow's and Fairburn's verse, one can 'hear' the cadences of New Zealand speech, almost for the first time in the literature.

It was perhaps inevitable, during the depression, that the writers should emphasise the lives of the poor. R. A. K. Mason, whose poems contain little explicit local reference, had earlier written about 'the

Beggar' (who was Christ). He hoped – in 1937 – 'to publish some reasonably decent proletarian stuff'.[47] He was a Marxist, but others who were not wrote much more about ordinary working people. Glover's Harry, Arawata Bill and Mick Stimson, like John A. Lee's 'the Shiner' are clearly 'men of the people'. So, too, is John Mulgan's 'Johnson'. Some of these characters scarcely belong to the work-force – they are marginal men. Frank Sargeson's men are generally not trade unionists, nor workers at all, but drop-outs, people on the fringes of society. Most of these men, as has often been remarked, were 'men alone', without women and often without friends – though sometimes, like Terry in Sargeson's story, 'That Summer', a man may have his mate.

Man Alone, Mulgan's novel, had come to symbolise this theme in New Zealand literature. It was not merely that Johnson was alone. Charles Brasch wrote that Mulgan 'was haunted by the sense of man's exile in the world of the Truce [the years between the wars?] – man homeless, without guidance, without allegiance.'[48]

In the article already referred to, Robin Hyde (Iris Wilkinson) thought that loneliness was a prevailing theme in New Zealand writing, in the work of Jane Mander and Katherine Mansfield, for instance. But it permeates everywhere like a spreading dye. It is clear that the 'man alone' was not only a legend: there had been thousands of pioneering bachelors. One may add to that the very real feeling of remoteness in New Zealand – not only from other lands, but in the bush and mountains, from any other people at all, past or present.

An allied theme dominates the literature of the time, mainly in poetry but also in prose. John Mulgan wrote, simply, in *Report on Experience*, 'The country is, in fact, so old in itself that none of us have dared to touch it; we have only just begun to live there. [He was in Great Britain.] The Maoris who came before us moved among the dark heavy trees like ghosts and could have sailed away at any time and never left a mark. We could leave it ourselves now.'[49] Haunting images of transience, impermanence, estrangement, exile abound in the literature.

Allen Curnow wrote in a critical essay that the idea 'that we are confronted by . . . a natural order, to which our presence in these islands is accidental, irrelevant; that we are interlopers on an indifferent or hostile scene; that idea, or misgiving, occurs so variously and so often, and in the work of New Zealand poets otherwise so different, that it suggests some common problem of the imagination.'[50]

The towns were seen as merely the encampments of nomads who

had broken into the natural order like robbers into a temple, blind to its beauties, proportions, or wisdom. Humanity in New Zealand feels insecure, oppressed, because it is rootless; it has failed to make the land its own. Such themes recur continually in the verse of Curnow, Ursula Bethell and other poets.

The plains are nameless and the cities cry for meaning ....

Homestead? Nay, halting-place, accommodation ....

Waiting for our songs, the woods are still,
The stones are bare for us to write upon.

Not I, some child born in a marvellous year,
Will learn the trick of standing upright here.

... what great gloom
Stands in a land of settlers
With never a soul at home.

The New Zealanders, it was said, had neither a past nor a future. D'Arcy Cresswell wrote ominously, 'As yet they have no future of their own; and when at length one confronts them, they shall awake to find where they lie, and what realm it was they so rudely and rashly disturbed.'[51] Man was alienated spiritually from Nature.

These writers seemed unaware that the ideas of 'man alone' and of the empty land had been adopted by writers of an earlier generation. Blanche Baughan had supposed that the country had no 'dust of the Dead'. Charles Brasch agreed: 'There are no dead in this land.' Man was not accepted; earth and man had not come to an understanding. He imagined improbable national ecstasies:

Man must lie with the gaunt hills like a lover,
Earning their intimacy ....

Some of these attitudes were expressed and explored in a series of essays by M. H. Holcroft.[52] 'Nature' was his central theme, and man's relationship with it. 'We are still strangers in the land', he wrote.[53] What impressed him most about his country was that it had rested so long in 'primeval silence'. When men arrived, they brought with them an 'unconscious memory' of the primeval forests surrounding their earliest ancestors. So, in New Zealand, Polynesians and Europeans were thought to have recreated scenes from the most ancient human environment.[54]

Like some of the poets, this essayist was impressed with the lack of human monuments in New Zealand. He made the astonishing assertion, 'There is no work here for archaeologists.'[55] Holcroft's essays seem now more 'dated' than the better poems of that time. Nevertheless, his mystical musings, his discussions of literary problems with the hills,[56] his postulation of a 'national soul', which we can only think of in terms of a work of art,[57] for many people stimulated nationalist thoughts at the time of the centenary and for some years thereafter.

The present writer once termed this congeries of attitudes a 'South Island myth'.[58] Most of the writers who expressed them lived in, or came from, the south, though similar observations were made by one or two North Islanders, like John Mulgan. The idea that man had no past in these islands was less likely to occur in the north, with its numerous pa (terraced forts), monuments to ancient Maori occupation.

Other writers have noted that nature poetry (or landscape poetry) which was, at least in the 1930s and 1940s, the dominant variety, was often inspired by William Wordsworth.[59] It seems that few of the writers had read Aldous Huxley's recent essay, 'Wordsworth in the Tropics', in which he pointed out that the pantheistic worship of nature might suit the 'cosy sublimities' of the Lake District but not the tropical jungle, which was 'fundamentally and utterly inimical to intruding man'.[60] The New Zealand 'bush' too, was primeval forest. Unlike the poets, the settlers had wanted to cut it down as fast as possible. They felt, not alienated from nature, but that nature was alien. Some writers had sensed that too. Holcroft referred to the 'sinister quality of the great rain forest'.[61] Though often for different reasons, both settlers and writers felt uneasy.

The writers discussed in this chapter were not the only ones who adopted the cause of nationalism. Eileen Duggan, for instance, an older woman, of Irish descent, often wrote in strongly nationalist terms. She wrote, in 'Invasion':

For if I held the freehold of this land
From Cape Reinga to Oreti Beach
I could not feel that it was more my own.

And in her 'Tribute to Jessie Mackay' she said:

Some say that they will sing for song's sake only
That passion, like the cuckoo, has no nation,
For everywhere a singer's heart is lonely . . . .

Much less successfully than Allen Curnow in his brilliant poems inspired by J. C. Beaglehole's histories, she, too, wrote of the explorers, and of:

> *. . . native faults: indigenous virtues,*
> *All those strange human elements,*
> *That collide to the chemical,*
> *We call nationality.*[62]

In 1945 Allen Curnow wrote in his preface to *A Book of New Zealand Verse 1923–45*, which first revealed to many people how New Zealand poetry was being transformed, 'The good poem is something we may in time come to recognize New Zealand by, not something in which we need expect to recognize obvious traces of the New Zealand we know.'[63] In his anthology, including his own 'House and Land' and his historical poems, 'The Unhistoric Story' and 'Landfall in Unknown Seas', this was now true for many people.

Charles Brasch wrote, some years later, 'A society can be said to have come of age when it begins to live by the light of an imaginative order of its own.' That 'order' was 'the spiritual form of the society that creates it.'

In older countries, where an imaginative order already exists, new works of art and literature need only embellish or extend or re-define that order. But in a raw colonial society much more is demanded of them; they have to create order for the first time, in a wilderness that is without form and very nearly void. Every work with even the mildest charge of imaginative vitality therefore assumes for the time being capital importance (which it will certainly lose later) as a new cell in the body of the embryo order.

He said that they now had 'the skeleton of an imaginative order'. Literary nationalism had added a new dimension to a New Zealand identity and to New Zealand culture.[64]

VIII

Epilogue

Protest on the return of 161 Battery from Vietnam, Auckland, 1971.
NZ Herald

Chapter Eighteen

INTO THE SECOND CENTURY

Readers over forty can roll their own final chapters to this book, making alternative endings from memories. Nevertheless, it seems worthwhile to conclude this account of the origins of New Zealand nationalism with a few reflections and suggestions on the evolution of national feeling since 1940, leaving a more searching inquiry to some future writer. A national identity is not a permanent and static possession; rather, the nation has from time to time to be reinvented. Indeed, the idea of the nation is changing all the time.

At first thought it might seem that another fifty or so years have brought only repetitions of what went before: more wars and more sporting achievements. And certainly those events have greatly strengthened New Zealand nationalism. John Mulgan wrote, of the New Zealand division in North Africa:

They were mature men, these New Zealanders of the desert, quiet and shrewd and sceptical. They had none of the tired patience of the Englishman, nor that automatic discipline that never questions orders to see if they make sense. Moving in a body, detached from their homeland, they remained quiet and aloof and self-contained. They had confidence in themselves, such as New Zealanders rarely have, knowing themselves as good as the best the world could bring against them, like a football team in a more deadly game, coherent, practical, successful.[1]

As in earlier wars, the New Zealanders won the respect of allied and enemy forces. One example must suffice. A distinguished British officer, European by birth, Vladimir Peniakoff, wrote, of the Long Range Desert Group fighting in North Africa:

I graded their squadrons, drawn from various parts of the Empire, on a scale of human excellence, which ranged from the New Zealanders high on top through the Rhodesians and the British Yeomanry down to the squadron drawn from the Guards Regiments. The New Zealanders, farmers in civil life, took easily to a roaming life in the desert. They had from the first a resourceful happy assurance and set a standard which the others tried to follow.[2]

The present writer, who served overseas in the navy, can certainly testify that the New Zealanders felt that they were as good as the British, and better than most. On a highly competitive course at a school for officer cadets, New Zealanders filled many of the top places.[3]

Since the Second World War, New Zealanders have excelled at the Olympics, to the delight of their compatriots. Jack Lovelock's 1500 metre gold medal at Berlin in 1936 has been followed by further 'golds' for middle distance races won by Peter Snell, Murray Halberg and John Walker. Yvette Williams won the long jump at Helsinki in 1952. New Zealanders have more recently won gold medals for rowing, yachting, canoeing, and hockey. Six 'golds' at Los Angeles in 1984 produced a national ecstacy. It was a considerable achievement for athletes from such a small nation.

The men have continued to excel at rugby and have become a force occasionally to be reckoned with at cricket and soccer. The women excel at netball, softball, squash, marathon and other sports. In short, the athletic emphasis in the New Zealander's sense of identity has been strongly reinforced.

New Zealand nationalism is, however, a much more complex topic and feeling than it was in the first half of the twentieth century. Anyone thinking about the Vietnam war and the disputes over playing rugby with South Africa might conclude that what used to unite the nation, war and sport, have come to divide it. Certainly, the war in Vietnam was very divisive, as the 'teach-ins' and public demonstrations showed.

It does appear that New Zealanders have become less militaristic. There is no longer – since 1958 – any compulsory military training. School cadets no longer exist in most secondary schools. Even more powerful evidence of changing attitudes is the fact that in the election of 1984, three of the four parties campaigned to oppose the entry of nuclear-armed vessels into New Zealand. The majority of voters supported those parties and the Lange Government banned the entry of nuclear-armed or propelled ships into our ports. Both the Government and the majority of people wanted to make New Zealand 'nuclear-free', while remaining a member of the ANZUS treaty with the USA and Australia. However, the USA refused to modify its 'neither confirm nor deny' policy with regard to the carriage of nuclear weapons. Leading American politicians and servicemen indulged in much threatening language, shocked, it seems, that a small democracy could have a mind of its own. ANZUS was put into moth-balls.

In 1949 a majority of those who voted in a referendum had voted in favour of peace-time conscription in the armed forces. It is doubtful whether any other nation has voted for conscription. That the same people – and their children – should in the mid-1980s ban the entry of

Demonstrators march against sporting contacts with South Africa, 1969. *NZ Herald*, 22 March 1969

nuclear powered or armed vessels into their harbours and make their country a nuclear-free zone was a remarkable transformation.

Attitudes towards rugby have not, however, changed as much as might be expected following the violent scenes during the Springbok rugby tour of New Zealand in 1981. Public opinion was again deeply split when the Rugby Union proposed, in 1985, to send an All Black team to play in South Africa. Public opinion polls showed in April that 63.5 per cent of people wanted the Rugby Union to stop the tour. At that time 56.3 per cent of people supported the Government's policy of opposing the tour. After the tour was stopped by a decision of a court, however, most people had not abandoned their support for rugby as a sport. An *Eye Witness* Heylen poll in July 1985 revealed that 80 per cent of people aged fifteen years and over had had some recent involvement in rugby, whether playing or watching the game on television. The majority of people interviewed said that they had positive feelings about rugby as a game. Some 33 per cent, however, had more negative feelings about the game than they had had in 1980.[4]

Some important changes may be referred to briefly. One is that, while maintaining a relatively high standard of living, New Zealand has dropped, since the first 'oil shock' of 1973, in the table of wealthy nations. In 1983, of OECD countries, it came eighteenth, ahead of only Ireland and the five Mediterranean countries, in gross national product per head of population. God had become more niggardly in responding to the request in the fourth verse of the national song, 'Give us plenty . . . .' Nevertheless, the New Zealand standard of living would still seem very high to most people on earth.

Another cause of national pride, for nearly a century, has been strongly sustained: that is, of belonging to a society which looks after all its citizens and regards welfare as an aspect of equality. The welfare state has changed, but it still thrives. The old age and other pensions introduced by the Liberals were enormously extended when the first Labour Government introduced Social Security in 1938. This was further extended by Walter Nash's Labour Government, in 1957–60, much more so under Robert Muldoon after the 1975 election. He introduced what may well have been the most expensive national superannuation scheme in the world, after what was the most costly election promise in New Zealand history. At the age of sixty people were given a pension of 80 per cent of the average wage, whether they were wealthy, still working for an income, or not. The Government of David Lange, in 1985, taxed this out of existence for the well-to-do elderly, restricting 'super' to those who needed it. They also 'targetted' a 'Family Care' programme to low income families with young children. It was still a people that cared for the old, the young, the sick. National self-regard could still stand up in front of the mirror and smile.

Another change deserves to be mentioned. In the late 1930s one of the Labour Government's favourite words was 'insulation'. The economy was, it was claimed, going to be insulated from the effects of overseas price changes and depressions. Rex Fairburn wrote, in 1932, of the aim 'to cut our international trade as far as possible'.[5] How a country so heavily dependent on world trade could achieve this goal was never clear, and probably no one now believes it possible. The fourth Labour Government, in 1986, is full of 'Free Marketeers', who believe in competition rather than in protective walls.

A further change, the subject of the previous chapter, has greatly accelerated. A number of New Zealand novelists and poets have achieved an 'overseas reputation' now, thanks to jet travel, as Janet Frame observed, referred to as an 'international reputation'. (When she returned Frank Sargeson told her, 'You know, I'm not jealous. I'm not jealous.')[6] Keri Hulme, Sylvia Ashton-Warner, James K. Baxter,

Maurice Duggan, Allen Curnow – the country was now home to some major writers.

An even greater change, beginning in the 1960s, was the surprising appearance of a large group of professional painters. Toss Woollaston, Colin McCahon, Don Binney, and Ralph Hotere have been followed by numerous younger artists. At the same time, in a number of towns and cities, private galleries were established to exhibit and sell pictures.

The New Zealand self-regard is less physical now than it used to be. At least, that is true for educated New Zealanders – and all New Zealanders have, at least, attended secondary school since about 1944. The stereotype of the New Zealander, as he or she sees it, is both less militaristic and less tough, less macho. The image is a softer one than it was fifty years ago.

War influenced New Zealanders' view of themselves, as we have seen, partly because travel afforded the possibility of making national comparisons. In recent years the increase in international travel has had a similar effect. Someone once observed that the traveller, like a snail, carries his house – his nation – on his back. A journalist wrote that a young sheep-farmer who had been abroad for a year had learnt only that Romney sheep in Kent were too big in the bone and the wool was coarse.[7] Janet Frame wrote of the change forced upon everyone who travels overseas, that of 'examining not the place of arrival but the place of departure'.[8]

The New Zealanders have become great travellers. In 1979 – a year chosen at random – nearly one person in nine of the entire population left the country on temporary visits. Certainly New Zealanders have more opportunity to compare themselves with other nations than do most people. Before the Second World War New Zealand travellers usually visited Australia or Great Britain. Now large numbers visit – and enjoy – Asia and North America.

What effect travel has on people's world-view is debatable, but one effect seems to be to make New Zealanders more confident of their distinct identity. It may seem a strange remark in a book on nationalism, but New Zealand nationalism has become more international, not in the sense of becoming anti-national, but in the sense of taking a broad internationalist view of the role of the nation. At the same time, it has become, at least in aspiration, less British and Maori and more multi-cultural. About 9 per cent of the population consists of Maoris and Pacific Islanders, who migrated here in large numbers after the Second World War. There are also 20 000 Chinese and Indians.

The question, how far these people of different origins form one

'The Birth of a Nation' by Bromhead. *Auckland Star*, 17 Sept. 1984.

community is an open one. There can be little doubt that most of the Pacific Island immigrants are 'joiners', and that many of their New Zealand-born children have joined. There is no question that large numbers of Maoris and Pakeha feel that they share a nation. When the Second World War broke out, Sir Apirana Ngata said simply in the House, 'it would be a waste of words to give any assurance that the Maori will be with the pakeha [in fighting], as the Maori is so much a part of the New Zealand nation now that that can be taken for granted . . . .'[9] On the other hand, nearly fifty years later, a minority of Maori radicals, some of whom have only a small proportion of Maori genes, and little Maori language or culture, continue to protest against their ineluctable fate, to share a country whether they feel part of the nation or not.

Maori demonstrations (joined by Pakeha too) have called into question an attempt to establish a new national day. The Waitangi Day Act of 1960 established 6 February as a day of commemoration and thanksgiving for the signing of the Treaty of Waitangi. In 1973 the Labour Government made Waitangi Day a national public holiday,

'"David", by Michael Langelo', by Minhinnick. *NZ Herald*, 17 Sept 1985.

New Zealand Day. The next National Government changed it back to Waitangi Day. Neither move was a success. In any disguise, 6 February provided annual occasions for lamentation, for the wrongs suffered by the Maoris. In 1986 the function at Waitangi was transferred to Wellington, where protest was more muted. It was not the first time that a national day has proved divisive.

The role of women within the nation is subject to rapidly changing perceptions. In the 1970s a number of United Women's Conventions were held. For the women who attended they were an exhilarating experience. However, their interests and opinions, for instance on issues such as abortion, proved too diverse for them to remain united. Nevertheless, the women's movement has proven a powerful influence on society. Women are no longer placed on the pedestal of motherhood. With an increasing proportion of women in the permanent work-force, the idea of careers for women has received widespread acceptance. The introduction of 'equal pay' is another sign that women are gradually achieving equality. The women's movement has strongly influenced the attitudes of men – though not of all men – and has altered the idea of the nation. New Zealand nationalism has become less 'male chauvinist'. In this respect, too, the image of the nation is softer than it was.

As these lines are written the 'Rainbow Warrior' is refloated on the

Waitemata harbour, after being sunk, and a crew member killed, by French Government agents. From time to time leading American politicians put pressure on the New Zealand Government to abandon its anti-nuclear policy. French bomb tests and limpet mines and American bullying stir up New Zealand's national feeling as no events have since the Second World War.

References

The following abbreviations are used:
AJHR Appendices to the Journals of the House of Representatives
ATL Alexander Turnbull Library
NZJH New Zealand Journal of History
PD Parliamentary Debates

CHAPTER 1: NATIONAL MODELS

1. See Gaetano Salvemini, *Mazzini*, London, 1956, for a discussion of Mazzini's ideas.
2. Paul C. Nagel, *One Nation Indivisible. The Union in American Thought 1776–1861*, New York, 1964, and Jay Fliegelman, *Prodigals and Pilgrims. The American revolution against patriarchal authority, 1750–1800*, Cambridge, 1982, afford many examples. I am indebted to Dr John Stagg for these and other references.
3. See, e.g., John Lynch, *The Spanish–American Revolutions 1808–1826*, London, 1973.
4. Benedict Anderson, *Imagined Communities. Reflections on the Origin and Spread of Nationalism*, London, 1983, pp. 49ff. This is the most interesting recent discussion of nationalism that I know of. I am much indebted to it.
5. For a discussion of Jebb's ideas, see J. D. B. Miller, *Richard Jebb and the Problem of Empire*, London, 1956.
6. *Empire Review*, IX, 52, May 1905, pp. 350–53.
7. *Indirections. A Memoir 1909–1947*, Wellington, 1980, p. 20, cited in John Geraets, *Islands*, 33, July 1984, p. 72.
8. *Report on Experience*, Oxford, 1947, p. 2.
9. p. 14.
10. 20 Aug. 1910.
11. Peter Russell (ed.), *Nationalism in Canada*, Toronto, 1966, p. 4.
12. These examples are quoted in Keith Sinclair, *The Origins of the Maori Wars*, Wellington, 1957, p. 3; *A History of New Zealand*, Harmondsworth, 1959, pp. 94–5; and *William Pember Reeves*, Oxford, 1965, p. 14.
13. *Kia Ora Coo-ee*, 15 Aug. 1918, p. 16.
14. A press clipping in ATL, MS Papers 522, T. W. Brown, item 21.
15. A. Rugby Pratt, *The Pioneering Days of Southern Maoriland*, London, 1932, p. 11.
16. W. P. Morrell, *The University of Otago. A Centennial History*, Dunedin, 1969, pp. 52–3; *New Zealand Magazine*, VI, 1876.
17. R. E. Irvine and O. T. J. Alpers, *The Progress of New Zealand in the Century*, London, 1902, p. 421.
18. *Evening Post*, 4 Dec. 1884.
19. London, 1890, p. 6.
20. D. M. Potter, *People of Plenty. Economic Abundance and the American Character*, Chicago, 1954.
21. Cited in Anderson, *Imagined Communities*, p. 15. I cannot find the source of this passage quoted by Anderson but Gellner expresses the same idea in *Thought and Change*, London, 1969, p. 174 and in *Nations and Nationalism*, Oxford, 1983.
22. Sinclair, *The Origins of the Maori Wars*, Ch. VI.

CHAPTER 2: PROPHECIES

1. See, e.g., J. M. Bumsted, 'Things in the Womb of Time: Ideas of American Independence, 1633–1763', *William and Mary Quarterly*, 3rd series, XXXI, Oct. 1974, pp. 533–64. I owe this reference to my colleague, Dr John Stagg.

2. *Ultima Thule; Or, Thoughts Suggested by a Residence in New Zealand*, London, 1854, pp. 3–4, 324–5.
3. C. C. Eldridge, *England's Mission. The Imperial Idea in the Age of Gladstone and Disraeli 1868–1880*, Chapel Hill, 1973, p. 26.
4. Cited in K. Sinclair, *The Origins of the Maori Wars*, Wellington, 1957, frontispiece. For two other early prophecies, see *New Zealand Magazine*, I, 1876, articles by David Bruce and John H. Shaw; *New Zealand Schoolmaster*, v, 7, Feb. 1886, article by W. Rolleston.
5. Vol. 1, May 1863, p. 100. The issue was further discussed in the June issue and in September 1865.
6. Pp. 3, 155.
7. Ibid., p. 6.
8. Grey/Cardwell, 20 Aug. 1864, CO 209/182/10544, Public Record Office, London.
9. On the situation in New Zealand, see J. Rutherford, *Sir George Grey*, London, 1961, and Jeanine Graham, *Frederick Weld*, Auckland, 1983.
10. Graham, *Frederick Weld*, pp. 80–1.
11. Macandrew/Bowen, 22 Dec. 1868, enclos. Bowen/Buckingham and Chandos, 26 Jan. 1869, CO 209/210/4284.
12. Fox/Bowen, 6 July 1869, Governors Series 7, 4–5, National Archives; Cardwell/Granville, 20 May 1869, filed with Bowen/Granville, 8 March 1869, CO 209/210/5531.
13. For a summary of these views, see Eldridge, *England's Mission*, Ch. 1.
14. Ibid., p. 72; W. D. McIntyre, *The Imperial Frontier in the Tropics*, London, 1967.
15. E.g., Eldridge, *England's Mission*, pp. 72–3.
16. Memo, 28 March 1870, enclos. Bowen/Granville, 2 April 1870, *AJHR*, 1870, A–1, no. 51.
17. 18 June 1869, cited in Michael Burgess, 'Imperial Federation . . .', *NZJH*, 17, 1, April 1983, p. 69.
18. H. A. Atkinson/A. S. Atkinson, 21 May 1869, in G. H. Scholefield (ed.), *The Richmond–Atkinson Papers*, II, Wellington, 1960, pp. 286–7.
19. H. A. Atkinson/A. S. Atkinson, 25 March 1870, ibid., p. 302.
20. 25 March 1870, McLean Papers, ATL, MS 32, 147.
21. Bowen/Granville, 2 Sept. 1869, *AJHR*, 1870, A–1B, no. 14; *PD*, v, 1869, p. 254.
22. *PD*, VII, 1870, pp. 8ff., 237ff.; 320ff.
23. Ibid., p. 242.
24. *PD*, 1868, III, p. 64.
25. *Evening Herald*, cited in T. J. McIvor, 'On Ballance: a Biography of John Ballance, Journalist and Politician, 1839–93', PhD thesis, University of Auckland, 1984, pp. 89–90.
26. *PD*, 1887, 58, pp. 305, 313.
27. *PD*, 1904, 128, pp. 304–9.
28. 20 April 1905.
29. 3 June 1905.
30. 15 Nov. 1905, Secret, CO 209/267/44677.

CHAPTER 3: THE RISE AND FALL OF THE NEW ZEALAND NATIVES ASSOCIATION

1. *Canterbury Old and New 1850–1900. A Souvenir of the Jubilee*, Christchurch [1890] (published by the New Zealand Natives Association), Preface.
2. R. Jebb, *Studies in Colonial Nationalism*, London, 1905, pp. 92–3.
3. Benedict Anderson, *Imagined Communities*, London, 1983.
4. *Zealandia*, 1 Jan. 1890.
5. J. E. Menadue, *A Centenary History of the Australian Natives Association 1871–1971*, Melbourne [1971], p. 162.
6. *Lyttelton Times*, 19 March 1890, reporting from the *Westport Times*, 27 Feb. 1890. No copies of Westport newspapers of that time seem to have survived.

7. K. Sinclair, *William Pember Reeves. New Zealand Fabian*, Oxford, 1965, p. 81.
8. *NZ Herald*, 20 Sept., 10 Oct., 18 Oct., 4 Nov. 1892.
9. Ibid., 24 May 1894; *Auckland Star*, 24 May 1894.
10. *Evening Post*, 15 April, 15 May, 28 May, 29 May, 11 June, 18 June 1896.
11. Ibid., 29 May 1896.
12. Ibid., 29 May, 11 June, 18 June 1896.
13. Ibid., 2 May, 9 May, 12 May 1896.
14. Ibid., 4 June 1896; *NZ Times*, 14 April, 27 April, 28 April, 29 April 1896.
15. *NZ Times*, 15 April, 16 April, 16 May 1892.
16. *NZ Mail*, 30 April 1896.
17. *Lyttelton Times*, 3 Dec., 9 Dec., 11 Dec. 1897, 27 Jan. 1898; *Press*, 6 May 1898. The branch did not become active until early in 1898.
18. *Lyttelton Times*, 17 May, 18 May 1898.
19. *Southland Times*, 24 January 1898.
20. Ibid., 5 Feb. 1898.
21. *Otago Daily Times*, 29 March, 28 April, 30 April 1898.
22. For Hawera, *NZ Times*, 24 Sept., 8 Oct. 1897; for Timaru, *Press*, 3 March 1898; for Gisborne, *NZ Mail*, 5 Aug. 1897 and *Constitution of the 'New Zealand Natives Association', Poverty Bay Section, adopted at Gisborne, Dec. 1900*, Alexander Turnbull Library, Wellington. This is the only known surviving copy of an NZNA constitution, though they were reported in the press, in part and at various times and places.
23. *Otago Daily Times*, 30 April 1898.
24. *NZ Graphic*, 6 March 1897.
25. *NZ Herald*, 12 Sept. 1894.
26. *NZ Graphic*, 6 March 1897; *Southland Times*, 5 Feb. 1898 (J. A. Hanan speech).
27. *Southland Times*, 5 Feb. 1898.
28. Ibid., *Lyttelton Times*, 3 Dec. 1897.
29. E.g. *Southland Times*, 5 Feb. 1898.
30. Ibid.
31. Ibid., 2 Feb. 1898.
32. *Lyttelton Times*, 17 Dec. 1898.
33. *NZ Herald*, 14 Nov. 1894.
34. E.g. *Evening Post*, 12 Nov. 1897.
35. Ibid., 15 April 1896.
36. *NZ Times*, 10 May 1898; *Evening Post*, 26 Nov. 1897; *NZ Herald*, 31 Aug. 1898.
37. *Evening Post*, 31 May, 7 June 1898.
38. Ibid., 10 May, 11 May 1898.
39. Ibid., 22 Jan., 31 Jan. 1898.
40. *NZ Times*, 9 Aug. 1897.
41. Ibid., 2 Aug., 8 Aug. 1898; *Lyttelton Times*, 26 April 1898.
42. *Evening Post*, 29 March 1898.
43. *Otago Daily Times*, 13 July 1898.
44. *Lyttelton Times*, 3 Dec. 1898; *Press*, 26 March 1898; *NZ Times*, 14 May, 23 May 1898.
45. *Lyttelton Times*, 17 Dec. 1898.
46. *NZ Mail*, 19 Aug. 1897; *NZ Times*, 12 Aug. 1897.
47. *Otago Daily Times*, 27 May, 15 June 1898.
48. *Southland Times*, 4 Feb. 1898.
49. *Lyttelton Times*, 6 May 1898.
50. *Evening Post*, 4 June 1896.
51. Ibid., 30 Sept. 1915.
52. Anderson, *Imagined Communities*, pp. 57–9, 102–3.
53. *Weekly Graphic and New Zealand Mail*, 7 Oct. 1908.
54. W. A. Chapple, *The Fertility of the Unfit*, Melbourne, [1903].
55. Evening Post, 25 Aug. 1898.
56. Ibid., 1 March, 2 March, 25 Aug. 1898.
57. 30 April 1898.
58. *Evening Post*, 1 Oct. 1897.
59. Ibid., 1 February 1898.
60. For reports on the conference see ibid., 15, 16, 17, 18 Aug. 1898; *NZ Mail*, 25 Aug. 1898; *NZ Herald*, 23 Aug., 31 Aug. 1898 (a lengthy interview with Baume on 31 Aug.); *Lyttelton Times*, 17 Aug. 1898; *Press*, 19 Aug. 1898. Christchurch forgot to send a delegate and belatedly ap-

pointed a person in Wellington.

61. *Evening Post*, 25 Aug. 1898; *NZ Herald*, 23 Aug. 1898.
62. *Lyttelton Times*, 19 June 1901.
63. *NZ Times*, 14 Oct. 1908; *Evening Post*, 23 Sept., 16 Oct., 23 Oct. 1908; 27, 30 Sept. 1915; Menadue, *Centenary History of the ANA*, p. 163.
64. *Evening Post*, 16 Aug. 1915.
65. Ibid., 21 Sept., 22 Sept. 1915; 23 Sept. 1916; *Quick March*, 1, 4 Aug. 1918.
66. *Quick March*, 1, 4 Aug. 1918.
67. *Auckland Star*, 12 June, 13 June 1906; Menadue, *Centenary History of the ANA*, pp. 163–4. Auckland City Council Archives, MB 29, 1 March 1928; *NZ* (a journal), 25 Aug. 1926.
68. There are no known references to it in historical works except in the author's Pelican *History of New Zealand*, 1980 edn, p. 226.
69. *Evening Post*, 15 May 1896; *NZ Herald*, 31 Aug. 1898.

CHAPTER 4: THE EMPTY LAND: LITERARY NATIONALISM

1. VII, 14, 4 April 1891 (later *The Weekly News*).
2. *Southern Monthly Magazine*, 3, November 1864.
3. *Atea*, I, 1, June 1899.
4. I, 1, 6 Oct. 1866.
5. I, 1876.
6. I, 1, pp. 2, 3.
7. Dec. 1889, p. 331; May 1890, p. 660.
8. June 1890, p. 730.
9. I, 1, 1899, p. 2. On the Association, see *New Zealand Magazine*, 12, 2, Nov.–Dec. 1933.
10. R. Chapman and K. Sinclair (eds), *Studies of a Small Democracy*, Auckland, 1963, p. 173 (article by F. Rogers).
11. *Quick March*, 10 Feb. 1921.
12. Ibid., 11 April 1921.
13. E.g. 'M.H.', in the same issue, p. 36.
14. *NZ Graphic*, 13 Sept., Christmas number, 1890; 3 Oct. 1891; *NZ Illustrated Magazine*, Dec. 1901, May 1903.
15. *NZ Illustrated Magazine*, I, 1, 1899.
16. C. Stuart Ross, *Early Otago and some of its Notable Men*, Dunedin, 1907, p. 145.
17. Arthur Adams, *Tussock Land*, London, 1904, pp. 148–9. I am indebted to Kendrick Smithyman for directing my attention to this novel.
18. *NZ Illustrated Magazine*, Dec. 1901.
19. Keith Sinclair, 'Reunion', in *Manuka*, Auckland, 1941. This theme is discussed in Bruce Nesbitt, 'Aspects of Literary Nationalism in Australia and New Zealand with Special Reference to the *Bulletin*, 1880–1900', PhD thesis, Canberra, 1968 and, most recently, by J. O. C. Phillips, 'Musings in Maoriland–or Was There a *Bulletin* School in New Zealand?', *Historical Studies*, 20, 81, Oct. 1983.
20. Nesbitt, 'Aspects of Literary Nationalism', p. 459.
21. Mary Colborne-Veel/E. Currie, 28 July [1904], E. Currie MS Papers 413, ATL.
22. Nesbitt, 'Aspects of Literary Nationalism', p. 234. The author's father used to speak about how generally the *Bulletin* was read in New Zealand in the early twentieth century.
23. 29 June, 8 July 1899.
24. *NZ Herald*, Supplement, 10 Sept. 1910.
25. Geoffrey Serle, *From Deserts the Prophets Come. The Creative Spirit in Australia 1788–1972*, Melbourne, [1973], pp. 60–8.
26. Nesbitt, 'Aspects of Literary Nationalism', pp. 500–1.
27. *Quick March*, 10 June 1922.
28. P. 98.
29. The expression is used by another New Zealand expatriate, James Philp, in 1890. Cited in Nesbitt, 'Aspects of Literary Nationalism', p. 452.
30. 8 Feb. 1913, Alpers Papers 86/14, ATL.
31. Pp. 29–34.

32. 28 July [1904], E. Currie MS Papers 413, ATL.
33. *New Zealand Verse*, p. xxi.
34. *The Collected Verses*, Melbourne, [1913], p. 53.
35. A. Wall, 'The Empty Land', in *A Century of New Zealand's Praise*, Christchurch, 1912, p. 6.
36. Jessie Mackay (ed.), *New Zealand Rhymes Old and New*, [Christchurch], n.d., p. 34.
37. E. Tregear, *'Shadows' and Other Verses*, Wellington, 1919, p. 22.
38. *Atea*, 1, 3, Oct. 1899.
39. London, 1891, pp. 87, 95.
40. For these examples, see 'The Rabbiter', *NZ Graphic*, 21 Sept. 1895 (anonymous); Thomas Cottle, 'The Boundary Rider', ibid., 23 Aug. 1890; 'Bill Martin's Notch', ibid., 1 June 1895.
41. *NZ Graphic*, 29 Dec. 1894.
42. Jane Mander, *The Story of a New Zealand River*, Christchurch, 1974 edn, p. 51.
43. July 1889.
44. *NZ Graphic*, 12 Aug. 1893.
45. *The Heart of the Bush*, London, [1911], pp. 21–2, 41–2, 109, 281.
46. Pp. 25, 57.
47. A. Wall, *A Century of New Zealand's Praise*.
48. P. 34.
49. Frank S. Anthony, *Follow the Call*, Auckland, 1975 and *Gus Tomlins*, Auckland, 1977, both edited by Terry Sturm.
50. Anthony, *Gus Tomlins*, p. 10.
51. *Maoriland and Other Verses*, Sydney, 1899, p. 89.
52. T. Cholmondley, *Ultima Thule*, London, 1854, p. 344.
53. E. H. Brown/chicks, 2 June, 28 Dec. 1914; E. H. Brown Papers, ATL.
54. E. H. McCormick, *Letters and Art in New Zealand*, Wellington, 1940, p. 125.

CHAPTER 5: CENTRALISATION AND SOCIAL REFORM

1. *The British-Australasian*, 29 March, 31 May 1906.
2. Frank Parsons, *The Story of New Zealand*, Philadelphia, 1904, pp. 722–3.
3. VI, 1876, pp. 174–5, 180.
4. *Evening Post*, 18 April 1894, cited in *The Cyclopedia of New Zealand*, I, Wellington, p. 435. The author does not certify the accuracy of all of these dates of foundation. Most are from A. H. McLintock (ed.), *An Encyclopaedia of New Zealand*, or from the *Cyclopedia*.
5. *Census of New Zealand*, 1886, 1901.
6. Lawrence Stone, 'Literacy and Education in England 1640–1900', *Past and Present*, 42, February 1969, pp. 119–21.
7. Rollo Arnold, *The Farthest Promised Land*, Wellington, 1981, p. 352.
8. Bruce Nesbitt, 'Aspects of Literary Nationalism in Australia and New Zealand', PhD thesis, Canberra, 1968, p. 89.
9. *Census of New Zealand*, 1901.
10. 'Local Community or Atomized Society? The Social Structure of Nineteenth Century New Zealand', *NZJH*, 16, 2, Oct. 1982.
11. Margaret Tennant, 'Elderly Indigents and Old Men's Homes', *NZJH*, 17, 1, April 1983.
12. Fairburn, 'Local Community or Atomized Society?', pp. 150, 159ff.
13. Ibid., p. 160.
14. In this respect I agree with E. A. Wrigley's opening comments in 'The Process of Modernization and the Industrial Revolution in England', *The Journal of Interdisciplinary History*, III, 2, Autumn 1972. I am much indebted, in the following paragraphs, to this lucid discussion. I was also greatly helped by Richard D. Brown, *The Transformation of American Life 1600–1865*, New York, 1976

and Daniel W. Howe (ed.), *Victorian America*, Pennsylvania, 1976, essays by the editor and R. D. Brown. These and related themes have been explored in New Zealand by Erik Olssen, 'Towards a New Society', in W. H. Oliver (ed.), *The Oxford History of New Zealand*, Wellington, 1981. Some of this discussion is also influenced by a very original book by Robert Weibe, *The Search for Order 1877–1920*, London, 1967. For references to literature on modernisation I am indebted to Professor Clyde Griffen and Dr Raewyn Dalziel.

15. Raewyn Dalziel, 'Popular Protest in Early New Plymouth. Why Did it Occur?' *NZJH*, 20, 1, April 1986.
16. Rollo Arnold, *The Farthest Promised Land*, pp. 349–53; Arnold, 'English Rural Unionism and Taranaki Immigration, 1871–1876', *NZJH*, 6, 1, April 1972, p. 31.
17. Wrigley, 'The Process of Modernization', p. 227.
18. Ibid., p. 231.
19. Keith Sinclair (ed.), *A Soldier's View of Empire. The Reminiscences of James Bodell*, London, 1982.
20. *PD*, 1870, VII, pp. 441–2.
21. 'Towards a New Society', in Oliver (ed.), *The Oxford History of New Zealand*, p. 253.
22. *The Story of New Zealand*, p. 715.
23. See J. A. Dowie, 'A Century-old Estimate of the National Income of New Zealand', *Business Archives and History*, VI, 2, Aug. 1966. The Report is in *AJHR*, 1866, D–7B.
24. R. F. Irvine and O. T. J. Alpers, *The Progress of New Zealand in the Century*, London, 1902, p. 425.
25. 13 Oct. 1900.
26. *The Story of New Zealand*, pp. 656–7, 727–8.
27. Cited in Rollo Arnold, 'English Rural Unionism and Taranaki Immigration, 1871–1876', *NZJH*, 6, 1, April 1972, p. 30.
28. W. Allan Lloyd in *NZ Graphic*, 8 Jan. 1898.
29. Elizabeth Hansen's *The Politics of Social Security*, Auckland, 1980, is the first scholarly study.
30. 13 Nov. 1897.
31. 5 Dec. 1900.
32. 29 Sept. 1894.
33. 29 Feb. 1896.
34. *The British-Australasian*, 26 July 1906.
35. *NZ Graphic*, 27 June 1891.
36. *The Triad*, 1 June 1907.
37. 1, 4 Oct. 1900.
38. 8 March 1906.
39. E.g. *NZ Graphic*, 12 March 1898, on Texan citizens building their own railway.
40. London, 1902, pp. 40–1.
41. See vol. I, ch. 2.

CHAPTER 6: 'IS THERE A NEW ZEALAND TYPE?'

1. *NZ Herald*, 26 March 1910, 18 March 1911.
2. William Lane, *Selections from the Writings of 'Tohunga'*, Auckland, 1917.
3. *PD*, 1887, 57, p. 230.
4. *NZ Times*, 9 Sept. 1899.
5. Cited in ibid., but published in the *Review of Reviews*, 15 August 1899.
6. C. M. H. Clark, *Select Documents in Australian History*, Sydney, 1955, II, 477.
7. *PD*, 1884, 50, p. 517.
8. XV, 1882, pp. 493ff.
9. *NZ Graphic*, 3 July 1897.
10. Ibid., 12 Dec. 1896.
11. *Quick March*, 10 Sept. 1919.
12. *Weekly Graphic and New Zealand Mail*, 19 Aug. 1908.
13. Ibid., 12 Aug. 1908.
14. *NZ Graphic*, 11 Oct. 1890; *Lyttelton Times*, 17 March 1890.
15. 18 April 1896.
16. National Association of New Zealand, Taranaki Branch, Taranaki Museum MS 128/0; *NZ Herald*, 2 Dec. 1905, editorial discussing this

opinion.
17. *NZ Times*, 1 March 1906 and 2, 3, 5, 8 March.
18. *NZ Herald*, 27 Aug., 3 Sept. 1910.
19. 4 Nov. 1911.
20. 10 July 1920, 10 May 1919.
21. 10 Feb. 1921.
22. W. P. Reeves, *New Zealand* and *The Long White Cloud*, London, 1898.
23. See the Tables in J. C. Firth, *Nation Making*, London, 1890, pp. 339ff.
24. Reeves, *Long White Cloud*, p. 403; R. F. Irvine and O. T. J. Alpers, *The Progress of New Zealand in the Century*, London, 1902, p. 429.
25. Minutes of Third Session, Wanganui, 1898, pp. 14–15.
26. Two recent articles discuss this subject: C. McGeorge, 'Hear Our Voices We Entreat: Schools and the "Colonial Twang", 1880–1930', *NZJH*, 18, 1, April 1984; and E. Gordon, 'New Zealand English Pronunciation: an Investigation into some Early Written Records', *Te Reo*, 26, 1983. On 1 April 1925 *National Education* published an article, 'Is there a New Zealand Accent', reviewing a recent controversy.
27. Thomas McKenzie, 1901, cited in McGeorge, 'Hear Our Voices We Entreat', p. 8.
28. *The Triad*, 10 Aug. 1910.
29. E.g. 11 April 1910.
30. *PD*, 1899, 108, p. 370, cited in McGeorge, 'Hear Our Voices We Entreat', p. 9.
31. G. P. Williams and W. P. Reeves, *Colonial Couplets*, Christchurch, 1889.
32. *NZ Graphic*, Christmas number, 1890.
33. *New Zealand Magazine*, VI, 1876.
34. *Farmers' Union Advocate*, 23 July 1910, Supplement p. 11.
35. 11 April 1910.
36. *Otago Daily Times*, 7 Nov. 1931.
37. McGeorge, 'Hear Our Voices We Entreat', p. 6.
38. *NZ Times*, 17 March 1925; McGeorge, 'Hear Our Voices We Entreat', p. 15.
39. C. B. K. Smithyman, 'Attitudes to Immigration in New Zealand 1870–1900', MA thesis, University of Auckland, 1971, pp. 50, 182. I am considerably indebted, in this section, to the late Christopher Smithyman's thesis.
40. The *Press*, 20 Sept. 1916.
41. Smithyman, 'Attitudes to Immigration', pp. 100–1, 196.
42. *NZ Herald*, 9 Feb. 1906.
43. Smithyman, 'Attitudes to Immigration', p. 69.
44. *Weekly Graphic and New Zealand Mail*, 12 Aug. 1908.
45. *Quick March*, 1 July 1918, 10 May 1919; 10 May, 10 July, 11 Oct. 1920 and other dates; Jacqueline Leckie, 'In Defence of Race and Empire', *NZJH*, 19, 2, Oct. 1985.
46. E.g. Humphrey McQueen, *A New Britannia. An argument concerning the social origins of Australian radicalism and nationalism*, Harmondsworth, 1970.

CHAPTER 7: 'HOME' AND 'HOMIES': THE EMPIRE

1. Alan Mulgan, *Home*, London, 1927, pp. 8–14; *The English of the Line*, Christchurch, [1925], p. 37.
2. E. H. McCormick, *New Zealand Literature*, Oxford, 1959, p. 85.
3. 16 Feb. 1905, E. Currie, MS Papers 413, ATL.
4. *Votes and Proceedings of Legislative Assembly of Victoria*, 1867, IV, no. 45, p. 26.
5. G. W. Russell, *New Zealand Today*, Christchurch, 1919, p. 115.
6. Vol. II, no. 10, July 1901, pp. 735–8.
7. Cited in K. Sinclair, *Imperial Federation: A Study of New Zealand Policy and Opinion, 1880–1914*, London, 1955, pp. 28–9. New Zealand politicians' views are discussed at greater length in this Commonwealth Paper.
8. Raewyn Dalziel, *Julius Vogel, Busi-*

ness Politician, Auckland, 1986, pp. 178–82, 294–5.
9. Thomas Cholmondley, *Ultima Thule*, London, 1854, pp. 225–7.
10. 8 June 1905.
11. Sinclair, *Imperial Federation*, pp. 35ff.
12. W. Gisborne, *Imperial Federation*, London, 1887, p. 10. He was formerly an MHR in New Zealand.
13. *British Australasian*, 7 June 1906.
14. Sinclair, *Imperial Federation*, pp. 41–4. See also, J. E. Kendle, *The Colonial and Imperial Conferences 1887–1911*, London, 1967, pp. 171ff.
15. Sinclair, *Imperial Federation*, pp. 44–5.
16. I argued this case thirty years ago in *Imperial Federation*. The distinguished Canadian historian, Carl Berger, wrote in 1970, 'Canadian imperialism was one variety of Canadian nationalism . . . .' *The Sense of Power. Studies in the Ideas of Canadian Imperialism 1867–1914*, Toronto, 1970, p. 9.
17. Sinclair, *Imperial Federation*, p. 13; *Lyttelton Times*, 5 March 1890.
18. *NZ Times*, 30 April 1891.
19. *The Weekly Budget*, 24 April 1886.
20. I, 1, 1 July 1925; I, 2, 1 Aug. 1925.
21. *NZ Herald*, 1 Nov. 1912.
22. Ibid., 30 Dec. 1912.
23. *Evening Post*, 1 May 1898; K. Sinclair, *A History of the University of Auckland, 1883–1983*, Auckland, 1983, pp. 175–6.
24. "*NZ*," I, 2, 1 Aug. 1925.
25. André Siegfried, *Democracy in New Zealand*, London, 1914, pp. 45–6.
26. *NZ Graphic*, 16 Aug. 1890.
27. 31 May 1890.
28. *Kai Tiaki*, July 1924.

CHAPTER 8: THE 'AUSSIES': AUSTRALIAN FEDERATION

1. These points are discussed in Keith Sinclair, 'Travellers' Tales: Some Comments on Australasian History', *World Review*, 11, 3, Sept. 1972.
2. See Rollo Arnold, 'Some Australasian Aspects of New Zealand Life, 1890–1913', *NZJH*, 4, 1, April 1970.
3. K. Sinclair, 'Australasian Inter-Government Negotiations 1865–80: Ocean Mails and Tariffs', *Australian Journal of Politics and History*, XVI, 2, Aug. 1970.
4. *PD*, 1890, 69, p. 607.
5. *NZ Times*, 17 Nov. 1900, discussing Stella Allen's article, quoted in Chapter 5.
6. J. M. Dargaville, *New Zealand and the Proposed Australasian Federation*, Auckland, 1884.
7. Wellington, 1885.
8. A. K. Newman, 'The Approaching Birth of a Nation in Australasia', *The Monthly Review*, 1891 (Wellington).
9. *NZ Illustrated Magazine*, VI, 1, 1 Nov. 1899 (Mahon and Newton).
10. *Otago Daily Times*, 27 Nov. 1889.
11. Ibid., 12 Dec. 1889.
12. *PD*, 1899, 107, p. 631.
13. CO 418/8, Minutes of a Conference of Australian Delegates, p. 143, Public Record Office, London.
14. *NZ Herald*, 13 July 1899. Reports, articles and letters were published every day or two until early October.
15. 15, 18 Aug. and every day or two from August to October, 1899.
16. *NZ Times*, 12 Sept. 1899.
17. *Lyttelton Times*, 1 Jan. 1901.
18. Ibid., 17 July, 8 Aug., 11 Aug.; *Evening Post*, 15 Aug., 6 Oct.; *NZ Herald*, 10, 18, 21 Aug., 7 Oct. 1899.
19. *Evening Post*, 15 Aug. 1899.
20. Ibid., 10 Oct., 17 Nov., 27 Nov. 1899.
21. Papers in CO 209/261, Public Record Office, London.
22. 20 March 1900.
23. Rollo Arnold, 'New Zealand in Australasia 1890–1914', MA thesis, University of Melbourne, 1952, pp. 132–3.
24. CO 418/8, draft Minutes, Public Record Office, published in *Accounts and Papers* (Great Britain), Cd. 158, 1900.
25. Keith Sinclair, *William Pember Re-*

eves. *New Zealand Fabian*, Oxford, 1965, pp. 291–2.
26. Reeves/Seddon, 5 May 1900, also 31 May 1900; Seddon/Reeves, 7 July 1900, Seddon MSS, National Archives, Wellington.
27. Arnold, 'New Zealand in Australasia', pp. 130–2.
28. Report, *AJHR*, 1901, A-4. Some people give two or more occupations. For this and other reasons it is not always simple to allocate an occupational group. Similarly, it is not always quite clear whether a person is pro, anti or non-committal. For these reasons, my totals differ slightly from those of E. J. Tapp, 'New Zealand and Australian Federation', *Historical Studies*, v, 19, p. 254, 1952 and Arnold, 'New Zealand in Australasia'. His totals were 50:112:24. Tapp's totals were 50:112:23. My summary of occupations also differs from Tapp's, though his had a different basis.
29. Report, *AJHR*, 1901, A–4, p. xviii.
30. Miles Fairburn, 'New Zealand and Australasian Federation, 1883–1901', *NZJH*, 4, 2, Oct. 1970, p. 154.
31. *PD*, 1890, 69, p. 787.
32. *The Critic*, 30 Sept. 1899. This remarkable effusion was discovered by the Canadian scholar, Bruce Nesbitt, 'Aspects of Literary Nationalism in Australia and New Zealand', PhD thesis, Canberra, 1968, pp. 632–3.
33. E.g. Sir Robert Stout, *PD*, 1884, 50, p. 515. Grey contradicted him, p. 518.
34. *NZ Times*, 14 Dec. 1900.
35. v, 2, Nov. 1901.
36. *PD*, 1906, 138, pp. 36, 96, 98.
37. 16 Jan., 23 Jan., 4 June 1912.
38. *PD*, 177, 1916, p. 149.
39. *PD*, 1922, 195, p. 595.
40. Keith Sinclair, 'Fruit Fly, Fireblight and Powdery Scab: Australia–New Zealand Trade Relations, 1919–39', *Journal of Imperial and Commonwealth History*, I, 1, Oct. 1972.
41. Angus Ross, *New Zealand Aspirations in the Pacific in the Nineteenth Century*, Oxford, 1964, p. 251, and *passim* on this topic.
42. E.g., *PD*, 1885, 53, pp. 528ff.
43. 29 Sept. 1900, 5 Oct. 1900.
44. *PD*, 1900, 114, p. 391.
45. *Evening Post*, 23 May 1902.

CHAPTER 9: NEW ZEALAND VOICES FROM SOUTH AFRICA, 1899–1902

1. Richard Jebb, *Studies in Colonial Nationalism*, London, 1905, pp. 87, 92–3.
2. *NZ Times*, 3 Oct. 1899.
3. *Lyttelton Times*, 6 Oct., 9 Oct. 1899; *NZ Times*, 6 Oct. 1899, letter from 'Peace', a woman. Another woman, Rose Atkinson, wrote a letter published in the same newspaper on 18 Oct. 1899. There are other examples.
4. See Thomas Pakenham's splendid history, *The Boer War*, London, 1982 edn, pp. xvi–xvii and *passim*. On the Jamieson raid, see pp. 27–30.
5. *Otago Daily Times*, 20 Jan. 1900; K. Sinclair, *William Pember Reeves*, Oxford, 1965, pp. 283–5.
6. Ian McIver, 'New Zealand and the South African War of 1899–1902', MA research essay, University of Otago, 1972, pp. 46–7.
7. K. D. Sampson, 'Chief Among the Children', MA thesis, University of Otago, 1970, p. 48.
8. 3 Oct. 1899.
9. Pakenham, *The Boer War*, pp. 169, 247–52.
10. *PD*, 1899, 110, p. 97.
11. D. O. W. Hall, *The New Zealanders in South Africa 1899–1902*, Wellington, 1949, pp. 11 and 97. This official history of New Zealanders at the war is a most inadequate narrative.
12. *Lyttelton Times*, 17 Oct. 1899.
13. Cited in ibid., 17 Jan. 1900.
14. J. G. H. Moore, *With the Fourth New Zealand Rough Riders*, Dunedin,

1906; Hall, *The New Zealanders in South Africa*, p. 35.
15. *Press*, 30 Jan. 1900, where the term 'Maorilanders' is used by a Special War Correspondent. For a protest, see *NZ Times*, 24 Jan. 1900.
16. Sampson, 'Chief Among the Children', p. 81.
17. Ranfurly/Chamberlain, 1 Jan. 1900, cited in McIver, 'New Zealand and the South African War', pp. 61–2.
18. *NZ Times*, 23 Oct. 1899.
19. Sampson, 'Chief Among the Children', p. 82; *NZ Times*, 26 July 1900; *Lyttelton Times*, 25 April, 26 July 1900; *NZ Illustrated Magazine*, Feb. 1902, p. 431.
20. F. L. W. Wood, *The New Zealand People at War*, Wellington, 1958, Chapter 14.
21. T. W. Brown to Jack, 25 December 1899, T. W. Brown MS Papers 522.1, ATL.
22. I have relied on New Zealand newspaper accounts of this action. See, e.g., *Otago Daily Times*, 21 Feb. 1900; *NZ Times*, 17 March 1900, a letter from Private Fred Wood, who was there.
23. Major Robin's clipping book, 1897, in the possession of Mr P. O'Shea, Wellington.
24. *NZ Times*, 17 March 1900.
25. Both quoted in Hall, *The New Zealanders in South Africa*, p. 88, but widely reported in books and newspapers.
26. *Auckland Star*, 24 Jan. 1900.
27. *NZ Times*, 25 Jan. 1900.
28. *Otago Daily Times*, 20 Jan. 1900.
29. *Evening Post*, 22 Jan. 1900.
30. *Lyttelton Times*, 8 March 1900.
31. Ibid., 26 Jan. 1900.
32. *Otago Daily Times*, 20 Jan. 1900.
33. Ibid., 18 Jan. 1900.
34. *NZ Times*, 13 June 1900.
35. Ibid.; *Press*, 26 Jan. 1900.
36. *Lyttelton Times*, 26 Jan. 1900.
37. *NZ Times*, 1 Nov. 1900.
38. *Press*, 23 Jan. 1900; *Otago Daily Times*, 24 Jan. 1900; *Lyttelton Times*, 17 Aug. 1900.
39. *Lyttelton Times*, 1 Feb. 1901.
40. Ibid., 10 May 1901; F. Twistleton, *With the New Zealanders at the Front*, Skipton, [1902], p. 94.
41. *Lyttelton Times*, 5 June 1900, citing the *Colesburg Advertiser*; [Mrs Hawden], *New Zealanders and the Boer War or Soldiers from the Land of the Moa*, Christchurch, [1907], p. 20.
42. Joseph Linklater, *On Active Service in South Africa with 'The Silent Sixth'*, Wellington, [1904], pp. 35, 75.
43. Twistleton, *With the New Zealanders at the Front*, p. 183.
44. *NZ Mail*, 15 Nov. 1900.
45. *NZ Herald*, 23 Jan. 1900.
46. *Lyttelton Times*, 27 Nov. 1900; *NZ Times*, 25 July 1900.
47. *Lyttelton Times*, 19 March, 24 July, 13 Dec. 1900; Sampson, 'Chief Among the Children', p. 77.
48. *Lyttelton Times*, 22 Sept. 1900.
49. *NZ Herald*, 24 Jan. 1900.
50. *NZ Times*, 17 March, 27 Oct. 1900.
51. Diary of W. H. Buckland, 13 Aug. 1900, ATL, MS BUC.
52. Twistleton, *With the New Zealanders at the Front*, pp. 64–7 and *passim*.
53. *Lyttelton Times*, 16 May 1901.
54. *Press*, 1 Feb. 1900, cited in Simon Johnson, 'Sons of Empire', research essay, Massey University, 1974, p. 35.
55. Cox minute, 10 July 1904, CO209/267/23101, Public Record Office, London.
56. *NZ Times*, 25 Jan. 1900; Trooper Frank Perham, *The Kimberley Flying Column*, n.p., n.d., p. 29.
57. *Press*, 25 Jan. 1900, cited in Johnson, 'Sons of Empire', p. 35.
58. *Lyttelton Times*, 20 Jan. 1900.
59. Ibid., 18 Jan. 1900.
60. Joseph Linklater, *On Active Service*, p. 91.
61. 20 Jan. 1900.

62. *NZ Times*, 24 Aug. 1900.
63. On the influence of newspapers, see Benedict Anderson, *Imagined Communities. Reflections on the Origin and Spread of Nationalism*, London, 1983.
64. 17 Feb. 1900.
65. A Wall, 'South African War and the Dreadnought', in *A Century of New Zealand's Praise*, Christchurch, 1912.
66. Sampson, 'Chief Among the Children', pp. 71–2.
67. *Lyttelton Times*, 2 April 1900; *NZ Times*, 27 Dec. 1900.
68. Pakenham, *The Boer War*, p. xvii.
69. Lord Onslow minute, 3 Feb. 1902, CO209/264/4601, Public Record Office, London.
70. *Lyttelton Times*, 26 May 1900; *NZ Times*, 23 March 1900.
71. Mr Philip O'Shea of Wellington kindly showed me his collection.
72. 18 Jan. 1900.
73. *NZ Times*, 2 May 1900.
74. Ibid., 23 Oct. 1899.
75. *Lyttelton Times*, 28 Sept. 1900.
76. *PD*, 1900, 114, pp. 57ff.
77. *New Zealand Journal of Education*, 1 September 1903, p. 157.
78. Ibid., 1 July 1905, p. 113.
79. *Press*, 5 Dec. 1900.
80. NZNA, *Canterbury Old and New*, Christchurch, 1900.

CHAPTER 10: 'PEACE HATH ITS VICTORIES': SPORT

1. *British-Australasian*, 3 May 1906.
2. Feb. 1864.
3. June 1890.
4. 16 Oct. 1897, 21 May 1898.
5. Cited in J. O. C. Phillips, 'Rugby, War and the Mythology of the New Zealand Male', *NZJH*, 18, 2, Oct. 1984, p. 95.
6. *Evening Post*, 19 Oct. 1915.
7. *Press*, 4 Oct. 1915.
8. Ibid., 11 April 1889. See also Tom Ellison, *The Art of Rugby Football*, Wellington, 1902.
9. *NZ Times*, 6 Aug. 1889; *NZ Herald*, 7, 9, 10 Aug. 1889.
10. W. McCarthy and Bob Hewitt, *Haka–the Maori Rugby Story*, Auckland, [1983], pp. 66ff.
11. *NZ Times*, 5 Aug. 1893.
12. Ibid., 31 July 1893.
13. Ibid., 25 Aug. 1903.
14. Ibid., 15 Aug. 1904; *Press*, 15 Aug. 1904.
15. *Press*, 25 Nov. 1905.
16. Ibid., 18 Dec. 1905.
17. Ibid., 24, 26, 27 Jan. 1906; *NZ Herald*, 20, 24 Jan. 1906; *NZ Times*, 18 Dec. 1905; *Why the 'All Blacks' Triumphed*, London, 1906, p. 84.
18. Terry McLean, *Great Days in New Zealand Rugby*, Auckland, 1959, shows a facsimile of Deans's telegram to the *Daily Mail*. Gwyn Nicholls's version was published in the *Official Programme* for 1924 New Zealand *v.* Wales game. There are innumerable other accounts of the episode.
19. 23 Jan. 1906.
20. *NZ Times*, 3 Jan. 1906.
21. Ibid., 7 March 1906.
22. Ibid., 9 March 1906
23. Ibid., 10 March 1906.
24. Ibid., 9 Jan. 1906.
25. It was reviewed in the *British-Australasian*, in London, on 3 Jan. 1906. It was written by Gallagher and journalists.
26. *NZ Times*, 9 Jan. 1906.
27. Cited in the *NZ Herald*, 21 March 1906.
28. *Press*, 24 Nov. 1905.
29. Cited ibid., 22 Nov. 1905.
30. Cited in the *NZ Times*, 2 Dec. 1905.
31. *Why the All Blacks Triumphed*, pp. 7–8.
32. 9 March 1906.
33. Ibid.
34. *NZ Herald*, 25 July 1932; *NZ Times*, 13 Aug. 1904.
35. 10 March 1923.
36. Cited in the *Evening Post*, 2 Jan. 1925; *NZ Times*, 18 March 1925.
37. *NZ Times*, 18 March 1925.

38. 12 July 1924.
39. 20 August 1910.
40. Anthony F. Wilding, *On the Court and Off*, London, 1912, p. 70.

CHAPTER 11: CAIRO TO LE QUENOY, 1914–18

1. Christopher Pugsley, *Gallipoli. The New Zealand Story*, Auckland, 1984, pp. 38–46, 55, 360–1.
2. *The Orari Tatler*, 1914 (a troopship magazine), p. 77.
3. Cited in Pugsley, *Gallipoli*, p. 12.
4. Reminiscences, ATL Microfilm MS 847.
5. MS Papers 1374, ATL, 16 Feb. 1915.
6. C. E. W. Bean's diaries, *Gallipoli Correspondent*, ed. K. Fewster, Sydney, 1983, p. 38.
7. G. W. Bollinger, MS Papers 2550/3, ATL.
8. *Evening Post*, 11 Dec. 1915, 'The Spirit of Anzac'.
9. Bean, *Gallipoli Correspondent*, pp. 29–48.
10. See, e.g., the comment of one of the New Zealand Engineers, J. Williamson, Memoirs, p. 35, Imperial War Museum, London, that they did not salute.
11. F. J. Foote, Reminiscences, Sunderland Archives.
12. P. S. O'Connor, 'Venus and the Lonely Kiwi. . . .', *NZJH*, I, 1, April 1967.
13. Bean, *Gallipoli Correspondent*, p. 47. See, e.g., C. S. Algie diary, Sunderland Archives.
14. Letter to his mother, 26 April [1915], Sunderland Archives.
15. *New Zealand at the Front 1918*, Written and Illustrated by Men of the New Zealand Division, London, 1918, p. 15; Bean, *Gallipoli Correspondent*, p. 83.
16. *New Zealand at the Front 1918*, p. 15.
17. Pvt L. G. Taylor diary, Sunderland Archives.
18. G. W. Bollinger, MS Papers 2550/3, ATL, 5 Feb. 1915.
19. H. H. S. Westmacott, Reminiscences, Micro MS 847, ATL. He copied this remark from his sergeant's diary.
20. Pugsley, *Gallipoli*, pp. 15–16.
21. E. C. Clifton diary, ATL (no reference number), dated 'Monday' and 'Saturday'.
22. F. R. Voitre Kofsky Papers, MS 199/0, Taranaki Museum.
23. Pugsley, *Gallipoli*, p. 361.
24. Lt. A. A. Currey to Capt. R. V. Bevan, 23 June 1915, Sunderland Archives.
25. Diary, p. 70, in possession of Mr E. P. Malone, Auckland.
26. Paul Fussell, *The Great War and Modern Memory*, Oxford, 1975, p. 9.
27. E.g., Private S. Blackmore, diary, 10 Aug. 1915, 3 DRL 6413, Australian War Memorial, Canberra; Geoffrey Serle, *John Monash. A Biography*, Melbourne, 1982, p. 243.
28. Letter to a friend, 24 April 1917, Sunderland Archives.
29. Cecil Malthus, *Anzac: A Retrospect*, Christchurch, 1965, p. 152.
30. See, e.g., Pugsley; Peter Liddle, *Men of Gallipoli*, London, 1976; Robert Rhodes James, *Gallipoli*, London, 1965.
31. Overton letter, 24 May 1915, WA 10/2/2, National Archives. On the Maoris, see O. E. Burton, *The Silent Division. New Zealanders at the Front: 1914–1919*, Sydney, 1935, p. 69.
32. *Press*, 14 Oct. 1915.
33. Pugsley, p. 312.
34. Ibid., p. 312; H. E. Browne (New Zealand gunner), diary, Imperial War Museum, London.
35. Stanley Natusch, letter, 26 Aug. 1915, Imperial War Museum, London.
36. E. H. Honnor/Mother, 9 Sept. 1915, Sunderland Archives.
37. Diary and Reminiscences, Sunderland Archives.
38. Diary, p. 27.

39. Reminiscences, Micro MS 847, ATL.
40. Pugsley, pp. 24, 332; *Press*, 9 Oct. 1915, a letter from Private J. W. Holmes, who fought on Chunuk Bair.
41. *Press*, 30 April 1915.
42. E.g., ibid., 18 June 1915.
43. *New Zealand Herald*, 19 May, 28 June 1915.
44. Pugsley, p. 360.
45. *Evening Post*, 19 May 1915; *NZ Herald*, 12 May 1915.
46. P. J. O'Regan/Minister of Defence, 26 July 1918, re Private William Ackerman; lawyer's letter in possession of Mr Ian Kidman, Wellington.
47. *Evening Post*, 25, 26, 27 Nov. 1915.
48. Ibid., 2 Dec. 1915.
49. Ibid., 17 Aug. 1915.
50. Marie-Louise Simich, 'Women in Employment in New Zealand 1911–1926', research essay, University of Auckland, 1978.
51. See, e.g., *Evening Post*, 4 June, 30 Nov. 1915.
52. *Press*, 11 Oct. 1916.
53. J. McK. Graham, 'The Voluntary System: Recruiting 1914–16', MA thesis, University of Auckland, 1971, p. 138.
54. See, e.g., *Evening Post*, 16 Dec. 1915.
55. *Manawatu Daily Times*, 10 March 1917.
56. H. Stewart, *The New Zealand Division 1916–1919*, Auckland, 1921, pp. 9, 57; J. B. Condliffe, *Te Rangi Hiroa*, Christchurch, 1971, p. 137; J. Cowan, *The Maoris in the Great War*, Auckland, 1926, pp. 81 ff.
57. W. F. Mandle, *Going it Alone: Australia's National Identity in the Twentieth Century*, London, 1978, p. 4. For the New Zealanders' part, there are accounts in New Zealand newspapers: e.g., *Evening Post*, 26 July, 27 July, 28 July 1916; *Press*, 22 Sept., 12 Oct. 1916.
58. *Chronicles of the NZEF* (an army journal), 31 Oct. 1917.
59. 8 Oct. 1917.
60. For a newspaper account see, e.g., *Evening Post*, 20 Oct. 1917.
61. B. D. Stokes diary, Imperial War Museum, London.
62. O. E. Burton, *The New Zealand Division*, n.p., n.d., p. 104; also see his longer book, *The Silent Division*, pp. 268 ff.
63. *Chronicles of the NZEF*, 29 Sept, 1916; W. S. Austin, *The Official History of the New Zealand Rifle Brigade*, Wellington, 1924, pp. 568–9.
64. Burton, *The Silent Division*, p. 307.
65. *NZ Herald*, 8 Nov. 1918.
66. G. St. J. Barclay, *The Empire is Marching. A Study of the Military Effort of the British Empire, 1800–1945*, London, 1976, pp. 74–5; *Press*, 14 Feb.
67. *PD*, 1917, 179, pp. 28–30.
68. This estimate is based on the census of 1911, when 198 594 men were aged fifteen to thirty-five. The war-time census did not, of course, count the men overseas.
69. *Evening Post*, 6 Aug. 1915.
70. Cited in Pugsley, *Gallipoli*, p. 13.
71. Ibid., p. 13, note 25; *Chronicles*, 14 Feb., 14 March 1917; private communication from Colonel Pugsley.
72. Austin, *Chronicles*, p. 568. See also, C. E. W. Bean, *The Australian Imperial Force in France*, Sydney, 1933, pp. 732–3.
73. *The Orari Tatler*, 1914, p. 35: 'the "Kiwi" begrudges the "Kangaroo" his daily allowance of grog.' For a cartoon see *New Zealand at the Front*, London, 1918, p. 85.
74. Reminiscences, ATL Microfilm MS 847. See William H. McNeill, *The Pursuit of Power*, Oxford, 1983, pp. 131–8, for a discussion of the effects of military drill.
75. ATL, MS Papers 1676.
76. Letter, 14 Sept. 1915, in private possession, cited in essay by Christopher Pugsley.

77. *Evening Post*, 2 Nov. 1915.
78. Letter, Sunderland Archives.
79. Fitzmaurice/Queenie (his cousin), 10 Jan. 1915, Sunderland Archives.
80. John Masefield, *Gallipoli*, London, 1916, p. 19; *NZ Herald*, 25 April 1919; *Evening Post*, 24 April 1920.
81. O. E. Burton, 'A Rich Old Man' (autobiography), MS Papers 438:59, p. 138, ATL.
82. Pp. 15, 47, 81, 121, 179, 190.
83. W. P. Morrell, *New Zealand*, London, 1935, p. 112.
84. AD1/10/471, National Archives.
85. E.g., Richard Price, *An Imperial War and the British Working Class. Working Class Attitudes and Reactions to the Boer War 1899–1902*, London, 1972; John M. MacKenzie, *Propaganda and Empire: the Manipulation of British Public Opinion, 1880–1960*, Manchester, 1984.

CHAPTER 12: HOLY DAYS

1. 25 May 1907.
2. 24 May 1905.
3. *NZ Herald*, 24 May 1911; *Press*, 24 May 1920.
4. *Evening Post*, 3 Jan., 15 Jan. 1890; *Lyttelton Times*, 22 Jan. 1890; *NZ Herald*, 17 Jan., 18 Jan., 25 Jan., 28 Jan., 29 Jan., 31 Jan., 1 Feb. 1890.
5. *PD*, 1907, 139, pp. 371–81; *Lyttelton Times*, 27 June 1907.
6. *PD*, 1907, 139, p. 379.
7. Ibid., p. 375.
8. Ibid., pp. 378, 383, 386; *Lyttelton Times*, 3 Aug. 1907.
9. 28 June, 13 July 1907.
10. 26 Sept. 1907.
11. 19 Sept., cited in the *Lyttelton Times*, 20 Sept. 1907.
12. *NZ Times*, 21 Sept., 24 Sept. 1907.
13. Ibid., 20 Sept., 24 Sept. 1907.
14. *PD*, 1907, 141, p. 216.
15. *NZ Times*, 27 Sept. 1907.
16. Ibid.; *Lyttelton Times*, 27 Sept. 1907; *NZ Herald*, 24, 27 Sept. 1907.
17. *Lyttelton Times*, 28 Sept. 1908.
18. *NZ Times*, 26 Sept., 28 Sept., 1908.
19. *NZ Herald*, 26, 28 Sept. 1908.
20. 26 Sept. 1911.
21. E.g., *NZ Times*, 24 Sept. 1912; *Lyttelton Times*, 28 Sept. 1909.
22. See the views of the trade unionists, *NZ Times*, 24 Sept. 1907.
23. This section on Anzac Day, while largely based on independent research, is much indebted to Maureen Sharpe's MA thesis, 'Anzac Day in New Zealand, 1916 to 1939. Attitudes to Peace and War', University of Auckland, 1981 and to her article, 'Anzac Day in New Zealand: 1916 to 1939', *NZJH*, 15, 2, Oct. 1981.
24. Sharpe, 'Anzac Day in NZ', thesis, p. 33; *Kia Ora Coo-ee, The Magazine for the ANZACS in the Middle East, 1918*, May 1918, p. 8.
25. *Press*, 24 April 1920.
26. Sharpe, 'Anzac Day in NZ', thesis, p. 5.
27. Ibid., p. 44.
28. Sharpe, 'Anzac Day in NZ: 1916–1939', article, p. 103.
29. *PD*. 1921, 191, p. 385.
30. 24 April 1922.
31. Sharpe, 'Anzac Day in NZ', thesis, p. 24.
32. *Quick March*, 10 March 1920.
33. Sharpe, 'Anzac Day in NZ', thesis, pp. 1ff.
34. *Evening Post*, 24, 26 April 1922.
35. *Press*, 26 April 1922.
36. *Otago Daily Times*, 26 April 1922.
37. *Evening Post*, 26 April 1922.
38. *NZRSA Review*, Nov. 1937.
39. For examples of this idea see *New Zealand Nursing Journal*, 15 Jan. 1930, on the opening of the Auckland War Memorial (on glory) and *Press*, 26 April 1920 (on the victory).
40. *Press*, 25 April 1919.
41. Ibid., 26 April 1921; *NZRSA Review*, Nov. 1937 (Pastor Nichol).
42. *NZRSA Review*, Nov. 1937.
43. *Press*, 26 April 1922.
44. T. Dunbar Moodie, *The Rise of Afri-*

kanerdom. Power, Apartheid, and the Afrikaner Civil Religion, California, 1975.

45. Hugh Jackson, 'Churchgoing in Nineteenth-Century New Zealand', *NZJH*, 17, 1, April 1983, p. 47.
46. Sharpe, 'Anzac Day in NZ', thesis, pp. 35, 103–5, 112–13.
47. Ibid., pp. 72–6.

CHAPTER 13: SIGNS AND SONGS

1. For small boys see the *NZ Graphic*, 1905–6; for a lion cub see *Weekly News*, 1 April 1909.
2. E.g., 21 Sept. 1895, p. 361.
3. Stella Bartlett in *New Zealand Life and Forest Magazine*, III, 4, 15 March 1924.
4. D. A. Corbett, *The Regimental Badges of New Zealand*, Auckland, 1970, p. 126.
5. *NZ Herald*, Supplement, 20 Dec. 1905.
6. K. Sinclair, *A History of the University of Auckland*, Auckland, 1983, pp. 31, 67.
7. *Chronicles of the NZEF*, 8 Aug. 1917, p. 272.
8. See *The Story of the Kiwi* [Philadelphia, *c*. 1950], a pamphlet in the ATL.
9. A. E. Tonson in *The Coat of Arms*, IX, 67, July 1966, p. 101.
10. For the entries, see file in National Archives.
11. *NZ Graphic*, 30 Nov. 1895, p. 675. See also, Arthur Boult's 'National Anthem', *NZ Graphic*, 18 Sept. 1897.

CHAPTER 14: MAORIS

1. See discussion in K. Sinclair, 'Travellers' Tales: some Comments on Australasian History', *World Review*, 11, 3, Sept. 1972.
2. Dec. 1889, 1, 6, pp. 388–9.
3. M. P. K. Sorrenson, *Maori Origins and Migrations. The Genesis of some Pakeha Myths and Legends*, Auckland, 1979, p. 14 and *passim*. I am much indebted to these lectures by my colleague on the question of Maori origins.
4. E. Tregear, *The Aryan Maori*, Wellington, 1885, p. 105.
5. Sorrenson, *Maori Origins and Migrations*, pp. 28–9, 83–4.
6. *Southern Monthly Magazine*, 3, Jan. 1865, p. 297.
7. *New Zealand Life and Forest Magazine*, III, 1, 1 Dec. 1923, 'The New Zealand Grace Darling'.
8. Augustus Earle, *A Narrative of a Nine Months' Residence in New Zealand in 1827 . . .*, London, 1832, p. 161. See also, pp. 8–9, 33.
9. *New Zealand Graphic*, 24 Dec., 26 Dec. 1891; 16 Jan. 1892; 20 Dec. 1894.
10. Ibid., 24 Dec., 26 Dec. 1891; 25 March, 29 April 1893.
11. 7 June 1906.
12. *Kai Tiaki*, July 1909, April and July 1910, Jan. 1911.
13. July 1901, May 1903.
14. *NZ Herald*, 27 May 1905.
15. G. W. Russell, *New Zealand Today*, Christchurch, 1919, p. 133.
16. Frank Morton article, *NZ Herald*, Supplement, 16 April 1910. The busts now look bronze.
17. 12 Dec. 1917; cf. 30 May 1917, 16 Aug. 1918.
18. Bruce Biggs, 'The Maori Language Past and Present', in Erik Schwimmer, *The Maori People in the Nineteen-Sixties*, Auckland, 1968, pp. 74–5.
19. 26 Sept. 1907.
20. Conference report, 1901, (6th Session), pp. 13–14.
21. *Evening Post*, 4 Sept., 20 Sept. 1915.
22. Ibid., 11 Sept. 1915, article by 'Arawa'.
23. Te Rangi Hiroa's war diary, cited in J. B. Condliffe, *Te Rangi Hiroa. The Life of Sir Peter Buck*, Christchurch, 1971, pp. 127–8.
24. A. Aitken, *Gallipoli to the Somme*, London, 1963, pp. 47–8.
25. Cited in Condliffe, *Te Rangi Hiroa*, p. 126.
26. Sunderland Archives. The translation

given here is by Professor B. G. Biggs.
27. *PD*, 1914, 169, p. 662 (Ngata); 1915, 174, p. 644 (Parata).
28. Ibid., 1916, 175, p. 519.
29. Ibid., 1917, 179, p. 590.
30. E.g., Ibid., 1916, 177. p. 942; 1918, 183, p. 1033.
31. Ibid., 1916, 175, p. 613.
32. For details, see Judith Binney, Gillian Chaplin and Craig Wallace, *Mihaia. The Prophet Rua Kenana and his Community at Maungapohatu*, Wellington, 1979.
33. *PD*, 1917, 180, p. 145.
34. On this issue see P. S. O'Connor, 'The Recruitment of Maori Soldiers, 1914–18', *Political Science*, 19, 2, Dec. 1967.
35. *PD*, 1915, 174, p. 612.
36. Ibid., 1939, 254, pp. 689 and 726.
37. See Keith Sinclair, *The Origins of the Maori Wars*, Wellington, 1957, p. 69.

CHAPTER 15: WOMEN
1. 15 April 1896.
2. 21 May, 4 June 1909.
3. *Evening Post*, 1, 2 Dec. 1915.
4. Ibid., 7 Aug. 1915.
5. Ibid., 1 Dec. 1915.
6. This paragraph is largely based on J. C. McLeod, 'Activities of New Zealand Women during World War I', research essay, University of Otago, 1978, pp. 43–8.
7. 1901 Conference, 6th Session, p. 14.
8. Doris Gordon, *Backblocks Baby Doctor*, London, 1945, p. 70.
9. *New Zealand Nursing Journal*, 15 March 1937; *Kai Tiaki*, Oct. 1912, Jan. 1910.
10. *Kai Tiaki*, July 1909, Jan. 1910.
11. Ibid., Jan. 1915, Oct. 1916; Joan Rattray, *Great Days in New Zealand Nursing*, Wellington, 1961, p. 135.
12. Rattray, *Great Days in NZ Nursing*, pp. 136–8.
13. *Evening Post*, 24 Nov. 1915.
14. Diary of Nurse Elsie P. Grey, Imperial War Museum, London.
15. *Kai Tiaki*, October, 1912.
16. Ibid., Jan., April 1920, July 1921.
17. *The Witness Christmas Annual 1907*, Dunedin, 1907.
18. 2 Aug., 18 Oct., 22 Nov. 1890.
19. A. Wilding, *On the Court and Off*, London, 1912, pp. 232–3.
20. 1 Sept. 1923.
21. Anna P. Stout, 'What the Franchise has done for the Women and Children of New Zealand', *The English Woman*, VI, 17, June 1910, p. 128 (I owe this reference to Dr Raewyn Dalziel).
22. Mrs Mactier, *Miranda Stanhope*, Auckland, 1911, p. 71.
23. Sophie Osmond, *Ponga Bay*, London, 1922, p. 35.
24. Gordon, *Backblocks Baby Doctor*, p. 133.
25. This section is based on Raewyn Dalziel, 'The Colonial Helpmeet: Women's Role and the Vote in Nineteenth Century New Zealand', *NZJH*, 11, 2, 1977, pp. 112–23.
26. See ibid., p. 112 for an 1839 example of this view.
27. Erik Olssen and Andrée Levesque, 'Towards a History of the European Family in New Zealand', in Peggy G. Koopman-Boyden (ed.), *Families in New Zealand Society*, Wellington, 1978, pp. 1–25.
28. *Ladies' Mirror*, I, 1, 1 July 1922.
29. 24 June 1893.
30. Dalziel, 'The Colonial Helpmeet', p. 122.
31. G. W. Russell, *New Zealand Today*, Christchurch, 1919, p. 110.
32. Patricia Grimshaw, *Women's Suffrage in New Zealand*, Auckland, 1972, p. 84.
33. Gordon, *Backblocks Baby Doctor*, pp. 68–9.
34. May 1904, pp. 139–42.
35. P. 125.
36. Doris Gordon and Francis Bennett, *Gentlemen of the Jury*, New Ply-

mouth, 1937; *Kai Tiaki* XXIX, 6, 16 Nov. 1936; XXX, 1, 15 Jan. 1937.
37. *NZ Graphic*, 15 July 1908.
38. *Kai Tiaki*, VIII, 3, July 1915.
39. Erik Olssen, 'Truby King and the Plunket Society . . .', *NZJH*, 15, 1, April 1981, pp. 4, 6; Jock Phillips, 'Mummy's Boys . . .', in Phillida Bunkle and Beryl Hughes, *Women in New Zealand Society*, Sydney, 1980, p. 229.
40. Margaret Tennant, 'Mrs Grace Neill in the Department of Asylums, Hospitals and Charitable Institutions', *NZJH*, 12, 1, April 1978, p. 12.
41. *NZ Graphic*, 8 Oct. 1892.
42. *New Zealand Official Handbook*, 1892, p. 161.
43. *AJHR*, 1890, H–5, pp. 32–5.
44. This section is based on Erik Olssen, 'Women, Work and Family: 1880–1926', in Bunkle and Hughes, *Women in New Zealand Society*, pp. 170, 178–9.
45. Ibid., p. 179.
46. Gordon, *Backblocks Baby Doctor*, pp. 161–2.
47. *NZ Graphic*, 28 Oct. 1893.
48. See Emily Gibson, 'The Position of Women in New Zealand', *NZ Herald*, 17 Feb. 1912 and Laura Bunting, on the same theme, in *The Ladies Mirror*, 2 July 1923.
49. *NZ Graphic*, 10 April 1897.
50. 15 June 1895.
51. *The Ladies Mirror*, 1 Sept. 1923.
52. *The Triad*, 1 April 1908.

CHAPTER 16: CHILDREN
1. These remarks are based on Erik Olssen, 'Truby King and the Plunket Society', *NZJH*, 15, 1, April 1981, pp. 3ff.
2. T. King lecture, *NZ Herald*, 9 Aug. 1912.
3. *NZJE*, 1 June, 1 Oct. 1906, 15 April 1907.
4. Lima and Samuel Lamert, *The Science of Life*, 1883, cited in David Walker, 'Continence for a Nation. Seminal Loss and National Vigour', *Labour History*, 48, May 1985.
5. 16 May 1906.
6. Olssen, 'Truby King', pp. 6, 21; Olssen, 'Women, Work and Family', P. Bunkle and B. Hughes, *Women in New Zealand Society*, Sydney, 1980, p. 167.
7. *Observer*, 13 March 1915.
8. *NZ Graphic*, 29 Jan., 26 Feb. 1898.
9. *NZJE*, April 1917, p. 73.
10. Margaret Tennant, 'Natural Directions: the New Zealand Movement for Sexual Differentiation in Education during the Early Twentieth Century', *New Zealand Journal of Educational Studies*, 12, 2, 1977.
11. *NZJE*, Feb., Sept., Oct., 1917.
12. Ibid., April, May 1917.
13. Ibid., Feb. 1918.
14. *New Zealand Capital and Labour Review*, 1 Oct. 1917.
15. *Wanganui Weekly Herald*, 16 March 1872, cited R. D. Arnold, 'The Country Child in Later Victorian New Zealand', *Comment*, April 1982.
16. 15 Aug. 1884.
17. *NZJE*, 15 May 1915.
18. Ibid., 15 June 1909.
19. J. A. Larsson, *Zealandia Song Book*, n.p. [New Zealand], 1915.
20. Roger Openshaw, 'The Patriot Band–the School Cadets from their Evolution to the Great War', MA thesis, Massey University, 1973, p. 28; *New Zealand Gazette*, 15 May 1902, pp. 1508–9.
21. *National Education*, 2 June 1919.
22. *The School Journal*, Part III, Sept. 1908, p. 334.
23. *NZJE*, Feb. 1917.
24. 24 March 1906.
25. *National Education*, 2 May 1927. There is a similar detailed comparison of English and New Zealand children in *AJHR*, 1915, E–2, Appendix F.
26. *NZJE*, 25 Nov. 1915; *National Education*, 1 Dec. 1920.

27. *NZJE*, Aug. 1917.
28. *National Education*, 1 April 1921.
29. *NZJE*, 15 Aug. 1911.
30. NZEI Annual Report, 1924.
31. I. L. G. Sutherland article, 'A Contentious Measure', in *National Education*, 1 Sept. 1928. For the debate, see *PD*, 1928, 217, pp. 605ff.
32. 25 Oct. 1911, 31 July, 22 Oct. 1912.
33. W. A. Chapple, *The Fertility of the Unfit*, Melbourne, 1903, p. 108.
34. See Phillip J. Fleming, 'Eugenics in New Zealand 1900–1940', MA thesis, Massey University, 1981.
35. *NZJE*, 15 Feb. 1909, May 1916; New Zealand Educational Institute, presidential addresses, 1919, 1920, 1923, 1929; NZEI Annual Report, 1918, statement from Executive.
36. *National Education*, 1 June 1931.
37. E.g., *Quick March*, 10 May 1922; *Evening Post*, 26 April 1922.
38. Roger Openshaw, 'Patriotism and the New Zealand Primary School. The Decisive Years of the Twenties', D.Phil. thesis, Waikato University, 1978, p. 123.
39. For an example, see *National Education*, 1 Aug. 1940, p. 271.
40. *NZJE*, 1 Oct. 1903.
41. D. R. Jenkins, *Social Attitudes in the New Zealand School Journal*, Wellington, 1939, p. 4; E. P. Malone, 'The New Zealand School Journal and the Imperial Ideology', *NZJH*, 7, 1, April 1973.
42. Openshaw, 'Patriotism', pp. 75–7.
43. *NZJE*, 15 April 1910, 15 April 1911.
44. For the most recent study of this subject see John M. MacKenzie, *Propaganda and Empire. The Manipulation of British Public Opinion*, 1880–1960, Manchester, 1984.
45. Malone, 'The NZ School Journal', p. 24.
46. *National Education*, 2 July 1934; 1 Nov. 1935; 1 June 1936.
47. Ibid., 1 Aug. 1940.
48. See K. Sinclair, *A History of the University of Auckland*, Auckland, 1983, Ch. IX.

CHAPTER 17: THE SINGERS OF LONELINESS

1. *NZ Herald*, 6 Feb. 1940.
2. Ibid., 7 Feb. 1940.
3. Ibid., 3 Feb. 1940.
4. *New Zealand Centennial News*, 6 Feb. 1941, 15 Aug. 1938.
5. 7 Feb. 1940.
6. 6 Dec. 1939.
7. *Art in New Zealand*, March 1940, p. 164.
8. E. H. McCormick, *Works of Frances Hodgkins in New Zealand*, Auckland, 1954, p. 10.
9. *New Zealand Art. A Centennial Exhibition* (Catalogue), Wellington, 1940.
10. Geoffrey Serle, *From Deserts the Prophets Come*, Melbourne, 1973, p. 89.
11. See Douglas Robb, *Medical Odyssey*, Auckland, 1967, pp. 18–19; Keith Sinclair, *A History of the University of Auckland 1883–1983*, Auckland, 1983, pp. 73–4.
12. De Montalk/Fairburn, 22 Jan. 1929, 6 June 1930, A. R. D. Fairburn, MS Papers 1128, ATL.
13. 5 April 1929, 29 March 1930, *loc. cit.*
14. Denys Trussell, *Fairburn*, Auckland, 1984, pp. 120–1; Leonard Woolf, *Downhill all the Way*, London, 1967, pp. 134–8.
15. C. Lahr/Fairburn, 18 March 1932, Fairburn Papers, University of Auckland Library.
16. Fairburn/de Montalk, 6 Aug. 1926, 21 April 1927, Fairburn Papers, University of Auckland Library.
17. A. R. D. Fairburn, *He Shall Not Rise*, London, 1930, p. 85.
18. Trussell, *Fairburn*, pp. 78, 83.
19. Fairburn/D. Glover, 6 May 1936, Glover MS Papers 418/15, ATL.
20. Lauris Edmond, *The Letters of A. R. D. Fairburn*, Auckland, 1981, p. 77.
21. Frank Sargeson, *Once is Enough*, Wel-

lington, 1973, pp. 110–12.

22. Charles Brasch, *Indirections. A Memoir 1909–1947*, Wellington, 1980, p. 360.
23. Edmond, *Letters*, pp. 62–3.
24. Trussell, *Fairburn*, pp. 144–5.
25. Helen Shaw (ed.), *Dear Lady Ginger*, Auckland, 1983, p. 118.
26. *New Zealand Railways Magazine*, 2 April 1934, 'Maoriland Posy'; *Tomorrow*, 28 Oct. 1936.
27. Cited in T. H. Beaglehole, '"Home"? J. C. Beaglehole in London, 1926–1929', *Turnbull Library Record*, Oct. 1981, p. 76.
28. Ibid., p. 77.
29. J. C. Beaglehole, *The New Zealand Scholar*, Christchurch, 1954, p. 8.
30. Lowry/Glover, 25 Feb. 1932, Glover MS Papers 418/1-5, ATL.
31. Lowry/Glover, 24 July 1932, Glover MS Papers 418/15, ATL. For a brief description of the journal, see Keith Sinclair, *University of Auckland*, pp. 165–6.
32. Charles Brasch, *Indirections*, Wellington, 1980, pp. 185–7.
33. O. E. Burton, 'Reminiscences', MS Papers 438/59, ATL.
34. *T'ien Hsia Monthly*, VII, 1, Aug. 1938.
35. Edmond, *Letters*, p. 246; Fairburn/de Montalk, 21 July 1926, Fairburn Papers, University of Auckland Library.
36. Fairburn/Glover, 27 Aug. 1934, Glover MS Papers 418/15, ATL.
37. Helen Shaw, *The Letters of D'Arcy Cresswell*, Christchurch, 1971, p. 101.
38. 10 Oct. 1937, Denis Glover MS Papers 418/15, ATL.
39. Edmond, *Letters*, pp. 88–9.
40. *Press*, 21 Aug. 1923.
41. *Art in New Zealand*, VI, 4, June 1934; see also Fairburn review of Sargeson's *Conversation With My Uncle*, *Tomorrow*, 8 July 1936.
42. *Press*, 10 Nov., 17 Nov., 22 Nov., 1 Dec., 8 Dec., 15 Dec. 1934. Ngaio Marsh joined in–equally out of touch–on 22 Dec. 1934.
43. Ruth E. Harley, 'Politics and Public Themes in New Zealand Literature 1930–1950', PhD thesis, University of Auckland, 1980, pp. 8–9 and *passim*. I found this thesis very helpful while working on this chapter and acknowledge my indebtedness.
44. Allen Curnow, *Enemies, Poems, 1934–36*, Christchurch, 1937, 'Author's Note'.
45. Fairburn Papers, University of Auckland, 26 Oct. 1926.
46. *Tomorrow*, 29 March 1939.
47. Cited in Harley, 'Politics and Public Themes', p. 159.
48. Brasch, *Indirections*, pp. 362–3.
49. Oxford, 1947, pp. 2–3.
50. *A Book of New Zealand Verse 1923–45*, Christchurch, 1945, p. 52.
51. *Present Without Leave*, London, 1939, p. 6.
52. M. H. Holcroft, *The Deepening Stream. Cultural Influences in New Zealand* (2nd edn), Christchurch, 1946 (but written before September 1939 and first published in 1940); *The Waiting Hills*, Wellington, [1943]; *Encircling Seas*, Christchurch, 1946.
53. Holcroft, *The Deepening Stream*, p. 21.
54. Ibid., pp. 25–7. For a study of Holcroft's writing, see D. M. Anderson, 'Mr Holcroft's Islands', *Landfall*, March 1952.
55. Holcroft, *The Waiting Hills*, p. 62.
56. C. K. Stead, in Keith Sinclair (ed.), *Distance Looks Our Way*, Auckland, 1961, p. 84.
57. Holcroft, *The Deepening Stream*, p. 16.
58. *History of New Zealand*, Harmondsworth, 1959, p. 301.
59. Kendrick Smithyman, *A Way of Saying. A Study of New Zealand Poetry*, Auckland and London, 1965, pp. 80–1.
60. *Collected Essays*, London, 1960, pp. 1–10.
61. Holcroft, *The Deepening Stream*, p. 22.

62. For a study of her work, see F. M. Mackay, *Eileen Duggan*, Wellington, [1977].
63. Curnow, *A Book of New Zealand Verse*, p. 22.
64. *Landfall*, VIII, 4, Dec. 1954, pp. 248–9.

CHAPTER 18: INTO THE SECOND CENTURY

1. *Report on Experience*, Oxford, 1947, pp. 14–15.
2. *Popski's Private Army*, 2nd edn, London, 1953, p. 56. I owe this reference to Dr J. Belich.
3. At 'King Alfred', Hove, and at other naval bases.
4. The Heylen Research Centre, Auckland, kindly provided me with a copy of this report and of an earlier report, of June 1985, on the proposed tour.
5. Edmond, *Letters*, p. 77.
6. Janet Frame, *The Envoy from Mirror City*, Auckland, 1985, pp. 160–2.
7. O. N. Gillespie, *National Education*, 1 March 1940, p. 61.
8. Frame, *The Envoy*, p. 5.
9. *PD*, 1930, 724.

Index